Also by Nikki Van Noy

So Much to Say:
Dave Matthews Band—20 Years on the Road

Five Brothers

and a Million Sisters

NEW KIDS
ON THE
BLOCK

Nikki Van Noy

A Touchstone Book
Published by Simon & Schuster
New York London Toronto Sydney New Delhi

Touchstone
A Division of Simon & Schuster, Inc.
1230 Avenue of the Americas
New York, NY 10020

First Touchstone hardcover edition October 2012

TOUCHSTONE and colophon are registered trademarks of Simon & Schuster,
Inc.

For information about special discounts for bulk purchases, please contact
Simon & Schuster Special Sales at 1-866-506-1949 or
business@simonandschuster.com.

The Simon & Schuster Speakers Bureau can bring authors to your live event.
For more information or to book an event, contact the Simon & Schuster
Speakers Bureau at 1-866-248-3049 or visit our website at
www.simonspeakers.com.

Designed by Joy O'Meara

Manufactured in the United States of America

1   3   5   7   9   10   8   6   4   2

Library of Congress Cataloging-in-Publication Data

Van Noy, Nikki
New Kids on the Block: five brothers and a million sisters /
Nikki Van Noy.—1st Touchstone hardcover ed.
p. cm.
1. New Kids on the Block. 2. Rock musicians—United States—Biography.
I. Title
ML421.N5V36 2012
782.42166092'2—dc23
[B]
2012020893

ISBN 978-1-4516-9522-9
ISBN 978-1-4516-6787-5 (ebook)

To Dad and Mom,
who taught me everything
I needed to know about magic

contents

Coming Home

There's just no words to describe it. I guess the
only thing similar is a Super Bowl quarterback
winning it for his hometown.

—Danny

On June 11, 2011, under a dramatic gray sky that threatens to
open up at any moment, one hometown band is getting ready to
stage the concert of a lifetime. For the Boston-bred New Kids on
the Block (NKOTB), *this* is the moment that defines success—
eighty million records, multiple sold-out world tours, and American Music Awards notwithstanding. Band member Joe McIntyre
explains, "You really feel the bricks and the mortar of Fenway Park.
You *really* feel that presence of who you are. Growing up in Boston, it's such a part of who we are and our story."

Though Boston is home to residents of all faiths and creeds,
there's one church that everyone considers sacred in this town:
Fenway Park, home of the Boston Red Sox. A deep loyalty for
both the quirky, historic ballpark and the baseball team that calls
it home is practically encoded into every resident's DNA. "Listen,"
band member Danny Wood says, "we don't have any Grammy
Awards. I couldn't care less about any of that stuff. Nothing will
ever top Fenway. Not playing any other stadium anywhere else
around the world."

Fenway inspires both comfort and awe in locals. It conjures up memories of sticky summer afternoons, hyped-up crowds, and eighth-inning sing-alongs to Neil Diamond's "Sweet Caroline." But even with this familiarity, a sort of reverence for both the park and the team is always there too—Fenway is where the magic happens. It makes sense that if anything were to serve as a pinnacle of success for a Bostonian, it would most likely somehow involve Fenway Park.

Though most of the New Kids grew up in the rough-and-tumble neighborhood of Dorchester, no more than four miles from Fenway (with the exception of Joe, who hails from the more middle-class Jamaica Plain), the journey to this ballpark has been a long and improbable one, comprised of one breakup, six albums, and twenty-seven years. For even the most successful music groups, the odds of playing Fenway are slim, since the park invites only one or two acts to play upon its painstakingly preserved field per summer. In fact, musical performances weren't permitted at the stadium until 2003. By then, NKOTB were not only long past their early-1990s heyday but also had been disbanded for nearly a decade. Nonetheless, NKOTB are here tonight, gearing up to join the ranks of just a handful of artists who hold claim to rocking forty thousand fans under the Green Monster. This exclusive roster includes iconic acts such as Bruce Springsteen, the Rolling Stones, Paul McCartney, and Aerosmith.

As the minutes tick by on the afternoon of NKOTB's sold-out show, park staff and the band's road crew buzz about, frenetically preparing for the gates to open and fans to come flooding down Yawkey Way. The roar of leaf blowers echoes throughout Fenway as groundskeepers valiantly attempt to wash pooled water off the tops of the chairs set up on the field for tonight's show. NKOTB management has alerted all personnel that the band will take the stage a bit earlier than planned in an effort to beat the brunt of the storm rolling toward Boston. A sense of focused determination permeates the venue as the staff sets its collective jaw in an attempt to batten down the hatches. There will be no rain delay in Fenway tonight.

Backstage, NKOTB bandmates Jon and Jordan Knight, Joe McIntyre, Donnie Wahlberg, and Danny Wood would expect nothing less than a dramatic downpour for their Fenway show. Waking up to a rainy Boston that morning, Donnie says, "Everyone was freaking out about the rain. It's rained every time we've done something big outside. I was like, 'Here we go again.'" However, even with the addition of weather-related hurdles to overcome, Jordan will be the first to tell you, "Our best things have happened in the rain."

In the three years since their inaugural reunion performance in 2008, Mother Nature has contributed her own signature flair to NKOTB's milestone moments. This streak began with the band's live comeback performance on NBC's *Today* show, where the New Kids performed for the first time in fourteen years before millions of viewers on a slippery stage soaked by sheeting rain. A definite theme has emerged since then, and it seems appropriate that it would continue on a night as monumental as this. It's gotten to the point where, to some degree, NKOTB *welcome* such circumstances. While the impending storm is a main topic of conversation around the park, Danny says that most of the band members "didn't even talk about the rain. We knew it would add some character to the night, and we thrive on improvising. We spent our whole life improvising and adapting." Over the years, NKOTB's members have become masters at going with the flow and relaxing into any situation, from spur-of-the-moment performances on street corners and in cramped dressing rooms during their early days, to creating a sense of connection with a vast audience in the humongous stadiums that came later on.

That doesn't mean the rain isn't causing some stress as the minutes tick by, especially for Donnie, who has been hard at work attending to even the most minute details of this gig for the past several months. Specifically, the dramatic entrance—which is set to feature the band running out from the home-team dugout in typical Red Sox fashion—is in danger because of the ominous clouds and the field's already wet grass. According to Donnie, "Early the morning of the show, I had to come to grips with the fact that we may just lose the big, awesome opening, which every pop star really wants to have . . . For me, it was like, 'Are they gonna let us run on the infield now?' 'Is the stage gonna be too slippery?'"

The rain today is only the latest in a series of challenges that NKOTB have overcome throughout their career. This much is clearly evidenced by the simple fact that the Fenway performance is happening in the first place. "Fenway is crazy for me—I think crazy for *all* of us—because it just seemed like we were this boy band that faded into the sunset," Jon says. "I think this go-around, people respect us more. To do Fenway and sell it out was just *amazing*. It just made me feel like, 'Wow, we really did have an impact.'"

Prior to NKOTB's resurgence in 2008, never before had a pop band managed to leave the industry for an extended period of time only to reemerge stronger than ever, with its fan base still intact. Sure, other acts have reunited for one last taste of glory or to pick up a bit of extra cash, but what's happening here is something entirely different. This is a bonus round—a second chance for band and fans alike. An opportunity to return to a touchstone from earlier days, only this time with the benefit of lessons learned, life lived, and an abundant sense of gratitude on both sides of the stage. The chances of this happening were improbable at best— which makes the fact that it *has* happened all the sweeter. Even band members seem incredulous at times. "It doesn't happen," Jordan says, shaking his head. "I always say that: this does *not* happen."

The New Kids' lifetime to date has been divided into two distinct phases. The first phase, from 1984 to 1994, saw these five "every-guys" come together and rise to dizzying levels of fame on the basis of hard work, personality, determination, good timing, and a certain intangible chemistry—both between the guys themselves and between the New Kids and their fans. Though NKOTB enjoyed more success over the course of that decade than the average band will in a lifetime, by the time they disbanded, NKOTB's oldest member, Jon, was only twenty-five years old.

After years of paying their dues and some marketing misfires, when the New Kids finally hit the national music scene in 1988, their success took off at the speed of light. In just a matter of months, NKOTB became a bona fide phenomenon as ingrained in 1980s pop culture as *The Cosby Show* and Cabbage Patch Kids. Children and adolescents flocked to NKOTB, losing their minds at the mere mention of the band or one of its members. In less than three years, NKOTB were catapulted from near obscurity to the top of the charts, with earnings that pushed them to number one on the *Forbes* list of highest-paid entertainers for 1991.

The adulation was intense, and the spotlight was glaring. With so much success and such a young fan base, a certain amount of distance and inflexibility was inevitable. Though NKOTB's fans loved the band members passionately, and the band was appreciative of and dedicated to its fans, before long, it was nearly impossible for the two groups to comingle in a truly authentic way. When NKOTB were in the vicinity, fans were quick on their feet, tracking them down. The band was in a constant run too. International tours stacked up one after another as NKOTB rocketed around the world, moving from one city to the next, day after day, month after month, for more than three years straight. Jon recalls, "Back in the day, I remember doing shows on Thanksgiving and only having Christmas day off. It was constantly go, go, go, go, go. We couldn't breathe."

By 1994 both the New Kids and their fans had grown up and were ready to move on. The music scene had changed drastically, making it more difficult for the band to find its place in the market. And the media had long since burned out on them. On April 14, 1994, *Philadelphia Inquirer* music critic Tom Moon wrote that the group's hits were either "ballads of overweening sincerity or dance tracks dusted with a thin coat of prepubescent funk." He continued, "Everything about the multiplatinum New Kids [feels] manufactured . . . Once kings of pop, NKOTB is now an underdog attraction back in the business of winning fans, if not fighting for its artistic life." It was a common sentiment amongst the music media during the 1990s.

The band faced a one-two punch: first, the witch hunt that haunted all pop bands in the wake of the Milli Vanilli lip-syncing scandal of the early 1990s; and second, the heavy merchandising of NKOTB once they hit it big. Both these issues hung over their heads, often putting the band on the defensive. There was a pervasive lack of understanding in both the media and music industry about what NKOTB were really about. Moreover, after years of functioning in such a cloistered environment, it was important to the members of NKOTB that they try life on their own terms. Their fan base, which dwindled significantly as the 1990s wore on, was growing up too, shifting away from teen idols and on to personal endeavors such as advanced education, careers, and relationships. The tidal wave of frenzy that surrounded NKOTB receded, and life moved on.

The band members grew up too and established individual careers across a broad spectrum of fields, including everything from entertainment to real estate. Some fans stayed in the loop with NKOTB members' more low-key solo careers, while others' NKOTB memorabilia gathered dust in the deep recesses of their childhood closets.

Then in 2008, when even the most die-hard NKOTB fans had more or less given up on a reunion, the second chapter of the group's career began with a small buzz online. Quickly it gathered speed. Rumors began to spread throughout other media outlets as well. All of a sudden it was official: NKOTB were back. No one—not even the band—saw it coming.

NKOTB reunited with no expectations. In the four years since then, the New Kids have responded to fan demand—a demand marked by an intensity and abundance far more powerful than anyone would have ever dreamed possible. The NKOTB scene is largely crowd driven, with the band following its fans' lead rather than vice versa. For the most part, both band members and fans will tell you that the second time around is even sweeter than the first. It's a bit looser, NKOTB and their fans can interact on a level that was never possible before, and with fifteen years' distance between now and then, both parties can truly appreciate how much *fun* it all is. It's simultaneously a chance to go back and relive happy, carefree memories and to build new ones. On some level, there's a sense of victory to it all too—the fact that NKOTB staged such a resurgence proves once and for all that this band is far more than just an overmerchandised, manufactured teen act.

Though the chances of achieving such staggering levels of worldwide acclaim were minuscule the first time around, they were exponentially smaller nearly fifteen years later, when most of NKOTB's members were approaching age forty. In the fickle, youth-driven pop music genre, perhaps even more surprising than NKOTB's reappearance was the fact that their fans came back with such force. But, as NKOTB have proven time and time again, they revel in defying odds, expectations, and precedents. As is almost always the case with them, something else was going on here. Something *more*. Call it what you will, but as Jordan sees it, "There has to be a piece of magic in it. And that's what we always look for. What makes your hair stand on end? What brings on the emotion? It's not just about making a beat or playing music, it's about the magic."

Unexpected as this entire resurgence was, it could have been written off as a fluke, based on the initial flush of excitement of seeing all five New Kids together again. However, that doesn't explain how three years after the band's initial reunion—well after the novelty of NKOTB v. 2 has worn off—forty thousand people are gathered in Fenway tonight, anxiously awaiting the guys' arrival onstage.

Spirited female voices dominate Fenway's echoing hallway. Though the standard-issue Red Sox colors and patterns are emblazoned on many attendees' shirts and jackets, tonight's Sox-themed souvenirs have a special NKOTB slant. Tonight the Red Sox, Fenway, and hometown boys NKOTB have fused into one. The back of the event's signature T-shirt perfectly and succinctly sums up the general feeling in the air: Once in a Lifetime.

Fans chatter excitedly as they fill the field and grandstand. The vast majority are aware that for all the milestones NKOTB have enjoyed over the years, this is *the* watershed moment. This is a night that will never be repeated, an event that only this audience will ever have the chance to experience. Despite Fenway's size, there is also a certain intimacy to the whole affair—this loyal crowd understands exactly what the past twenty-seven years have entailed and why this moment is so magical. Fan Ali Lewis surmises, "This was more than a concert. It was an historic moment in the lives of the performers and the audience. It was a celebration of twenty-five years of togetherness, twenty-five years of believing in each other."

Every band will tell you that each and every show is just as important as the next, whether it's in Wichita, Kansas, or New York City. But, of course, that's not exactly true. Some nights mean more than others. And—if you're *really* lucky—one or two nights will stay with you forever. This is one of *those* rare, special, defining nights. Backstage, even these five guys who have seen it all are overcome at the surreal nature of playing this particular ballpark. For five men who have spent decades taking part in countless experiences that most of us can only dream of, this night is beyond even *their* wildest fantasies. Danny says, "I never even dreamed we would play Fenway—that was unobtainable. Our manager all along the way would joke, 'It's gonna go all the way to Fenway.' I never believed it, nor did I take it seriously. So when it happened, I had to look at the email a few times, and I had to call him and be like, 'Don't mess with me. This better be for real.'"

This gig was nearly a year in the making. On August 14, 2010, Donnie sat in this very ballpark, watching as fellow Boston-based band Aerosmith took the stage. Donnie remembers, "I started taking videos, and I sent one to our manager, Jared Paul. I said, 'We have to do this,' and planted the Fenway seed with him." Over the course of the next several months, that seed took root. In late 2010 Donnie received a call from Jared informing him that Fenway was up for offer.

Making those phone calls was a special experience for Jared. He says, "It was one of the greatest moments of my life. It wasn't even one of the best moments of my business life—it was one of the best moments of my *life*. It was such a milestone we had set for ourselves. To be able to accomplish it? It's the top of the mountain." Then the real work began, as months of preparation and planning commenced. From the beginning, Donnie says, he knew, "We *need* to make it an event. Everything has to be crazy and special for the fans."

The payoff comes tonight. The excitement sweeping through Fenway is electric. Like a kettle spouting steam to release built-up pressure, a roar tears through the crowd when Joe appears onstage shortly before showtime. The tone of the evening is officially set when he chokes up a bit while introducing the Neighborhood Children's Theatre of Boston. It's a very full-circle moment for Joe as a group of about forty boys and girls spread across the stage in red T-shirts, their little voices echoing throughout Fenway as they belt out a medley that includes "God Bless America" and "On a Wonderful Day Like Today."

"I was six years old when I sang my first song with the Neighborhood Children's Theatre," Joe explains, "literally miles away in Jamaica Plain. To be at Fenway with them was just phenomenal. As if that day could be any more emotional, I got to do that. The four other guys were so supportive. It's a simple thing, but to have their support is really special."

Shortly after the children leave the stage, Boston mayor Thomas Menino kicks off the festivities by announcing that June 11, 2011, has officially been deemed NKOTBSB Day in Boston in honor of both the New Kids and Backstreet Boys (BSB), which have joined forces this summer to form one massive pop spectacle. This announcement is followed by the ceremonial unveiling of a giant banner on Fenway's left field wall (affectionately dubbed "the Green Monster" by locals), which reads "NKOTBSB" in the traditional Red Sox font. Donnie says, "I went to Opening Day the year after the Red Sox won the World Series in 2004, and I remember they dropped the Red Sox banner down the Green Monster. I said, 'I wanna do *that* with NKOTBSB.'"

Once the banner is unfurled, a final special guest is brought onstage to introduce the band: Mark Wahlberg. The crowd roars deafeningly when the former musician, Academy Award nominee, producer, and—most important for tonight's purposes—younger brother of Donnie saunters onstage. Despite his inherent connection to NKOTB, Mark has rarely been overtly associated with the group since the earliest days of his own long-ago rap career. Tonight Mark is just a proud younger brother as he looks out over Fenway and his voice echoes through the stadium:

"I'm so glad that I got to be here to introduce these guys tonight because [twenty-seven] years ago I introduced them at their first show at the Lee School. It's pretty damn incredible, them going from the Lee School to Fenway Park. I'm very proud, especially of my brother, who I don't get to thank that often. But if it wasn't for him, I'd probably still be incarcerated somewhere right now instead of doing what I do and having the beautiful family that I have."

As Mark exits, the screens on either side of the massive stage stretched across Fenway's outfield come to life. The image pans down through the galaxy to Earth, then narrows in on tonight's epicenter of the universe, Boston, Massachusetts, and, finally, Fenway Park. A video montage follows, with pictures of the band's and Fenway's history alternately filling the screen. The video's narration, built around a line penned by Donnie, encapsulates not only the sentiment of the evening but also NKOTB's career: "Like most kids from humble beginnings, we all knew this: You push us, we push you back. You respect us, we respect you back. You doubt us, we will bleed to prove you wrong."

For as spectacular as those moments leading up to the show are for fans, the band is also drinking them in. Donnie remembers, "The truth is, as is typically the case, it all happens as it is meant to. The sun sort of crept through the clouds—just a hint of it—during the opening intros. We were packed in the dugout, sort of watching in wonderment. There were a couple of fans just outside the dugout . . . just looking at us. I was like, 'Are you excited?'"

The familiar voice of Fenway public-address announcer Carl Beane echoes throughout the park. For a second, one might almost expect to see the Red Sox take the field. But tonight's starting lineup is a bit different. One by one, Beane calls out each member of NKOTBSB. As each member emerges onto the field fully outfitted in Red Sox regalia, a new burst erupts from the crowd until it's almost ear splitting. As each band member takes the field, he moves down the line, slapping five with his "teammates." The excitement isn't just vibrating throughout the spectators—it's also dripping off the musicians. The anticipation is all encompassing and almost tactile.

The pop supergroup takes a lap around first base on the roped-off baseball diamond before running to the stage. NKOTBSB have managed to beat the brunt of the storm to Fenway, but the energy in the stadium is thunderous during the opening mashup of "Single" (NKOTB) and "The One" (BSB), both of which have been looped around Coldplay's "Viva La Vida." It's a surreal moment when, at the end of the opening number, NKOTB are lifted onto the riser at the foot of the stage ramp and hover over Fenway Park, Sox jerseys on, with the Green Monster serving as their backdrop. If there's a more fitting visual image of victory for any kid from Boston than this, it's difficult to imagine what it might be. Joe remembers, "The stage rises up, and both groups are going higher and higher, and we're in center field in Fenway. That's the first time I cried that night."

The show continues in a sustained mad burst of energy that even teenagers would struggle to rival. "There's just no words to describe it," Danny says. "I guess the only thing similar is a Super Bowl quarterback winning it for his hometown." A myriad of emotions are visible onstage as the night wears on. It's difficult not to be touched when Joe moves to the end of the stage ramp and stretches out the end of NKOTB's breakthrough hit, "Please Don't Go Girl," for what seems to be several moments as he soaks in the powerful sight of a packed Fenway spread out before him. Or as Danny takes a moment to tell the crowd how proud his deceased mother, Betty Wood, would be tonight.

Fans are emotional too. Longtime NKOTB fan and Dorchester native Jodi Mackie says, "The way the New Kids looked around Fenway, it was clear they were appreciating everything and taking it in. And that makes me love them even more because they appreciate where they came from. They *appreciate* the fans. Growing up in the Dorchester slums to becoming what they became, seeing them actually playing Fenway and being from the same place as I am made me feel great. The triumphs they've had and obstacles they've overcome are amazing to me."

A very different kind of energy overtakes the New Kids as the rain clouds finally open up dramatically, drenching Fenway almost instantaneously as NKOTB begin singing "Tonight." Though one might presume this would put a damper on the affair, strangely, it has the opposite effect. Donnie remembers it as a fortuitous case of impeccable timing. "It started to rain at the very moment where we have to walk down the catwalk—the moment when the New Kids are *most* connected to the audience. We walk down out into the teeth of the crowd, to the tip of the stage. I said, 'It feels like Fenway, it sounds like Fenway, it smells like Fenway. Show us if it looks like Fenway!' Right when those house lights went up, it started to rain. We walked down the catwalk, and I just could *feel* the guys all like, '*Yes!*' Jordan started to take off his clothes, I already had my shirt off. And then we do 'Tonight' and go into the crowd."

"We came alive as soon as it started raining. That's where I felt like, 'This is a moment,'" Jordan remembers. "For me, that was when the New Kids had a chance to come true to form. We played in front of basically all-black crowds in the beginning of our career, and we played in not the greatest places. We performed in executive offices—we would move a desk and perform right in people's offices. So it was kind of like we went back to our old New Kids tricks in the middle of Fenway. I think that's one of the great things about the group is that we play off each other, and we play off the moment. I think that's what makes us fun, spontaneous, good entertainers."

Entertain they do. Band members rip off shirts and jackets and gleefully strut out to the end of the stage to greet the rain, as though daring it to come down even harder. Joe adopts his thickest Boston accent for the occasion, dropping all of his *R*s and bellowing, "Oh my *gawd*! I caught pneumonia at the New Kids *con-caht* at Fenway *Pahk*, and I don't give a shit. It was fucking awesome, and I don't *ca-yah*!" The stage's long ramp is transformed into the world's largest Slip 'n Slide, with New Kids joyfully skidding up and down it, driving the sodden crowd into more of a frenzy. "I think it was one of the funnest shows that we did," Jon remembers, smiling. "We were just like, 'You know what? It's raining, let's make the best of it!'"

As the rain comes down during "Tonight," the band jumps off the stage and into the crowd. Joe decides to seize this moment as the opportunity to run a lap around the roped-off baseball diamond and get closer to fans sitting in the grandstand. "I mean, God bless the fans that were in the grandstand having just as much fun. I ran back there, and I did a lap and danced on home plate like an idiot. It was just another highlight," he remembers. As is often the case at NKOTB shows, there's a strong sense of youthful abandon, both on the stage and in the audience.

This is no warm, humid summertime rain. Icy pellets assault the crowd, but still no one runs for cover. Fans dance and scream and revel in the onstage antics as the show rolls on. "Our fans already came from all over the world—that already says they're special. But did the world need to know they were *that* special to stand in the rain like that and not one person left? If this is a niche audience, this is the biggest, greatest, most awesome niche *ever*," Joe marvels.

It is moments precisely like this that fans often cite as one of the primary reasons their love for this band is so deep and durable: no one is going to miss this, no matter what the weather serves up. Fan Amy Johnson tries to put the feeling in the air that night into words: "Something really wild happened during the 'Tonight' downpour. It was as if all the crazy high energy that the show already had suddenly lifted into a whole other dimension. . . . The crowd went—and believe me, this is saying something because it was already insane—but we went absolutely *mental* at this point. It became like one enormous party, and the energy was just astounding. From that point on, this concert became one for the ages. One of those 'I was there' moments. I've been to so many concerts in my life, but only a handful where I've actually had the experience that something miraculous is happening. This show achieved that sensation."

As the show draws to a close nearly three hours and several inches of rain later, the familiar introductory beats of NKOTB's closing number, "Hangin' Tough," blast throughout Fenway. Audience members look about in confusion as smoke pours onto an empty stage, with no New Kids in sight. After a few seconds, the crowd reorients itself slightly to stage right, realizing that NKOTB have abandoned the stage and invaded the Green Monster. More than twenty-five years after its release, "Hangin' Tough" takes on new life and energy as the band sings it from atop the deck looking out over Fenway.

Fan Amy Johnson says, "By the time the New Kids appeared on top of the Green Monster to start off the finale, I'm pretty sure the park had turned itself inside out into a whole other world of its own. A world where we the fans could literally—*literally*—see these guys' dreams coming true before our very eyes. I really cannot imagine what a thrill it must have been for all of them, not only to play this particular show but to do it in the most spectacular fashion, with rain pouring down in sheets and thousands of soaked-to-the-bones fans screaming as if they would never stop."

As if the evening hasn't been full circle enough, Joe brings his oldest son, three-year-old Griffin, with him up to the Green Monster. Joe's father, Tom McIntyre, marvels, "Griffin's great-great grandfather, Mr. Gleason, was the boss bricklayer on the Green Monster. Isn't that something?" For Donnie, this moment is the culmination of the vision he had at that Aerosmith Fenway show nearly a year before. "I knew we were gonna sing 'Hangin' Tough' from the Green Monster the day I saw Aerosmith. And we did it."

As "Hangin' Tough" draws to a close, NKOTB descend to the main stage as the crowd goes crazy and fireworks explode into the night sky above the park, bringing the exuberant, emotional show to a finish. Fan Christina St. Arnaud recounts, "Throughout my life, I have seen countless home runs fly across the Green Monster's massive wall. On that night, it was no different. Our boys hit the greatest home run of all. It truly was a once-in-a-lifetime show, and the firecrackers that lit up the Boston sky were nothing in comparison to the light in the eyes of thousands of Blockheads."

By the end of the night, NKOTB have taken an imperfect set of conditions, given it everything they've got, and allowed room for a little bit of magic to trickle in. As Donnie puts it, "There's always a moment in hindsight when it's like, I worked my ass off to get that Fenway show ready. But for as much work as I put in, I love that it started raining at that moment because it told me that we were being guided by the universe. I'm only doing my part, and it's something so much bigger than us." While the drenched, happy crowd shuffles out of Fenway, NKOTB gather in the home team locker room (which serves as the evening's dressing room), celebrating its own victory by dousing one another with champagne in the Red Sox's tradition. Joe sums up the entire evening simply: "It was just sublime. It really was."

For Donnie, the biggest victory wasn't in any of the more obvious elements of the show. "To play Fenway Park all those years later and to be one unit the way we were that night, *that* was the true magic," he says. "There were no moments of tension. There were no moments of discomfort. It was *all* good. We could've played Fenway Park before, but we wouldn't have been ready for it, and we couldn't have played it the way we did it. The five of us were unified. That may be the unspoken part of it all. Everyone knows about the rain, and they know about the fans, and they know about our homecoming and all these other things. But we were one. We all knew how important it was and how special it was, and we were *all* friends. That's real full circle."

What's a Nynuk?

I found the golden ticket, except the contest
hadn't started yet.

—Donnie

In many ways, Boston is a town of contradictions. It's rich with history and home to any number of pedigreed families that can trace their lineage back to the *Mayflower*. It's an intellectual hub where some of the world's best and brightest go to nourish their minds inside the imposing walls of Harvard and MIT. But that's only part of the story.

Boston is also home to many blue-collar families whose living wages are dependent upon manual labor and union jobs. Kids born into neighborhoods like Dorchester, Roxbury, Mattapan, and Southie are often forced to rely on their street smarts to prosper. Despite this, or maybe because of it, residents tend to have a strong sense of pride and allegiance to their neighborhood roots. In Boston, where each area has such a distinct, entrenched personality, your neighborhood is a part of what defines you.

Racial and socioeconomic divides between one neighborhood and the next were a particularly polarizing issue between 1974 and 1988, when bussing was instituted in Boston's public schools through the Racial Imbalance Law. Essentially, any school that had a student ratio consisting of more than 50 percent of one race was ordered to bus kids in from and out to other neighborhoods to diversify. Bussing had the greatest impact on low-income neighborhoods such as Dorchester, Roxbury, Southie, Roslindale, and Hyde Park.

For some parents, bussing was a controversial issue, since their children could potentially be forced to attend a lower-quality school farther away from home. It took kids out of their neighborhoods and flew in the face of that sense of community solidarity. For other parents, bussing was a whole lot of to-do over nothing. Donnie's mom, Alma Wahlberg, remembers being confused by the racial tension at the root of it. Living in Dorchester with her nine children at the time that bussing commenced, Alma was part of a group of parents who took the inaugural bus ride for a television news segment in support of the integrated schools. She remembers, "The newscaster asked me a couple of questions, and I thought I sounded stupid because I was like, 'I don't understand this. What is the *problem*?'" In this polarized atmosphere, some schools became hotbeds for protests and, at times, outbreaks of violence.

Alma remembers witnessing an incident at Dorchester's Woodrow Wilson Middle School, which two of her children were attending. "The black kids would be bussed in. When they were getting on the bus to leave, people were throwing rocks, and one kid got hit. One mother's standing there, and she's crying, and she said, 'Do you realize we bleed red also? We cry. We have feelings. I am so worried about my child.' You're worried to send your child *to school*? I was so ashamed for anybody who took part in this whole thing. It was awful."

Racial tensions weren't limited to the school system. Jordan and Jon's mom, Marlene Putman, remembers how the general climate of their integrated neighborhood disintegrated over time. She says, "Because of where we lived, when I first was there, I would go up to the square and be able to do grocery shopping and banking. But then it became a hostile environment in my own neighborhood. One day my son David and I were walking along the street. All of a sudden rocks and bottles and stuff came our way. I had my car robbed, my windshield broken. People were *really, really* angry."

Despite the social and political turbulence of the time, for most kids—especially younger ones who weren't pulled from schools and classmates to whom they were already accustomed—bussing was standard operating procedure. Because they weren't privy to the politics behind it, most children didn't give much thought to going to school outside of their neighborhood with classmates of other races and colors. They simply adapted to the people and the environment around them. It was what they knew.

It was in this late-1970s-and-early-1980s climate that Dorchester kids Jon and Jordan Knight (brothers separated by just eighteen months of age), Donnie Wahlberg, and Danny Wood were raised. According to Donnie, "I am—and I think *we* are as New Kids—the success story of bussing. The news clippings and the video of those people protesting and screaming at the busses, that was the trauma. But we were the by-product."

According to Jordan, "I was the youngest of six; and then there was at least six foster kids that lived in the house too. The house was teeming with life. It was a bit scary at times; these were Boston kids that we lived with, and we lived in Dorchester, which wasn't the greatest of areas." Because of the size of the house and so many mouths to feed, conditions weren't always perfect. Marlene Putman explains, "It was a six-thousand-square-foot, massive three-story Victorian house that wasn't insulated. We were very careful about electricity, water, and heat bills. So a woodstove was put in one of the rooms on the first floor, and we called it 'the Stove Room.' In the morning the kids would get dressed in front of the stove because that was the only warm room."

To pay all of those bills and feed the many mouths that occupied the Knight residence at any given time, Marlene, a licensed social worker, offered residential foster care services from within their home. She remembers, "I shadowed a mentally ill teenager for twenty-four hours out of the day, but what I made for that wasn't sufficient to provide for us. So I became a specialized foster parent for the elderly through Mass General Hospital. We basically had three people living with us, on top of my six kids, and on top of my mentee. We had tons of kids come through, housed in our family structure."

Despite the Knights' parents' efforts to maximize time with their kids by working at home, it was difficult to vie for attention in such a buzzing atmosphere. Jon muses, "I think it didn't work, because they were so busy with all these other kids that we didn't really get any more attention than we would have if they worked nine to five. It was cool because we were young, so a lot of these kids were like older brothers and sisters to us. A lot of them were nuts, too—my parents took in mentally ill kids, so that made it interesting. As kids we fought for our parents' attention all the time."

In the end, Jon thinks the environment was a good one to grow up in. "I'm actually glad that we grew up in Dorchester and in the inner city. I think my life would be a lot different if we didn't. At a young age, we were surrounded by so many different cultures. Being around that sort of diversity as a kid shapes you for the rest of your life." Jordan agrees that their upbringing made it easy to keep life and the success that would come later in perspective. "Even in childhood, if there's any crew of guys hanging out in Dorchester or in Boston and you get too big for your britches, you get your balls busted."

Growing up, Jon and Jordan shared almost everything. Jon remembers, "We didn't have our own bed; me and Jordan slept in a double bed, and my other brothers slept in another bed. I remember me and my brother sharing three pairs of jeans between us.

Me and Jordan would just switch the jeans back every other day, thinking nobody would notice." Marlene describes the brothers as "very, very bonded. They understand each other, and they're very, very loyal to each other. They understand each others' anxieties, appreciate each other, and, certainly, accept each other with tremendous love."

The family made the most of what they had, though it often involved scraping together limited resources. Marlene remembers, "When Jordan was really young, he really wanted a keyboard. I was dirt poor, and I thought, 'Oh God, a keyboard.' And yet I also thought, 'He deserves this.' So I borrowed some money, and found a used keyboard. Well, I got the used keyboard, and you would've thought I had given Jordan the world. He used to stay up really late playing the keyboard on mute."

Jordan wasn't the only Knight with musical inclinations. Jordan explains, "I don't know if all my siblings went at it with such fervor as I did. But my brother David is musical, Jon's musical, we were *all* in the church choir." Amongst their siblings, Jordan and Jon showed a particular propensity for musical endeavors from a young age. Jordan remembers, "In my church choir, I was in this all-star kind of choir, and we went to a summer camp at Princeton University. I did that when I was six or seven—I was just tiny." Jon too attended this special training camp at Princeton, organized by the Royal School of Church Music in London. In addition to the church choir, Jordan and Jon also participated in the chorus at their grammar school, Trotter Elementary.

Just a short distance away from the Knight home, Danny was growing up in a more traditional nuclear family as the fourth child of six and the eldest son. Though the Woods were certainly a working-class family, they lived a comfortable life in Dorchester and enjoyed a tight-knit, loving family bond. From day one, Danny had a particularly special relationship with his mom, Betty Wood. Of the influence she had on him, Danny says, "My mom always thought I was gonna be something special. She *always* thought that. She instilled a lot of good stuff in me. My confidence comes from her; she built that for me."

Meanwhile, Donnie was living in a very full household as the eighth of nine children. Even amongst all of these children, Donnie's mom immediately saw something in him that set him apart from the rest. He says, "My mother tells me to this day—and will tell anyone that will listen—that she looked in my eyes as a baby and said, 'There's something special about him. And something wonderful is gonna happen.'" Indeed, Alma says, "I don't know what it was, but there was something about him. He was a people pleaser. He was the peacemaker of the family. He didn't want anybody arguing. I just knew—I really did always know."

Of his youth, Donnie remembers, "We were poor. My dad drove a truck, and my mom did all types of different jobs, usually working nights. I remember the water company coming to turn the water off a few times, and my dad would chase them away. We were up against it. It was a constant struggle." For the first several years of his life, Donnie was blissfully unaware of his family's financial standing. That is, until one day when Alma sent Donnie to the store to buy milk and soda for the family. Donnie remembers, "I was going to the store with my older brother and a friend from up the street. I said, 'I gotta get a half gallon of milk, and I gotta get a liter of Pepsi. And I got a dollar and I got a f—' And before the words *food stamp* came out of my mouth—because I didn't know it was anything to be embarrassed about—my brother punched me straight in the face because he didn't want our friend to know we were on food stamps. From that point on, I was totally ashamed of being on food stamps. They taught me how to be embarrassed, my older brothers. I was just a happy kid. I wish I could've been innocent about it a little longer."

Despite the stress that came with financial struggles, Donnie was a dreamer. As a child, he says, "I just believed that something good was out there for me. I never lost hope that something was out there."

The four Dorchester boys' paths crossed at Roxbury's Trotter Elementary School, although they were spread across different classes. Danny has fond memories of his time at Trotter. "Outside of school, it was a very controversial time because bussing started when Donnie and I went into first grade. We were surrounded by chaos, but in school it was amazing. We didn't feel all that. Everyone was open to being around everyone else." For Donnie, being bussed outside of Dorchester to Roxbury was actually a gift of sorts. "We lived in a racially diverse neighborhood, but on my street, it was mainly all white kids. In the white neighborhoods, we weren't really allowed to dream. It wasn't like, 'I'm gonna be famous one day.' That would get you punched in the face. But in school, it was okay to talk like that and think like that." Marlene believes Trotter created the perfect environment for kids to explore and embrace creativity and the arts. She remembers, "Trotter emphasized the performing arts, so they had a choir, and they did a lot of concerts. It was a wonderful school; it really was."

Donnie vividly recalls the first time he crossed paths with Jon at Trotter. "I met Jon when I was in first grade. Jon was in second grade, and him and my brother Bob were in the same class. I still remember where it was in the schoolyard that I met Jon—I can go there right now and *show* you. It was the first or second week of school, and Bob walked up to me and said, 'This is my best friend, Jon.' So, that was how I thought of Jon: he was Bob's friend, he was a little older than me." Looking back, the vibrancy of this memory is somewhat bizarre to Donnie, as are his childhood recollections of his other future bandmates. He says, "I don't remember meeting any of my brothers' other friends. Just Jon. I probably couldn't pick another face out of the school chorus. Just Jordan. I remember that Danny played Slightly Soiled in Mr. Artis's fifth-grade performance of *Peter Pan*. He was sitting in the front, and his shirt said 'Slightly Soiled.' I didn't know what that meant, but I remembered it."

Similarly, Jordan has distinctly fond memories of third-grade bus rides from Dorchester to Trotter that provide a peculiar sort of foreshadowing. "Donnie and I were on the same school bus route. He would always be in the back of the bus, and I would be one row ahead of him. On the way to school and on the way back, he would have songs that he would have the whole *entire* bus sing along with him. It's the same *exact* thing now in concert and at after-parties. It's the *same* person. It's unbelievable."

While on the one hand Donnie made a habit of getting everyone on the school bus riled up, Jordan remembers that he also made a point of ensuring that everyone was comfortable with the situation. "I'm a year younger than Donnie, but I was a lot smaller. He knew I was the vulnerable little kid, so he would always check on me. 'Hey, Jordan, you all right?' He would pat me and make sure I was good and stuff like that and then just go on and get everyone singing again. It's really cool to have that memory of him then and see him be the same person now. He's that sensitive guy."

Danny agrees that all the characteristics Donnie would go on to be known for were firmly in place at a young age. "A lot of people talk about how Donnie's such a character—about how he's always flirting with girls and doing this or that. But he's been like that since we were kids. He would do the same *exact* thing when we were kids. I tell people, 'That's just the way he's always been.' That's what I love about him."

Though he wasn't close to the Knights during childhood, Danny has foretelling memories of Jordan, dating back to their young years singing together in the Trotter chorus. "Jordan would be in the background singing the solos with the high soprano voice. I'd be in the front with all the baritones, then it would go to the solo parts, and you'd hear this voice coming from behind you—this amazing voice coming out of this little kid." Donnie, too, remembers Jordan as standing out from the pack. "Jordan was in the school chorus, and he was always dead center. He was 'the voice' in the school chorus. He was *that* kid. He stood out from the rest." Jordan laughs at the memory of those youthful solos. "I unleashed my vocal stylings on the kids there," he jokes. "They were like, *'What the hell is that?'*"

Donnie was engaging in activities of a less organized variety—wandering around the streets of Boston. "I was riding the subways at ten. My parents didn't know where the hell I was. Me and two of the older kids or one of my older brothers would hop the turnstiles, jump the train, go downtown, and spend the day—no money, not a dime in our pockets. Then we'd sneak back on the train and go home. As long as we were out of the streets and home by dinnertime, my parents didn't care. I think of that, and I think I must be the luckiest guy alive because I didn't end up in some random psychopath's arms and dead. Or in jail. We were stealing clothes. We had nothing. I was wearing my brothers' old, ripped jeans. I wanted my own jeans, so I'm gonna go in Filene's Basement and steal a pair of Calvin Kleins."

In sixth grade Donnie and Jon began to form a friendship. Donnie remembers, "I hadn't really come out of my shell. I was a little, insecure kid. That year I was in a reading class with Jon the period before lunch. And there was a girl, who dated my brother the prior year. So, her, me, and Jon started going to lunch together after class, and we would smoke cigarettes. She would take us in the girls' bathroom at lunch, and we would smoke cigarettes with her. Then we'd eat lunch together and go outside at recess and just talk. Then Jon went to a new school."

After Trotter, both Jordan and Jon received a grant to go to Thayer Academy in the suburb of Braintree, while Donnie and Danny remained in Roxbury to attend Phillis Wheatley Middle School and then Copley High in Boston's Back Bay neighborhood. Danny says, "Donnie and I were, like, the only white kids in our middle school. There was maybe one or two other white kids in our whole sixth-through-eighth-grade classes. But for us it was a great experience and built character." It was during this period that the two really began to form a friendship. "Donnie and I started hanging out more in middle school as we got older," Danny says. "We were getting more freedom at home and were able to hang out after school and stuff."

For Donnie, these middle school years marked a pivotal turning point. "Seventh grade came along. My parents broke up, and I started to be crazy. I started hanging around with Danny and these other guys: Elliot Jackson and David Thompson. These guys who were wild and fun and crazy and spontaneous. Danny was popular with the girls. He always had on Izod shirts with the collar up, and he was cute."

Though Danny would go on to play a very visible role in Donnie's life, Elliot had a life-changing impact on Donnie during those adolescent years. Donnie explains, "My parents splitting up and me meeting Elliot is *guaranteed* one of the reasons why I am where I am right now. He was so funny and spontaneous. I came out of my shell. Me and him were like a duo. He is probably—up until I finished high school—the most influential person in my life.

"I have two sides. I'm a total extrovert, and I'm a total introvert. I was *really* insecure at that point. Left to my own devices, I would just shell up and hide. But being around him, he was just so free and fun, and we became such good friends that I became that way too. He changed my life. To this day, I wake up in the morning and I can draw the curtains or I can take on the world with that same sort of free-spirited abandon that I discovered with Elliot."

Over at Thayer Academy, the Knights found themselves in a very different environment from what they had known during their elementary years in Roxbury. According to Jon, Thayer was "this real ritzy academy that gave grants to kids from the inner city. Me and my brother went there, and it was amazing. Talk about two different worlds! We went from an inner-city school to a place where kids were showing up in chauffeured limousines, and we were going to all these kids' bar mitzvahs and their parents' restaurants. It was really—it was *weird*. We were totally taken out of our element. We were there for two years, and the cultural and education difference was night and day."

When the Knights' grants ended, they returned to Boston for high school. It was during this time that their parents divorced, an event that Jon says "messed me up *really* bad." At age fifteen, in ninth grade, he dropped out and went to work full-time. Looking back on his decision to quit school, he says, "I always hated school. It was so hard to get up for school. I think the only time I liked school was the two years at Thayer Academy. My mother always says it was my anxieties that made me not want to get out of bed and go to school. I think that was part of it, because learning *was* fun for me. I always hated English class when we'd sit in a big square and go around, and everyone would have to read. I'd sit there the whole time waiting for it to come around and just go crazy." Although Jon ultimately obtained his diploma on the road at age twenty-one, he entered the working world full-time in those in-between years as a teenager.

Always an entrepreneurial soul, working was nothing new for Jon, who began selling Amway products when he was just ten years old. At age twelve came a job at the Burger King his sisters managed in downtown Boston, and then a number of jobs after that, including everything from restaurant work to serving as a health aide for a disabled teenager. Jon says, "When my parents got divorced, I felt like I was responsible for taking care of my parents and my brother. So I went to work, and I was giving my brother money, I was buying my mother clothes. I think that's when it started that I had to make sure everyone was okay. I was the caretaker. Still, to this day, I'm that way."

Meanwhile, Jordan bounced from one school to the next for

the duration of high school. He remembers, "My mom wanted me in a great school. It was kind of a tug-of-war between us because I really didn't want to be with different kids; I wanted to be with friends from my neighborhood. The schools that I went to, I didn't fit in—white kids did not dance back then. So me being in an all-white school, honestly, was weird to me because I felt really out of place. I went to Heights Academy in South Boston. For two weeks, I went to Boston College High School, then I refused to go any longer. It was *not* my scene, I couldn't take it. I thought, 'I will never be able to be myself here without being bullied.' Then I went to Catholic Memorial; it was the same type of thing. I did not like it, I was late every day, they kicked me out. One of my confessions to the priest was, 'I have to confess I don't like this school, and I don't want to be here. That's my confession.' Then I went to Newman Preparatory for a year. And I finally got my wish and went to English High School with all my friends for eleventh and twelfth grades."

Outside of school, Jordan kept himself busy with a variety of artistic endeavors. Aside from music and break dancing, he says, "I was into drawing. I was into graffiti too—I used to be a tagger in my teens. I was always into hip-hop culture. There was trouble to get into, for sure." Marlene remembers Jordan as being all over the place at that point in time. She says, "He was very busy—secretly busy. He was Mystery Man. He'd leave the house, you'd never know what he was up to. He kept running around town, spray painting. When I was in graduate school, I'd take the Red line into Harvard Square and be on the train, like, 'Oh, that's a new piece of graffiti. I wonder when he did that?' You'd see Jordan's tagger name 'Popeye' all over the place. Of course, so many other people were doing the same thing. It was a graffiti-crazed age. I have to secretly admire the work—he was talented, he really was. My son, the public defacer. I swear, I kept waiting for the cops to come to the door with him."

In addition to graffiti, Jordan was also displaying other artistic talents around town. Marlene says, "I remember him going downtown and around the corner with his cardboard and break-dancing. He would go into the subways and sing when he was really young. There were times I was concerned for his safety, but he was so darn charmed, he just got around the city smoothly. He was a young teenager and thought he knew everything. But he was fine. And his sense of confidence just allowed me to relax."

Meanwhile, Donnie and Danny were busy building up a repertoire of their own. According to Donnie, "Me and Danny used to do rap performances and shows. I would write rap routines for Danny and me. In ninth grade, Danny and I used to go to the Catholic school dances every Friday night. We would be the two hip-hop guys, and they'd be like, 'Where did these guys come from?' In those neighborhoods, the guys didn't dare do anything like that. That wasn't cool. But me and Danny came in and turned the place upside down. There'd be a big circle, and we'd be break-dancing in the middle of it, and all the girls loved us. One time my brother Paul was in culinary school. I saw his white double-breasted jacket and was like, 'Yo! Can me and Danny borrow one of those each?' And we made outfits. We had white gloves and the white culinary jackets."

Though they dwelled in somewhat separate circles, the four Dorchester kids' paths did cross at certain points. Most notably, Jordan and Danny interacted with each another as young teenagers because of their mutual break-dancing endeavors. "Back then," Jordan remembers, "dancing crews battled each other, so my crew battled Danny's crew. It wasn't some big, huge battle, but it was funny. We'd see in the movies where troupes would have these incredible battles, and we were just two dance crews trying to be cool. By the end of the quote-unquote battle, we were just sharing dance moves and talking." Of the battles, Danny says, "It was crazy. I remember we had this one battle at a roller skating rink and then after, we all rode the train home together."

While the guys were immersed in high school, over in Roxbury, producer Larry Johnson (more widely known as Maurice Starr) was getting ready to take on a new project in the wake of his recent ousting from New Edition. Though only in his early thirties at the time, Maurice already had a significant amount of music industry experience under his belt by 1984. Working as a musician in the 1970s and early 1980s, he found varying levels of success with his own two solo albums (which flopped) and as one-third of the more successful electro-pop group the Jonzun Crew ("Pack Jam" and "Space Cowboy"), alongside his brothers Michael and Soni Jonzun. Ultimately, Maurice turned his attention to writing music and producing other acts. To discover talent, he hosted frequent talent shows in the Boston area.

In 1982 Maurice struck gold when New Edition entered one of his competitions. The Roxbury-based pop group was composed of five black kids from the projects (Ricky Bell, Michael Bivins, Bobby Brown, Ronnie DeVoe, and Ralph Tresvant), and New Edition's 1983 album *Candy Girl* was released on Maurice's Streetwise Records label. The album broke onto international charts on the strength of contagious pop hits such as "Candy Girl" and "Is This the End." Though Maurice helped New Edition ascend to fame, they parted ways in 1984, following a nasty scuffle about an unbalanced contract.

With the demise of his relationship with New Edition, Maurice turned his attention to other projects. One of his ideas was to work with a group of kids somewhat similar to New Edition, only this time he envisioned a white group. In an effort to identify just the right kids, Maurice called in talent agent Mary Alford (who was previously involved with R&B acts such as Rick James and the legendary local singer Margo Thunder) to assist with the legwork of the search. In July 1984 Mary was turned on to then-fourteen-year-old Donnie on the basis of his frequent performances around Dorchester. She convinced him to audition for Maurice.

In an odd twist of fate, Donnie was already acquainted with Maurice's work. "On my thirteenth birthday, I got on the subway and I went to Strawberries Records in Downtown Crossing," Donnie remembers. "I think I had ten dollars for my birthday. I'm choosing between New Edition's *Candy Girl* and Jonzun Crew's *Lost in Space*." In an attempt to choose between the two albums, Donnie placed them side by side on the counter and looked over the credits. He noticed that the same names appeared on both the Jonzun Crew and New Edition records: M. Jonzun and M. Starr. Intrigued, he dug a little deeper and uncovered Maurice Starr's solo albums in a nearby record bin. He finally chose the Jonzun Crew album, but Starr's name stuck with him. Donnie reflects, "It's like *Willy Wonka*. I found the golden ticket, except the contest hadn't started yet."

Donnie received his first introduction to the eccentric producer upon arriving at Maurice's Roxbury home for the audition with his brother Mark and a couple of friends. "Maurice came in looking homeless. He had a ripped up T-shirt, a beanie on in the middle of summer, with holes in it, and little braids sticking out. And he was using a broomstick or a mop stick for a crutch; he had hurt his knee playing basketball or something. And his house was run-down. It was a brownstone, and the first three floors were decrepit. It was like where the Munsters lived. The top floor had a kitchen, a bedroom, and a living room, and it was nice and furnished. The rest of it was cobwebs and dust and blown-out walls, missing windows."

Donnie made two immediate first impressions on Maurice and his brother Michael Jonzun, who was also there. Donnie laughs, saying, "I lied and told him I was fifteen, because I had lied all my life and said I was one year older than I was because all the girls I liked were one year older. I even put an 8 on my birth certificate to make it 1968 instead of 1969. I actually got confused as to what age I really was. Maurice asked how old I was, and I said, 'Fifteen.'

He did the math, and I had to tell him, 'Look, I lied, man. I'm only fourteen.'"

Maurice and Michael were far more impressed when Donnie relayed the story about his Jonzun Crew record purchase the year before. "After I told them the story, they said, 'What album did you choose?' I told them I chose theirs. They were so glad because Maurice now didn't like New Edition anymore—he was fighting with them. I became Michael's instant little buddy. Suddenly these guys loved me."

After performing for Maurice, Donnie and Mark were immediately asked to join, while Donnie's other two friends were dismissed. And, thus, the nonsensically titled music group Nynuk (a meaningless name Maurice pulled out of thin air) was officially born. Though the Wahlberg brothers started going to singing lessons at Soni Jonzun's house and recording songs, the whole thing wasn't exactly the most organized endeavor. Donnie remembers, "We'd go every weekend to Maurice's house, and he would never show up. He was just out screwing around playing basketball. He wasn't focused on starting this group."

Despite Maurice's lack of focus and the general disorganization of the project, it nonetheless provided an escape for Donnie, who was in the thick of dealing with the fallout of his parents' divorce. While his dad remained in the Wahlbergs' old house, Donnie's mom moved to a different section of Dorchester, Savin Hill, with her boyfriend, effectively removing Donnie from his friends and the familiar environment of his childhood. Donnie says, "I *hated* it. I didn't have any friends there; I wanted to be at my dad's house where I grew up. I knew every inch of that neighborhood. I knew every shortcut, alley, crevice."

Because of this, Maurice's studio became a refuge for Donnie, although Mark started to drift away. Donnie says, "Mark had new friends in Savin Hill, so he didn't want to be in the studio with me. He wanted to go out and steal cars with his friends." So Donnie immersed himself in the studio and began to teach himself, even on those days when Maurice was nowhere to be found. He remembers, "I fell in love with being at the studio. I discovered the Roland 808 drum machine at Maurice's house. So I'd sit there and play with the drum machine all day. I found a Fender amp, I wired the drum machine, hooked it all up, and the next thing you know, I'm making the beats of all my favorite rap records. That was enough for me."

But for Mark, it *wasn't* enough, and soon he stopped going altogether. Although Maurice expressed some doubt about the future of Nynuk after Mark's departure, Donnie convinced the producer to stick with it. Donnie remembers, "Maurice said, 'You wanna quit or keep going?' I said, 'I wanna keep going! I'm having fun!' Maurice was like, 'All right, we'll keep going. Me and you.'"

Donnie continued showing up for rehearsals and occupying himself in the studio, even though Maurice's supervision and guidance were sporadic. "I still was skeptical of Maurice because he was just *jive*. He was full of it." Had Donnie's circumstances been different, he might well have walked away from the whole thing. However, as it was, Donnie says, "It was a perfect storm of life circumstance and opportunity. I didn't like where I slept at night, I didn't like the smell of the apartment, I didn't like the neighborhood, I didn't like the kids in the neighborhood. I was all about getting out of that neighborhood. Even though I was the only member of the group for the first year, even though Maurice wasn't around and it wasn't much of a group, *I* still wanted to be around the studio and the music. I didn't care if he didn't show up half the time. Sometimes when he did show up, I was nervous. I was like, 'I gotta sing.' I'm afraid. I might not sound good. I didn't know if I could do this. I was a little kid putting on headphones and just singing, and I was never a singer before."

This distraction during a dark time helped Donnie avoid many of the pitfalls that were so readily available to him. He says, "For me, it wasn't *if* I'm gonna steal a car, it's *when*. That's what it was like for us. And that's no reflection on our parents. My older brothers drank and smoked pot. If I bumped into one of my older brothers in the park on a Saturday night, I could get high with them if I wanted to when I was eleven. It always seemed an inevitability. But then this *thing* came along. For me it was like, 'Nah, I'm gonna go to Maurice's house.' Why? Because I'm gonna be doing the coolest stuff ever. The engineer's gonna ask me to do stuff if I go to the studio *and* Mary Alford's gonna be there, and she's gonna take me to Kentucky Fried Chicken. She's gonna take care of me—I'm gonna eat good food, I'm not gonna be scrounging for food on the street corner or going hungry. I'm gonna have fun! Me and Mary are gonna listen to music and talk about basketball on the way to the studio. That was a lot for me. That was *a lot*."

One day about a month after Mark quit the group, Donnie happened to watch *Saturday Night Live*. On that particular night, Peter Wolf, former lead singer of the J. Geils Band ("Centerfold") and a long-time high-profile figure on the Boston music scene, was the musical guest. All of a sudden Donnie noticed a familiar face onstage playing the bass: Maurice Starr. Of the moment, Donnie remembers, "I saw him, and I was like, 'Okay, this is real.' Seeing that really gave me reassurance."

Reinvigorated by Maurice's *Saturday Night Live* appearance, the next day Donnie approached his dad to inform him of his musical pursuits. "He was sitting on the couch with a Schlitz beer in his hand. This was, like, one in the afternoon—he drank beer from the moment he woke up," Donnie says. "I walked in, and I said, 'Dad, I'm gonna start a band.' And he was like, 'Yeah, yeah, okay.' And I said, 'No, Dad. This is real. This is gonna be a real band, and I'm working with this music producer. This could be something really special.' And he said, 'I'll tell you what: if you ever make it big, and you come home and you've changed, I'm gonna kick your ass.'" For Donnie, this exchange was monumental. He explains,

"That was the greatest endorsement that I've ever gotten. Knowing my old man and the way he treated us, the only response he should've had was, 'Go get a job' or 'Give me a break.' But he didn't say it. In the early going, when I was establishing who I was with fans, that always rang in my head. But, more importantly, that meant 'I believe in you.'"

For the next six months, Maurice and Donnie pressed forward, writing and recording songs. After laying down four tracks, one day Maurice turned to Donnie and said, "You gotta find some other guys now." With this, Donnie began the process of rebuilding, utilizing his schoolmates and neighborhood circle as a talent pool. He first approached Jamie Kelly, a friend of Mark's. The very same day as the audition, Maurice made Jamie the second member of Nynuk.

Driving around with Mary one day, Donnie's mind suddenly turned toward his friend Chris Knight's brothers Jordan and Jon. Donnie remembers, "At the start of tenth grade, I was driving around Dorchester with Mary Alford. She was like, 'You gotta know some white kids.' I said, 'My friend Chris Knight lives on this street, and his brothers Jordan and Jon used to sing.' So we drove up the street. They had this old Victorian house with a barn in the back. I saw the barn, and I said, 'That's their house!' I knocked on the door, but Chris wasn't home, so I called him."

Although Chris forewarned Jordan, the phone call from Donnie was still somewhat out of the blue, considering that it had been a couple of years since the two last spoke. Jordan remembers, "Donnie called me and said, 'I met this producer, Maurice Starr, who does great music. He produced New Edition and got them off the ground.'" Like most other teenagers at the time, Jordan was well aware of New Edition and the success it had attained. He says, "Everyone knew 'Candy Girl' and 'Is This the End.' I knew all about New Edition and thought they were wonderful."

In that initial conversation, Donnie made it clear to Jordan that

Nynuk had the potential to make it big. "One of Donnie's quotes was, 'This ain't no church choir. This is real. This is a pop star kind of thing—we could become famous.'" For Jordan, Donnie and Maurice's large-scale vision was in many ways more of a deterrent than an incentive to join. "I didn't jump at the opportunity, but I thought it was interesting. I'm naturally kind of a shy guy, so I wasn't like, 'What? I can be famous? Sign me up!' But I thought it would be cool to go to an audition and meet Maurice."

The day of the audition, Donnie and Mary picked up Jordan and took him to Maurice's house. Like Donnie, Jordan clearly remembers being a bit taken aback by what he saw. He says with a laugh, "It was this city house, halfway done, the construction's still going on. It was tidy, but it wasn't nice—there was makeshift things all over the place, including some of the clothes Maurice wore."

After taking a few minutes to adjust to this rather peculiar new environment, Donnie and Mary left the room to give Jordan and Maurice some privacy for the audition. Maurice played Jordan a couple of falsetto lines from songs he'd written, including "Stop It Girl" and "Be My Girl." After a couple of plays to familiarize him with the tunes, Maurice asked Jordan to sing the lines over the top. When Jordan finished, Maurice's feedback was succinct. Jordan remembers, "As I sang, he was just bobbing his head, like, 'Yeah, man.' Then he told me, 'I think you'll be good. I think you'll be good.' And, really, that's all he said."

With the rather anticlimactic singing portion of the audition out of the way, it was now time for Jordan to display his dancing chops. "We went downstairs, and Maurice had an open area next to the studio that was halfway done, halfway not done. There was a space where I could dance, so I did some dancing—break dancing, stuff like that." Shortly after, Jordan says, "Maurice was like, 'You got it, man! You're in the group.' That was that."

Once Jordan joined Nynuk, the puzzle pieces fell together

quickly—beginning with Jon, who says, "When Jordan came home and started talking about Nynuk, that's what spurred me to go join the group. I remember the first thing was, 'No! You're not leaving me. You can't do something without me!'"

Shortly after, Jon went to meet Maurice for the first time, although he says what occurred that day wasn't really an audition. "It's so weird how fate is," Jon muses, "because if Maurice wasn't so jive and laid-back, this never would have happened. Any other producer would've been like, 'No, you're not good enough to be in this group.' He's so cocky that if somebody came in and was totally tone deaf, they would've made it. I think Maurice had a vision, but I also think his cockiness was such that he figured he could make anybody anything. Whatever vision he had, he thought he could make you into that."

Although Donnie had already approached Danny about joining Nynuk multiple times to no avail, once Jordan and Jon entered the mix, Danny finally decided to throw his hat into the ring. "When the auditions for the group came up, I remember Donnie coming to me and asking me to try out. I was like, 'I haven't sung in so long, dude, I have no idea what you're talking about.' Donnie kinda had to come at me two or three times. Finally, he told me he had Jordan in the group and Jon was coming to audition the next day. And I was like, 'All right, I'll go.' I finally went, and my singing was obviously a little rusty, but when Maurice saw me break-dance, he was like, 'All right, we gotta have him.'"

With five slots now filled, it was time to get down to business. The group began meeting after school, with rehearsals held alternately at Dorchester's Lee Elementary School and in the basement of the Knights' home. Danny remembers the intensity of taking those first paces down the long road ahead of them. "Working with Maurice was kind of like boot camp. We rehearsed at a place called Lee School, which was in a really rough neighborhood of Dorchester, and we were the only white kids there. They used to call us 'the crazy white boys.' We'd come in there and act like we owned the place. We were around a lot of really good dancers and singing groups and really talented people."

Even though the group was officially together, not all members were fully committed to the project. Jordan admits that even after joining, "I wasn't incredibly keen on it. I was still wondering, 'Do I really want to be famous?' I didn't really want to be famous. But my mom kinda talked me into going to rehearsals. I skipped one of the rehearsals, and my foot was halfway in and halfway out, and my mom said, 'You should definitely go for it. Do it!' After that, I started going to more."

Marlene remembers encouraging Jordan to commit to Nynuk. "All the boys would practice in my basement and they'd be raiding my pantry for cereal and milk, and where's Jordan? Here rehearsal is at my house—Jonathan's here, and *where is* Jordan? I would find him down at the local youth center. I remember going down there one time and almost taking him by the scruff of the neck and say-ing, 'Listen, you made a commitment to this group, you have to make a commitment to rehearsal. They're there!'"

It sounds somewhat strange to hear Jordan's concerns about being famous at that early point—after all, the band consisted of not much more than an eccentric personality like Maurice and a group of scrappy kids. But according to Jordan, there was never any doubt in his mind that he was making a decision to do much more than participate in a run-of-the-mill after-school project. "Fame was the end goal, and I believed Maurice right from the start. Even though he lived in kind of a run-down house in Roxbury, I felt the magic. I felt it with Maurice, and I felt it with Donnie, and I felt it as far as the music Maurice had me singing. I fell in love with it." Jon's expectations for the group were a bit more tempered. He says, "Maurice had just come off his success with New Edition, so we knew it could be something more than an after-school project, but I think initially it started as an after-school thing for us. Jordan and all them were doing break dancing and spray painting, so this was just one other piece of that. I don't know what I was thinking back then other than that I knew it was fun."

From a parent's perspective, Marlene says she liked the band because it provided a safe place for her sons, away from the lure of the streets. "You know where they are, they're doing something productive, something they love. It was great. But, once again, there was no anticipation, no 'You gotta be great,' no 'You gotta be a star.' There was none of that on a scale that made us parents uncomfortable. The boys liked doing it, they felt like they were accomplishing something."

Nynuk's first live appearance was scheduled at a talent show at the Lee School. Jordan vividly remembers how nervous he was performing before that first audience of approximately two hundred kids. "I didn't grab my mike and go in front; I stayed behind the mike stand. Even on my lead parts."

Shortly after, Nynuk had one of its first major lessons in dealing with adversity onstage, while playing a show at the Franklin Park Kite Festival that was hosted by a local radio station. Thousands of rowdy fans packed into the park as a series of bands played. In attendance that day, Donnie's mom, Alma, remembers, "I almost had a heart attack. It was just a lot of people. A *lot* of people." As Nynuk came onstage, audience members started throwing some of the 45 records that were being handed out that day directly at the stage. "Somebody threw a record, and it cut Danny," Alma says. "It just whizzed right by him and cut him. The bodyguards are grabbing the kids off the stage and making them go in the car. Donnie kept saying, 'No! No! We're here. We're going on.'"

Of what compelled the band to get back onstage, Donnie says, "Here's the simple truth: the records was flying. The security guards dragged us offstage, and the song kept playing. The crowd was laughing because the song kept playing and the voices were on the tape *and* we were singing. The mikes were on. There was, like, ten thousand people. But my classmate, Cristin, who I'd been going to school with since first grade, was standing dead center in the front row looking at me. And Danny knew her too. The minute they pulled me offstage, all I thought was, 'Cristin's gonna tell everyone in school what happened. I can't let this happen.' And I ducked under the security guard, and I ran back onstage, and I looked back and said, 'Come on!' and all the other guys came back onstage."

Alma vividly remembers watching the crowd turn around once the guys reemerged and continued performing. "They all started clapping and yelling for them. I got in the car after and said, 'That was the best thing you ever could've done.' As scared as I was, that was the right thing to do, and I knew it. Believe me, it took courage on their part."

The group's collective willingness to fight for acceptance set it apart from the pack. Donnie explains, "In those times when race relations were so tense in Boston, you couldn't drop another white kid in Franklin Park at the Kite Festival and expect them to perform in front of ten thousand black people. They would've ran. We were like, 'This is awesome.' We *loved* it. We thrived on it. And it felt natural to us—it wouldn't have been natural to other white kids. Going back onstage was simply about us believing in ourselves and wanting to stand our ground. In retrospect, it was probably one of the moments that taught us we could overcome any challenge. It certainly endeared us to a community that could have easily disregarded us. In the climate of the eighties, that was no small feat."

After just a few performances, it became clear that Jamie was not fully committed to Nynuk. Jon says, "He was just conflicted. He didn't stick around long enough to wait it out." Rather than having Donnie identify a new member through his circle of acquaintances, this time Maurice decided to take a new approach and incorporate a boy younger than the already existing band members. Although the members of Nynuk auditioned a few younger kids on their own, they couldn't find someone both they and Maurice agreed on. Simultaneously, Mary kept her ear to the ground, expanding her search beyond the confines of Dorchester and contacting schools throughout Boston in hopes of obtaining a lead.

The search was officially on for the fifth and final New Kid.

Cruising from Kabul

While deployed in Afghanistan in 2009, soldier Robert Smith received an email from his wife, Amber, a longtime NKOTB fan. Stationed in Germany at the time, she found out that Jordan was running a contest for European fans to win a trip to see NKOTB in Chicago. To win, fans had to answer a list of questions. Amber was hoping Robert could help her with some of them. In a hurry because of an upcoming three-day mission, Robert decided it would be quicker to just submit his own entry.

Robert remembers, "One of the questions was, 'Why do you deserve this trip?' I wrote that my wife deserved it because the life of an army wife is sometimes more difficult than that of a soldier. Here I was in Afghanistan while she was living alone in a foreign country." Robert sent the email and went on his mission. When he returned, he found an email from Jordan. Assuming it was an auto response for the contest, he didn't open it immediately.

Once Robert did read the email, he realized it wasn't a template message at all. "It was a personal email from Jordan saying that he was not going to send us to Chicago because we were not European, but the guys wanted to do something for us. I thought, 'Hey, a free CD or something—great!'" Robert was wrong again. "About two weeks later," he says, "Jordan announced that the guys were bringing us on the annual NKOTB cruise free of charge!"

This cruise meant a lot to the Smiths. Robert explains, "It had been a difficult deployment for both of us. I was not with my regular unit and did not have any close friends I felt I could depend on. As a result, we were both suffering difficult times, but the cruise gave us just the lift we needed to finish the deployment."

Prior to the cruise, Amber sent Robert five flags. He carried each one on his body armor on a mission, then flew them over his headquarters in Kabul. The couple hoped to give each of the guys a flag as a token of gratitude on the boat. Robert says, "Our chance came after the concert on the ship when we met Jordan and Joey and gave them the flags. Then they took us downstairs to meet Danny, Jon, and Donnie. That moment made the cruise for both of us. The guys were all great, and I will be forever in debt to them for helping us through a tough time."

We're the New Kids on the Block . . .

Oh shit! We're on the radio.

—Jordan

Though just a few miles apart, Jamaica Plain (JP) was significantly more genteel than Dorchester. Joe McIntyre remembers
the Jamaica Plain of his childhood as "this amazing neighborhood. It was the seventies and eighties, and everything was very
blissfully normal." The youngest of nine and one of only two
sons, Joe was raised in a lively household. As the last of so many
children, Joe says, "I've always been quote-unquote special. After
nine kids, my father actually had time to come up for air, so of
course the last one is going to get a little bit more attention. And
my family always pointed that out." Looking back on his childhood with the McIntyre brood, Joe says, "I had a blast, and it
was so much fun. I grew up in a family that loved to entertain,
loved to joke around. Sarcasm was our greatest weapon, and that
played out in theater."

Residing just four blocks away from the Footlight Club (the
oldest community theater in America), the McIntyre kids and

Joe's mom frequently took the stage. During these family-affair performances, Joe's dad served as the troupe's biggest fan. Joe remembers, "My dad loved it—he would always do fund-raisers for the bricklayers union there. He was never involved but would always sit in the back with the biggest smile in the world, watching his kids and wife perform." So it was that a love of theater and performance was already deeply ingrained in Joe by the time he was twelve. "It's everything to me, whether you're doing Shakespeare or George M. Cohan or New Kids on the Block."

Music and performance of a more pickup variety was a part of life for Joe's family offstage too. Tom McIntyre remembers, "We had a beach wagon in those days. We'd hop in there, all of us. Today you'd be arrested because of seat belts and all that. We did that shtick with Nat Cole and Sinatra and Tony Bennett. Joe was weaned on that kind of stuff." Before Mary Alford's search led her to this Jamaica Plain theater kid, Joe was living the life of a typical middle-class twelve-year-old. If he wasn't in school or onstage with his family at the Footlight Club, he was performing with the Neighborhood Children's Theatre of Boston or hanging out with his friends.

When Mary began calling around schools in search of white kids who could sing and dance, Joe's name came up repeatedly. But initially, Joe was not enthused. "I remember getting Mary's number, and I was like, 'Yeah, whatever,' and didn't think of it, didn't want to call."

Despite Joe's ambivalence, Mary persisted. The difference was that in her second attempt, she dangled Maurice's previous involvement with New Edition in front of Joe. That did the trick. "New Edition was my favorite group; that was the music we listened to," Joe says. "I always say I'm different than the other New Kids because I grew up in Jamaica Plain, and they grew up in Dorchester. But I grew up with a lot of soul. I grew up with seven sisters who had a lot of soul and wanted to dance in the kitchen.

They were into disco and soul music and Elton John and the Gap Band and all that stuff. So New Edition was right up my alley."

On Father's Day 1985 Joe auditioned at Maurice's. (A happy coincidence, since, as Joe puts it, "It was quite a gift for my father because there's no bigger New Kids fan than him—he just thinks it's the most marvelous thing in the world.") "I went up to the third floor, and there Maurice was, a big bear. His place was kinda kooky-looking, but he was nice. He asked me to sing a song, and I sang a Nat King Cole song, 'L-O-V-E.' I brought a buddy of mine to the audition too, but they were never really interested in him. He was a very talented kid, but just not the *right* kid." As with the other members of Nynuk, Joe was immediately and unceremoniously brought into the fold. "It was like, 'Yeah, all right,'" Joe remembers of Maurice's response. "I sang nice enough, I was twelve years old. I think part of it was probably Maurice's ego going, 'Yeah, I can work with this guy. I can make him a star.'"

Joe doesn't remember the first time he met his bandmates because, as he puts it, "I guess it was too wild." His second gathering with the guys was more memorable. Just a week after his audition, Mary picked up Joe with the four other guys in tow. Joe laughs and says, "Danny always says I was in the front seat of Mary's car, and I would peek over. Like, I'd literally turn around to look and check everybody out, which makes sense as a little kid." Of the five members, there's no doubt that Joe was the kid. Not only was he younger than the others, but he was also much smaller. As Joe puts it, "I was twelve going on eight. I was twelve years old, but I was a *little* twelve years old."

With a three-year age gap between Joe and the next youngest member of Nynuk (Jordan), it was often difficult for the four teenagers to relate to the new guy. According to Jon, "We were talking about the olden days recently, and Joe said that he questioned it a lot. 'What am I doing here?' Just because we were so rough with him. Poor guy. But he persevered, and it paid off. It's crazy:

he was twelve, and I was seventeen. Joe went through a lot in the beginning because he was so young. I think we beat him up—not physically, but emotionally. We were not really too nice to him." Remembering Joe's entry into the group, Jordan says, "Honestly, Joe was always the outsider, and he had a rough time. He was tiny. *Tiny*. And from another part of town too, so he was just a total outsider."

While Joe concedes that in some ways he was "being thrown to the wolves," in other ways it was exciting to be around something so new and different. The way he remembers it, "I was going to a neighborhood where I didn't know any of the people. Dorchester definitely had a different vibe. JP was much more tranquil and congenial than Dorchester was. When you grow up in Boston, you have these ideas like, 'Fuck Dorchester!' 'Fuck Southie!' This was before political correctness, so you can understand the racial undertones of everything. Jamaica Plain was 'Jamaica Spain' because there was a lot of Spanish people there, and so on and so forth. All these stigmas before we knew how to quote-unquote work it out. And so for me to go to Dorchester, that was different. It was wonderful; it was exciting. And, listen, I grew up in a household that was, thankfully, not racist and not prejudiced. So I had that open-mindedness. It's just that I wasn't used to Dorchester."

There was also a bit of additional awkwardness because of Joe's high, prepubescent voice, which led him to assume some of the vocals previously allocated to Jordan. "Other guys would say, 'Who's this kid coming in taking the solos?' And some people got jealous," Joe remembers of the time. "But, first of all, I didn't even know who had what songs before I came in, so that was my perspective." According to Donnie, "Before Joe, it was just me and Jordan who were gonna sing all the songs. Then it became me and Joe singing a lot of the songs, and Jordan was getting bumped off records he had been singing on. So that was tricky. That didn't help Joe's cause." But, for Jordan, "I kinda kept my head down and kept going. That's *always* been my style, and it just motivates me more. I got the fact that they wanted a young kid."

According to Joe, over the years, stories of his persecution at the hands of the other New Kids have been exaggerated significantly. While it's true that he did quit the group at one point about a year after joining, the entire scenario was not as dramatic as it has been made out to be, nor was his threat to leave the band solely a result of being bullied by Donnie, also a commonly held notion. "It looked that way because Donnie and me had an argument," Joe remembers. "But, really, I was out of my comfort zone." Though, this is not to say that Joe and Donnie didn't butt heads. "I mean, it was tough," Joe says. "But not brutal. We always talk about how Donnie was tough with me, and, yeah, he was. It was that classic case of Donnie would kill anyone who ever messed with me, but he was awful to me himself. He was the one who saved me from leaving the group, but he was also the one who made me want to leave the group."

Although it took awhile for Joe to mesh with the rest of the guys, Donnie believes it was right around the time he attempted to quit the group that things began clicking into place. Donnie says, "I guess I never thought Joe would leave the group, so I didn't have to think about it until he was wanting to leave. I was only fifteen or sixteen myself at the time; there was no manual to tell me what to do. The little kid was gonna quit, and it was our fault. I told him the truth. I told him, 'You have to get out there and take over. You have to *wow* these people. Every time you go out there, you have to go for it. Don't just stay and be what you are now. Stay and be better. Stay and be the best. Stay and steal the show from us.' I don't think I would've said that to him had we not been pressed to the point of him leaving. He was leaving, and I know I probably felt like a good part of it was my fault. Sometimes life is like that: you don't know what you got till it's gone. Well, Joe wasn't gone yet, but I knew he was going."

Most of all, though, what Joe received was a lot of good old-fashioned razzing at the hands of the older kids, who would summon him out to Dorchester for rehearsals, then leave him waiting for hours on end or give him a hard time when he flubbed dance moves at practice. "I *was* good at learning choreography, so I would learn it at least as fast as everyone else," Joe explains. "It was competitive, and I did take some hits, and they would focus on me more if I messed up because I didn't usually. There was that natural instinct to kind of keep me down to size, but it wasn't constant." This is not to say that Joe didn't hold his own. According to Donnie, "Look, don't get me wrong. Joe was a fresh little wise guy too. He wasn't no innocent little baby. He had a big mouth, and he knew how to antagonize us. *A lot.* So it wasn't just us; we definitely started it all the time, but he was a wise guy."

Those early days of Nynuk consisted of a mixture of rehearsals, low-key (and sometimes offbeat) gigs, and recording. A lot of time was spent in the car as Mary (or "M. Lou," as they called her) shuffled them from one place to the next. Joe says, "The existence of the group was Mary picking us up, driving us around, taking us to rehearsal, and learning the steps for the show." Those car rides were an adventure in and of themselves. Joe remembers, "Somehow we fit in a two-door Mustang—six of us. I was always sitting on someone's lap."

"It was really great for us," Jordan says of that period. "We all fell in love with it, and we were just gung-ho and crazy for it." Ostensibly, the focus and time commitment also helped prevent the guys from falling into some of the more negative patterns their peers were privy to. Looking back, Jordan says, "That's another incredible reason why the New Kids is so special to me, because I had something to grab on to at a young age. By age fourteen, it was like: here's my trajectory, here's my clear path. Most kids at fourteen, they get lost in the shuffle. They don't know what they're gonna do. From a young age, I was pulled out of all that, pulled out of the muck, and set on my way. It really changed my life, big-time."

It certainly wasn't all work and no play. Though the group has become known for its work ethic, Joe explains that there was definitely a healthy dose of fun and games back in those early rehearsals of 1985 through 1986. "We would work hard when we needed to," Joe says. But at that point, it was also quite easy for the guys to balance school and Nynuk. According to Joe, "It was very doable to do school and do this. It wasn't like I was on some sitcom and had to do school at the same time. It didn't have that look at all."

In terms of time management, Joe says that the biggest issue was certain members' lack of it. In particular, Joe remembers one incident where he was summoned out to Dorchester for rehearsal. This time Mary couldn't pick him up, so Joe was left to his own devices, making his way from Jamaica Plain to Dorchester on an unfamiliar subway route. "It was sort of a challenge, those bastards," he remembers. "They were like, 'Yo, we need to rehearse, and Mary can't be here, so just take the train, man.' I was like, 'All right, cool,' and I took the challenge. The Orange line is one thing—I knew the Orange line like the back of my hand, but I had to take the *Red* line." After taking the train in the wrong direction and being forced to make an embarrassing phone call to his band-mates to get back on track, Joe finally arrived at the correct train station and then walked through Dorchester to the Knights' house, where Nynuk was allegedly rehearsing that day. "And, of course, we don't rehearse for four hours," Joe remembers, laughing. "There probably wasn't even a rehearsal at all that day!"

Generally speaking, Joe found himself in a fairly constant state of waiting. "That's the other thing that would *piss . . . me . . . off*, is waiting. They messed me up with the waiting thing," Joe says. As opposed to Joe's and Danny's more punctual habits, Jordan and Donnie would often be late for practice simply because they were busy being typical teenagers. Joe remembers, "I would sit there, and they'd be *so* late. And you can't blame Mary—she was late because Jordan and Donnie would be playing basketball and want to play one more game. They didn't care that I was sitting on my curb, waiting for them to come. Then once we got to rehearsal, we wouldn't even always rehearse—everyone would just be messing around. They were teenagers, so there was girls, there was basketball, there was hanging out." According to Joe, there was no way of remedying this situation, either. "Laid-back doesn't even begin to describe Jordan. He's so cool that you can't really get him to take the bait. He's not gonna care if you get mad at him about being late. Me and Danny were always on time, but Donnie, Jordan, and Jon—forget about it."

Although Mary served as the day-to-day manager, now that the full band was intact, Maurice was more reliable and consistent. In addition to being in the studio with the guys, he was often at the center of all the fun as well. "He was our friend," Donnie says. "That's probably one of the reasons we held it together, because there were times when we weren't doing anything. Maurice had a car, and me, Danny, and Jordan *loved* being with Maurice. He would take us to play basketball in the park, and he knew where the good games were. We'd be three crazy white kids playing basketball in some crazy-ass neighborhood. That would get us through the times when nothing was going on."

Of Maurice's demeanor and the environment he created for the young boys, Marlene Putman says, "He was full of life, that one. He was bigger than life. There were people coming and going from his place all the time—it was like Grand Central Station. There'd be this one over here working on some musical instrument, that one over there singing. I remember going there for the first time and just meeting this big hulk of a guy. I'm like, it doesn't seem like this man and this place are gonna propel these boys to stardom. He'd say, 'They're gonna be the biggest thing in the world.' *Okay*, Maurice, in your under-construction home.

"But, you know," Marlene continues, "you'd talk to him, and underneath the bravado was a very, very loving man. And shy—I found him to be shy. Just very giving and very talented. The boys started coming home and saying, 'Maurice says this, Maurice says that.' I told him once, 'Maurice, if you mess my guys up, if you hurt my sons, if you get them thinking they're gonna fly, and they come crashing down, I'll come and get you.'"

Along with Marlene, all of the New Kids' parents were in contact with one another (and Maurice and Mary) to keep an eye on what their sons were up to. Tom McIntyre remembers, "We met with the other folks over at Betty Wood's house. Betty was as fine a lady as ever came down the pike. She was just delightful; both feet on the ground, really, really indeed the epitome of stability and caring without being overbearing about it."

The end game of all of this was, of course, to better their performance and begin garnering some grassroots attention and recognition. The New Kids played any gig they could land, and each appearance they booked drove them to practice even harder. "The good thing about us is we set up shows," says Jordan. "Regardless of what sort of shows they were, we had shows scheduled, so we always were focused on that next show. Each show, we had something new to do that we were excited about. We *wanted* to be in rehearsal. It wasn't like you see today with all these Svengali-type producers at their compound and all those stupid things. We had a show schedule, and we would be talking and scheming and excited about doing new stuff in the show, no matter how small-scale it was. We were in it."

Some of these shows occurred at unlikely places, including everywhere from retirement homes to a jail where one of Donnie's brothers was incarcerated at one time. The group was clever enough to adapt to each audience it played by pulling little tricks out of its sleeves when necessary, such as tossing cigarettes out to the crowd of inmates. Of the decision to throw out cigarettes to win over their rough audience, Donnie says, "I just knew prisoners loved cigarettes, and I also figured it's the only way we wouldn't get humiliated. When we threw those packs of cigarettes out, that's it. We were *heroes*. The whole prison was going crazy. Any movie you've seen with a prison or, like, Marilyn Monroe singing at the USO, it was like that. Except we were boys singing at a man's prison."

Around that same time, the guys played an intimate show in a far less hostile environment: at Jon and Jordan's nephew Matthew's second birthday party. Marlene recalls, "We have all that on video, and it's just *hilarious*. Jon's got the mullet, Danny and Jordan have the long, skinny rattails. We watch that now and say, 'How did we ever have the faith that group was going to do anything?' There was nothing slick about them. *Nothing*."

Then there were the more standard performances such as talent shows, community gatherings, roller skating rinks, and nightclubs. Although they didn't receive any sort of compensation for these shows, the payoff was in the form of training. "Wherever we could perform and practice our chops, we were there," Jordan says.

In those days when Nynuk had little to no financial resources to allocate toward effects, they would get creative. For example, Donnie remembers, "There was a show we did at a club called Vincent's, where we used to always play. The DJ booth was about ten feet above the stage. I said, 'I wanna jump out of the DJ booth to enter the stage that way.' And I think I talked the guys into it. I know they all thought I was crazy. They're like, 'You're stupid. This is stupid.' But it was *big*. It was all we had; we didn't have any special effects. The point is, all those choices and all those times— it wasn't Maurice making all those choices. Maurice wasn't there with us every show. He'd be there, but he didn't decide this stuff. We did."

Every show presented *some* sort of opportunity, even when there weren't inmates to win over or large precipices to jump off.

Donnie remembers, "We used to wear these blue sequined jackets with white pants, and I said, 'Let's get those Patrick Ewing Adidas sweat suits that have buttons and rip them off. We'll rip them off, and the crowd will go crazy. It's like we're stripping, but we actually have boy band outfits under it.' And it worked. We tore the house down. Those little choices would work most of the time."

Of the impact all these maneuvers had, Donnie muses, "Did that go on to help us sell a million records? No, not necessarily. But it built up our resolve. It just was always something, trying to rise to the occasion. Every show presented a new opportunity to do something new and different."

Regardless of how successful each individual show was, more than anything else, it was the guys' willingness to actually show up and play that set them apart from the pack. According to Donnie, "The truth is, we were the only five people you were gonna find who dared to dream such a scenario could even happen. There was no white kids thinking like that. There was no white kids rapping and break-dancing and aspiring to be actors or singers or *anything*. It was just us. We kept showing up to the fight. It worked because Maurice was a black guy; he only knew how to get us gigs in black neighborhoods. We had gone to Roxbury for school on the school busses, so we all felt comfortable in that environment. No one else would do that."

Crowd reception varied from one gig to the next. According to Jon, "This city was very divided racially twenty years ago. If we went into certain environments, we were hated no matter what just because we were white. It was either, 'We hate you because you're white' or 'You guys are amazing for white kids.'" For the most part, though, performing was fun. Jon remembers, "We were Boston quasi-celebrities because we were always doing talent shows, and everyone knew Maurice." There were moments when the guys started to feel as though they were making progress. Danny says, "When you see the crowd reaction, and it's an all-black crowd, and there's five white boys up there, you start to think, 'Maybe we got something.' As that went on, the feeling got stronger."

Tom McIntyre remembers seeing the New Kids play one of these early shows. "The first show we saw was at the William School down on Blue Hill Avenue. It was a housing project. The only Irish in the joint was Alma, myself, and Betty. And out they came. They got a big hand, but it was nothing. But Alma, she never had an ounce of doubt. Never. To her, the whole thing was 'They're the greatest.'"

Alma *did* know the guys were on to something special from the very beginning. She laughs, remembering, "I figured everyone in Massachusetts is gonna know who they are. They're gonna be famous. But when I said famous, I meant everyone in Boston's gonna know who they are. I didn't mean the whole world, for God's sake. And I used to say, 'It's not that they're the greatest singers. There's just something about *them*. They're great performers.' There was always something about them, whatever it is." Marlene Putman saw this same quality in the five guys but explains it in a different way: "A spiritual choir without singing gospel, that's what they are," she says.

Nynuk recorded demo tracks at Mission Control Studio, owned by Maurice's brother Michael and located near Boston's Copley Square. Joe has fond memories of recording those early tracks. "It was *really* cool. You go into the studio, and it would be dark and cozy and air-conditioned, and you'd get to get McDonald's and watch TV or play video games, read *Billboard* magazine. We were working on the record, and I remember Run-DMC was huge at the time. They were on the back of the cover of *Billboard* magazine, like double platinum after a month."

Jordan, too, was enamored with the whole recording process. He says, "By the time we got into the studio, I was hooked. That's where the music was, and I saw Maurice play the keyboard and make music. I was really taken aback by the whole process."

Joe loved working in the studio with Maurice. "I remember being a kid and going into these dark, cool-looking studios, and Maurice would be there. We loved Maurice, you know? This was *long* before the days of him putting on a general suit and making an ass of himself. This was a guy who mortgaged his house to make it happen. This was just a guy who liked to play basketball with us, and laugh about girls, and laugh about our stories. But he was a very soft-spoken guy. *Very* soft spoken, very sweet, and very gentle as a producer. *Never, ever* would he think, 'Oh, I'm gonna get this line out of you by scolding you or saying "That's not good enough,"' which might work for some people. That was not his MO." Looking back, Joe recognizes the importance of the kind manner in which Maurice handled the band. "There was a lot of vulnerability in the studio. Not everybody was born singers. And even if they were, they didn't have the experience. There was a lot of 'What is this all about?'"

For as flighty as Maurice could be at times, there's no doubt in Donnie's mind that Maurice was invested in the group. "He did other projects, but that was just to get by. We were his everything. Now, that said, he was the kind of guy who would only give half of his time even to his everything because he was a very unfocused individual. He was probably our first experience with something like ADD—he had it bad."

With many of the tracks that would ultimately be included on the group's debut album in hand, Maurice searched for a record label to represent Nynuk. After a string of rejections, the five guys found themselves in the New York office of CBS Records's black music division. Joe remembers, "We went in for an interview, we all walk into a meeting there, which was hilarious because it was five kids stuffed into an office at the CBS building. Ruben Rodriguez, vice president of black music, got his shoes shined while we were doing the interview."

Although Rodriguez may have been distracted during his initial meeting with Nynuk, in January 1986 the band nonetheless inked a deal with the black division of CBS Records. Upon hearing the album, CBS suggested that the group's name be changed from Nynuk—a name the band members hated anyway—to the title of one of the album tracks: "New Kids on the Block."

The songs featured on this eponymous debut album were a combination of bubblegum pop ("Angel," "Popsicle," and "Stop It Girl"), lightweight rap ("New Kids on the Block" and "Are You Down?"), and ballads ("Be My Girl" and "I Wanna Be Loved by You"), with the subject of puppy love serving as the topic du jour. The album also included a cover of the Delfonics' 1970 soul hit "Didn't I (Blow Your Mind This Time)"—slightly retitled as "Didn't I (Blow Your Mind)"—which highlighted Jordan's falsetto, and closed with "Don't Give Up on Me," featuring local soul-R&B singer Phaedra Butler's mature voice juxtaposed with Joe's much younger one. Although Maurice was the primary writer of this album, Donnie served (and was credited) as a cowriter on the tracks "New Kids on the Block" and "Are You Down?" The lead vocals were split mostly between Joe and Donnie, with Jordan's falsetto often bringing home tracks, and Danny and Jon singing primarily backup.

In April 1986 the ballad "Be My Girl" was released as the group's first single. Joe laughs, remembering Danny's reaction to receiving the 45. "Danny has a thing where he gets really excited. Like, when something fun happens, he gets overly excited, almost like a comedian. He believes it, but it's way over the top. When he first got the 'Be My Girl' 45, Mary picked him up and gave it to him, and he was in the front seat of the car, and he flipped *over* the seat into the backseat. Because he was so athletic and a break-dancer, he could do goofy stuff like that. And he'll still do stuff like that today—you know, get really excited. He's silly like that, and fun."

Jordan remembers the milestone moment of hearing "Be My Girl" on the radio for the first time. "It was amazing. It was on an

AM station I listened to all the time, WILD. It was a black station—
that's what they called it back then, which is really funny. Anyway,
the first time I heard 'Be My Girl' on the radio, I was in my living
room. Anytime you hear your song on the radio, there's a certain
sound the radio gives your song that compresses it. Just to hear the
DJ announce it, to hear that radio sound, makes it sound like a hit.
I was blown away. I was like, 'Oh shit! We're on the radio.'"

Marketing the single to these black stations was the underly-
ing game plan for NKOTB. Both Maurice and CBS wanted to sell
the group first and foremost to black audiences, both through live
performances and on the radio. And therein lies another great
misconception about NKOTB. In the years that would follow, a
big part of the group's legend would involve talk of the marketing savvy that much of the media felt its success was rooted in.
Common lore holds that the corporate decision makers behind the
band were shrewd enough to identify a gap in the marketplace for
young white girls and specifically created NKOTB to capitalize on
and fill that void. In actuality, this was not the case at all. Jordan
explains, "Maurice had so many connections in the black market,
those are the channels we were marketed through in the early
days. Even when we went to CBS, we were in the black division.
No one ever thought, 'Um, these kids are *white*. Maybe white kids
would like 'em too.' "

Maurice and CBS's plan for NKOTB didn't exactly light the
music scene on fire. Though "Be My Girl" received some airplay
in Boston and managed to eke out the number 90 spot on the
Top Black Singles chart, it fizzled quickly. The album, with a
cover image of the five boys wearing brightly colored clothing and
hanging off of a streetlamp that looked as though it belonged on
Sesame Street, was released in October 1986 to little fanfare. The
second single, "Stop It Girl," suffered a similar fate, only this sophomore 45 failed to garner NKOTB any chart presence whatsoever.

Although the album didn't create huge waves or a significant following, a small audience did discover NKOTB through this initial release. Fan Tara Slang remembers coming across the album at a Sam Goody record store and being drawn into NKOTB fandom from there. "When I saw their cassette tape staring me in the face . . . I knew I was going to love it after I saw all of those hot boys on the cover. At the time when I bought the tape, I was immediately drawn to Joe, and I have been a fan of his ever since. I took it home and popped it into my Sony Walkman—immediately I was hooked! 'Popsicle' became my new favorite song, and I played it over and over until I knew the words in reverse."

Similarly, Elma Morales remembers, "I was a nine-year-old Duran Duran fan, eagerly awaiting their new album, *Notorious*. I pestered my mom until she took me to buy it. So there I was, clutching my new Duran Duran record, when out of the corner of my eye I see Donnie's face on the cover of the New Kids' debut album. After two minutes of staring at his picture, I focused on the rest of the cover. I just remember thinking 'Oh my God, they're so cute! Especially the one in that colorful sweater!' I didn't know who they were, nor had I heard a lick of the record, but damn it! I had to have it. I managed to convince my mom to buy it for me. We get home, I run to my room, rip the plastic off the album, and put the record on the player. It was love at first sound. I memorized the lyrics to each song better than my schoolwork. It would be a full week and a half until I listened to the Duran Duran record."

Despite lackluster sales, just having a record on the market was thrilling for the guys. At that point, they were living in the moment and more concerned with having fun and honing their craft than breaking records. According to Joe, "I certainly didn't have an attachment to needing a hit record. That wasn't my mind-set. We were excited once we got signed and it was actually on wax. It was for fun." Jordan expresses a similar sentiment, saying, "I wasn't disappointed. Maybe Maurice was. Maybe Mary Alford was. But I just figured, 'We're together, and we're gonna do more music, and we're gonna keep going.'"

Although they weren't exactly tearing up the airwaves, the New Kids *were* winning over fans slowly and steadily through the exposure their weekend gigs provided. In December 1986 they took their act outside of Boston for the first time, fanning out around the area. "We started just doing random shows wherever we could. Talent shows, this, that, and the other thing," Jon remembers.

Because CBS was unwilling to front the money for NKOTB to go on tour, conditions on the road were extremely sparse. Usually, travel consisted of Jon driving the rest of the group from place to place in a jalopy that Maurice had purchased with $500 the band had earned at a show. "It was a piece of crap," Jon says. "But I was the oldest one and had my driver's license, so I was chauffeuring everyone around for rehearsal, to school, this, that, and the other thing."

Even as a relatively unknown act, the effect of five cute, young white guys onstage was not lost on audiences. Fan Nicole Nunn still remembers the excitement of stumbling upon the group in 1987. "I was eleven years old. My friends and I thought we were so cool because we were headed to Boston for a talent show to perform with our all-girl dance crew." Though NKOTB were not competing in the actual talent show, they were the evening's special guest. Nicole remembers, "The boys hit the stage, and everyone was quiet. Then Joey's voice came through the speakers, and the screams were ear piercing. I was instantly in *love*! NKOTB was dancing, singing, and they were *so cute*. On the ride home that night, we all staked our claim to a member of the group. I was a Donnie girl from day one—in fact, in twenty-four years, none of us has traded our boy for another."

Around that same time, Jennifer Scali was inadvertently introduced to NKOTB while attending a dance at Catholic Memorial High School. She remembers, "During the dance, someone came onstage to tell us that a local group from Boston would perform a few songs. My first thought was, 'My girls and I came out tonight to dance to our favorite pop tunes, and we are stuck listening to some awful band.' The music began, and out run five local guys. As they sang, a swarm of girls bolted to the stage, throwing their hands in the air and squealing uncontrollably. My friends and I were standing toward the back of the room taking it all in. I remember wanting to be at the stage with the others—I was squealing on the inside. My friends were talking, and they didn't want to move, but I was truly mesmerized by these guys."

Unfortunately, CBS Records wasn't so impressed by these smaller victories and was ready to drop NKOTB altogether after coming out of the gate with a commercial flop. Jon recalls, "It was disappointing because we put so much into it, and it seemed like things were going really good. Then it just went downhill." Of their early relationship with CBS, Joe says, "There wasn't a lot of love, and Maurice was trying to find different ways. There was talk of another label, and a deal was on the table from RCA, but they wanted to bring in other producers, and we were like, 'No, man!' I must've been thirteen or fourteen—we all sat down and talked about it." It was only when Cecil Holmes, NKOTB's A&R rep (the person responsible for identifying talent for the label and overseeing the recording process) and founder of CBS's black division (who'd also worked with acts such as Michael Jackson and the late Marvin Gaye), went to bat for the band that the record company agreed to give it a second chance.

Despite the New Kids' lukewarm reception, the early days were good days. Not only were the guys growing as performers, but they also laid the groundwork for a solid foundation of friendship. Most of all, Joe says, "It was a *fun* time; 1985 through 1986 was really not a care in the world. In many ways, I was just a puppy trailing along behind everybody, but a lot of times there was a smile on my face. I was just happy to be around everybody.

At a certain point it stopped, because I couldn't go out with them, I couldn't meet girls with them because I was much further behind at that stage of my life. But it was awesome."

For as loose and carefree as the group members could be collectively, they also learned and grew a lot during this period, even if those strides and successes weren't reflected in record sales. Looking back on the period as a whole, Joe says, "There was a lot of vulnerability. There was a lot of figuring it out: getting out onstage and figuring that stuff out. I had enough confidence when I sang and danced and performed because I had been doing the song-and-dance-man thing for a long time. Whereas Donnie and Danny could dance, and they could rap and get a party going, but they didn't come from that more traditional thing. Jordan and Jon were more like choir. We all had soul, and they had great taste in music and all that stuff, but it was like everybody coming together and figuring themselves out. That's how I see that period. But it was light, and it was fun. I think it was sweet."

Team Betty

Since his mother, Betty Wood, succumbed to breast cancer in 1999, Danny has done a lot of work to raise money for Susan G. Komen for the Cure through his Remember Betty charity. Fans have rallied around this cause through events such as the annual fan-organized Batting for Betty softball game and by forming Team Bettys at Race for the Cure walks around the world. Team Bettys consist of NKOTB fans who participate in Race for the Cure walks as a group and donate funds raised in the name of Betty Wood. Fan Abbie Vicknair was compelled to start her own Team Betty in Nashville after hearing Danny speak about his mom and Remember Betty onstage in 2009. "It really got me interested because he was so passionate about it," Abbie says.

For Abbie, who had struggled with her weight since childhood, this initial 5K was a big deal. "At that point in time, I walked a quarter of a mile and felt like I was going to pass out. By the time October came around, I walked the 5K." Invigorated by the experience, the next year, Abbie did the three-day, sixty-mile Race for the Cure walk in Boston, raising $3,100 for charity in the process. In 2011 she did six 5Ks and the Boston three-day and served as the captain of three Team Bettys.

The experience has been transformative. Abbie says, "I am a different person than I was before I started participating in Team Betty. Once you get to a certain size, you're big, but at the same time, you're invisible. This was a way I could change that. It didn't seem like it was for me, since it was benefitting others, so I didn't feel that pressure." Not only that, but Abbie has become a central force in Remember Betty, working hand-in-hand with Danny to run the website and organize international teams.

Reflecting on all that Abbie has done in the past few years, Danny says, "She's incredible. I always tell her, 'You're like an angel who came into my life.' She helped me organize Remember Betty to the point where there's an army of girls out there fighting breast cancer in tribute to my mother. It's really special." In 2011 alone Remember Betty raised over $250,000 through more than eighty teams, including international efforts in Panama, Greece, Germany, South Korea, and the Netherlands. In 2012 Komen designated Team Betty as an official national team, putting it in the same category as the teams of major corporations, including American Airlines, Ford, and Bank of America.

You Got It

We're sitting there, and all of a sudden Jordan
said, "You know we're gonna be famous, right?
We're gonna be famous." And he was right.

—Joe

Despite the underwhelming success of *New Kids on the Block*
and NKOTB's shaky standing with CBS, the band soldiered on,
continuing to rehearse and play any gig that came its way. Perhaps
most important, they stuck together, even during those sometimes long stretches of time when it seemed like nothing was
happening.

Although NKOTB's situation didn't change much on the sur-
face in the time between the recording of *New Kids on the Block*
and the *Hangin' Tough* follow-up, their mind-set certainly evolved.
When the guys reentered the recording studio in the summer of
1987, they had more experience and swagger, and a new resolve.
Joe explains, "Everybody was older now. We had the first album
under our belts. We had more attitude, we had more perspective,
and we could see the whole picture." Donnie agrees, saying, "We
were young and crazy and going through something exciting, but
this was the second time around for us. We'd already had a record
come out in 1986. We'd already had a record go to about number

eighty on the R&B charts and stall. We'd already heard our record on the radio for the first time. It was two years later, and we wanted more."

Rather than a bunch of primarily fourteen- and fifteen-year-olds, the average band age was now eighteen. Moreover, the New Kids were armed with more experience and something to prove, with their near ousting from CBS Records in recent memory. All of these factors resulted in a new sense of confidence that was reflected as soon as the recording of *Hangin' Tough* commenced. While they were still very fresh, they were no longer novices.

Joe has a distinct memory of a particularly newly resolved Jordan for the album recording sessions. According to Joe, "Everyone always says Jordan doesn't say much, but when he does, you listen; he's like E. F. Hutton or something. I was maybe fourteen, and we walked into Mission Control and were going up the elevator, and Jordan was like, 'I wanna sing, man.' Like, I wanna sing more. I'm not singing, I want to sing."

Despite that trip to Mission Control Studios, most of the recording for *Hangin' Tough* was actually done in a makeshift recording studio Maurice was in the process of building in his perennially half-finished Roxbury home. Because of this, the recording atmosphere was much less professional for NKOTB's second album than it was for the first. "It was very third-world-ish," Danny says of their new setup. "We did it in Maurice's house when he was in the middle of building the studio. So, literally, you had the soundboard and no vocal room. We all had to wear headphones. It was like, Maurice is sitting there, and I'm standing two feet away from him. There was nothing separating anything." Jordan agrees with Danny's assessment. "It was very ghetto. But very fun. There was plastic on the windows. If you solo the tracks on *Hangin' Tough*, you'll hear babies crying, you'll hear sirens, you'll hear a lotta stuff in the background."

This time around, certain members stepped forward and assumed a more hands-on role: particularly Danny, Donnie, and Jordan. Jordan explains, "We were getting into the production of music, so we gave Maurice lots of ideas. Of course, Maurice was the master of it at the time, but he was really feeding off of our ideas. He had his finger on the pulse, but we *really* had our finger on the pulse because we were high school kids. We were the target audience, and we were into music. We called ourselves the Crickets—that was our little production crew." Of their investment in the project, Donnie says, "We were like a three-headed monster; me, Danny, and Jordan. And we *all* had Maurice's trust and respect in different ways."

For these three, being a New Kid was now a full-time occupation. In the summer of 1987, Danny, Donnie, and Jordan all worked summer jobs in downtown Boston. Donnie remembers, "Danny and me worked in the Shawmut Bank building, and Jordan worked right across the street in the mailroom in some other bank building. We'd take the subway into work in the morning, we'd meet for lunch, and then we'd probably go to Maurice's house at night after that. From the summer of '87 on, we were together *all* the time. We were with Maurice, or we'd go ride around and play basketball together. We'd go try to pick up girls together. Everything we did all day was related to the group. If we weren't with Maurice, we were at his house. We were just all about it. It was the group of us, and girls, and Ping-Pong, and playing the drums and the keyboards. If Maurice wasn't doing a song with us, we'd do a song on our own. It was *constant*."

Once school started again, Danny, now at Boston University on scholarship, was diligent about attending class. However, Donnie and Jordan, both in their senior years of high school, since Donnie stayed back a year, had a somewhat different philosophy. According to Donnie, "Jordan and me started skipping school a lot. Jon would pick me up with Jordan in the car, and they'd drive me to school in the mornings. Jordan and me would just say, 'Let's don't go to school—drop us at Maurice's house.' We'd get out of the car at Maurice's house at eight in the morning, and we'd go into one of the rooms on the first floor and crash. Jordan would be on one sofa with holes and dust and spiders on it, and we'd crash for a few hours. Then we'd wake up and have nothing to do. We'd stroll upstairs around eleven and start playing Ping-Pong. Maurice would come down and say, 'Why aren't you in school?' We'd say, 'Oh, we had the day off.' We found some old parts to drum sets, and Jordan had one of Maurice's keyboards, and we set them up in the lobby, in the front room downstairs where we'd sleep. Jordan and me would have jam sessions for *hours*. Then around evening time, we'd record with Maurice." Jordan remembers those jam sessions well. "We'd play 'Push It' by Salt-N-Pepa. We'd play Eric B. & Rakim songs, and we'd just jam out for the day."

When they weren't working on the album or sleeping, band members could often be found playing on Maurice's makeshift Ping-Pong table. Jordan recalls, "Our Ping-Pong table was a piece of plywood spread across two sawhorses left over from the construction." Though it was a simple way to pass the time, these Ping-Pong games are a standout memory of the recording process for many of the band's members. "Growing up in our neighborhood, there wasn't too many houses with Ping-Pong tables in them, so it was a pretty big deal," Jon explains.

For Joe, fourteen at the time, the recording of *Hangin' Tough* was more of a weekend endeavor during the summer after eighth grade and through the beginning of his freshman year of high school. When he was recording, it was primarily at Mission Control rather than at Maurice's. Of his slightly different experience, Joe says, "They were together all the time. They were all eighteen, so I could see that from afar, but I didn't really hang out."

Even when Maurice wasn't in the studio, the New Kids were able to keep working thanks to their increasing knowledge of the technical side of the recording process. Jordan remembers, "We were in the studio banging around on the equipment. I think when you have so much fun, good stuff happens. Back then the energy was so great with us just loving what we were doing. We didn't have much, but we were in it to win it. We were very enthusiastic about the whole process."

For Danny, the attention being put into the album was making it more difficult to balance New Kids with academics. "It was obvious to me that I just couldn't study *and* do everything New Kids were doing. We'd rehearse every day after school. My grades were fine at Boston University, but it was really hard. We had gotten to the point where I felt like things were starting to happen. Although our first record had flopped, from the stuff I was hearing on the second record, I just felt like it was going to happen." When the dean told Danny he could retain his scholarship and come back at any point, he decided, "All right. I'm gonna really focus on the group and give this a real shot."

Donnie remembers, "We really *talked* to Maurice. Like, Maurice played us a song he was writing for this band the Fantini Brothers called 'Cover Girl.' There was another called 'I Need You' and another called 'Hold On.' We had only recorded a couple songs for *Hangin' Tough* at the time, and those songs stuck out in my head. I called Maurice and was like, 'Why don't you give us those songs, Maurice?' He was like, 'Oh, they're not really right for you guys.'" Ultimately, Donnie convinced Maurice to bring the songs into the NKOTB stable. Donnie explains, "Maurice was very scattered. He'd record a song with some R&B group as a favor for a friend. He had these songs with the Fantini Brothers. He had a couple of songs for us. We just were sort of staking our territory, like, 'Hey, rather than giving that song to this other band, why don't you let us have it? *We* should record it.' He'd play us a new song, and we'd say, 'Mmmm, we don't like that one as much. Maybe we need a song that sounds more like this.'"

Though the New Kids only received writing credits on one

song on *Hangin' Tough*, they were certainly part of the process. Donnie remembers, "When we did 'Hangin' Tough,' we literally set out to do a song that could be a theme song for the Celtics. That was the idea: blatantly trying to sound like Queen's 'We Will Rock You.' Maurice would be working on the beat while we're sitting there in the studio messing around, two guys go down and play Ping-Pong. Just sort of a vibe session. Maurice is doing the beat, and guys are in and out, Maurice is in and out, we're running out for Chinese food, and coming back. But we're sitting there chopping out the lyrics with him: 'Instead of using that line, swap this one in. Do this, do that.' Maurice is the composer of the song. Could we have gotten some credit and probably deserved it for a song like 'Hangin' Tough'? Yeah. Am I angry about it or anything? No. I can see how it happened. I don't think he intentionally set out to be deceptive. And, look, I can be honest: when we were doing 'Hangin' Tough,' we thought it was kinda silly. So, in fairness to Maurice, it wasn't like, 'Dude, we need our writer's credit.' Nobody really thought the song was gonna be a number one record." Ultimately, the only official writing credit the New Kids received on the album was for Danny, Donnie, and Jordan's work on "My Favorite Girl."

Also included in the *Hangin' Tough* recording sessions was "I'll Be Loving You (Forever)," a sweet ballad that features Jordan's falsetto backed by group harmonies. Jordan recalls, "Maurice gave me a copy of the demo tape to practice, and I was like, 'This song's the bomb! This is a smash.' I knew it as soon as I heard it—it was like magic." When it came time to record, Jordan says, "My girlfriend came to the studio and was in the vocal booth with me. Maurice gave her a separate pair of headphones so she could listen while I was recording. I'd record a take, then turn around and look at her, and she'd give me thumbs-up or thumbs-down. That was pretty cool."

Danny served as the engineer for "I'll Be Loving You (Forever)" and remembers taking home the recording the night they finished it. "I made a demo tape and played it for my mom. That was the only time during those days when my mom was like, 'You guys are gonna make it.'"

Then there was "Please Don't Go Girl," featuring Joe's still unchanged voice. The song was recorded on consecutive Saturdays in the B studio at Mission Control. Though "Please Don't Go Girl" would go on to play a pivotal role in the band's trajectory, when asked if he had a good feeling about the song at the time, Joe responds, "No. Not compared to the reaction and even how I feel when I listen back to it. It's so pretty—but, no."

NKOTB ultimately recorded a number of songs that would go on to be virtual anthems for their fans over the next two-plus decades, including "Please Don't Go Girl," "You Got It (The Right Stuff)," "Hangin' Tough," and "Cover Girl." Although the album featured at least one lead by every band member except for Jon, in the end, Jordan definitively proved that he was, in fact, ready to sing, just as he had declared to Joe when they began recording. Songs like "The Right Stuff," "My Favorite Girl," and "What'cha Gonna Do (About It)," originally slated to feature Donnie on lead vocal, all transferred to Jordan. Of this change, Joe muses, "Jordan didn't sing a lot on that first album. Then, suddenly, things kind of shift a bit, and he becomes our lead singer. He's singing a *lot* on *Hangin' Tough*. We say everybody sings songs, but if we had a lead singer, certainly Jordan was our lead singer."

Despite all of the hard work NKOTB put into the album, Jordan gives Maurice a lot of the credit for having a good ear. "That Maurice guy, he had something. He grew up hearing that kind of sound with the Jackson 5, and he just knew what would touch people. Back then, Maurice was like a god to me. I was like, 'This dude is a magician.' He would get on the piano or the keyboard and play songs or come up with a new song. I was witnessing something incredible." But even with all the hard work and Maurice's and the band's combined talent, Jordan still believes there is an intangible element to *Hangin' Tough* that's just as critical as anything else. "Maurice just had it. The New Kids, we *had* it. You could just feel it. It's kind of spoiled me. From a young age, I saw the magic in us and in Maurice and in the combination. I know that it's not just about recording music."

"Please Don't Go Girl" was released as *Hangin' Tough*'s lead single on April 16, 1988. The song was distributed to black stations, utilizing the same marketing strategy put in place for *New Kids on the Block*. In conjunction with the single, the band recorded a low-budget music video, which was released to BET (Black Entertainment Television). Clearly made on a very slim budget, the video featured a still very young-looking Joe holding a yellow flower and imploring a significantly older woman not to leave him, with the four other guys in tow. The video was recorded on a frigid winter day, which is apparent by the group members' red faces in the outdoor scenes. Jordan remembers, "It was torturous. I don't know why we used that footage. It was downright freezing that day; it was really bad. That video was so whack. But you gotta start somewhere."

Maurice fronted the $9,000 needed to film the video—a lot of money for him to come up with, especially, as Joe points out, nearly twenty-five years ago. "That's why I always say, Maurice leveraged everything," he says. Looking back on those low-budget days, Jordan says, "You gotta do what you gotta do until it catches on and you have more funds. We didn't have no stylist or anything like that. We just dressed ourselves. We didn't have anything."

Around that time, Joe distinctly remembers sitting near a window in a diner with Jordan in Dorchester's Fields Corner in February 1988, shortly before "Please Don't Go Girl" was released. "Our album is coming out, our nine-thousand-dollar video was gonna be on BET, and we're sitting there, and all of a sudden Jordan said, 'You know we're gonna be famous, right? We're gonna be famous.'

And he was right. He just didn't have the right setup." Though Joe nodded in response to Jordan's prediction, he wasn't sold on the notion of fame. "I was just looking for the next round of applause," Joe remembers. "I wasn't looking to be famous. I was looking for love in a corny, fucked-up way. That's what I was looking for: instant, quick, what was the next thing? Not the long-term fame."

Maurice began taking the guys on frequent weekend trips to New York City to get them in front of radio station program directors and other industry types. Jordan remembers, "Maurice would have us dance and sing anywhere. We would audition on the street, anywhere. We carried a boom box with us everywhere. We used to just move furniture out of the way and were like, 'There's our dance floor!'"

Despite these excursions to New York City, NKOTB's progress remained modest. Donnie recalls, "We opened for Brenda K. Starr at some point at a club in New York. Maurice was pressing and pressing to find opportunities for us, but we were a floundering R&B act. It wasn't really happening." On one of these excursions, Maurice had the band perform for Hal Jackson, a broadcasting legend and then-director at New York's urban WBLS radio station. Donnie remembers, "That got us the slot at the Apollo's Amateur Night."

Ask almost any member of NKOTB what his happiest or most standout memory of those earlier days was, and he will cite that first Apollo Theater appearance. Located in Harlem, the landmark theater attracted a primarily black audience that was infamous for being unforgiving, frequently driving performers offstage with their tails between their legs. Although the New Kids had played plenty of tough crowds by this point, this was an entirely new level, and it put their potential failure up for display on a very visible platform. Of the anticipation leading up to it, Donnie says, "We weren't terrified that we were white and no one was going to like us because we were white. We kinda figured when these five white kids walk out onstage, they're gonna think we'll sing like a barbershop quartet. Then we'd start dancing and going crazy. I think by that point, we were aware that it was an asset. But there in the Apollo Theater, it was like, 'We can't fail. We can't be booed. This could be the end of us.'"

Looking back on their performance of "Please Don't Go Girl" and "The Right Stuff" that night, Jon says, "I think that was the scariest show I ever did. It was just nerve wracking. We're in the middle of Harlem at this show where they're so brutal." In this day before boy bands and crossover music, the New Kids were a novelty for the Apollo crowd. Donnie remembers, "They just couldn't believe it. It was so unexpected. I always tell people, you see 'NSync and all these groups now, but back then, no one was doing it. It was us. Only us. We were pre–boy band." As a testament to the audience's wonderment, Jon remembers that in the middle of the performance, "They started shouting, 'Go, white boys! Go, white boys!' It was just like, 'What the *hell* is happening?'" Even today, nearly twenty-five years later, Jon gets visible goose bumps when talking about those moments onstage at the Apollo.

Danny remembers that night as a big turning point. "The moment for me when I knew it was going to happen was when we did the Apollo and got a standing ovation. That was pretty big. It was the Apollo, so growing up, that was everything. I never thought we'd get to play there. Plus, it has a reputation for a rough crowd. We were not expecting it. We didn't do the TV show [the syndicated *Showtime at the Apollo*], we did the real Amateur Night, which has a crowd that's even more rowdy. I remember when Joe was singing 'Please Don't Go Girl,' and the crowd stood up and gave us a standing ovation. It was amazing."

Proud father Tom McIntyre vividly remembers watching the boys perform that night. "It was a gorgeous place—really and truly. I was there with my daughter Judy, and Alma, and Marlene. We were the only Irish people there. There was a break, and I went downstairs and smoked my cigar. I said to myself as I was smoking my cigar, 'Jesus, if these guys at Amrheins [a restaurant and bar in Boston's Southie neighborhood] could see me now.' So they were last, the New Kids. That was a question mark: they had done *stuff*, but the Apollo is the first thing they did with any kind of notoriety. They knocked 'em dead. It was marvelous."

After watching from backstage as her sons took the Apollo by storm, Marlene says, "We knew. They got over the Apollo, and we were like, 'Okay, this is it. They're successful.' And the parents, we were crying, and the boys were hugging each other. It was so *emotional*. Because, you know, you didn't know if they were going to get the hook and get pulled offstage or get booed, or what was going to happen to them. I mean, this audience could've been like, 'Who do you think you are, little guys? Get the heck out of here.' But they didn't. There's an authenticity about the New Kids, I swear. The Apollo just loved them. Nobody cared they were white. They admired it."

The crowd was so enthralled with the New Kids that that first performance led to repeat appearances. Donnie remembers, "The host of Amateur Night at the Apollo for years was this famous emcee, Ralph Cooper. He came onstage and said, 'Give it up for New Kids. Can we bring 'em back again?' And the crowd started cheering. He said, 'We're gonna do something we've never done. We're gonna bring you back next week and have you perform again.' And the crowd was going crazy. We came back and performed again the next week."

By the time he got off the Apollo's stage, Jordan says, "I was crying. I was bawling." In fact, with the exception of Joe, *all* the New Kids were crying. While Joe loved the experience just as much as anyone else in the group, he believes the combination of his theater background and age made his reaction to the experience a bit different. "Don't get me wrong, I loved it. Loved it, loved it, loved it. Remember every second of it. But I grew up on the stage, so there was no difference between the audience at the

Footlight Club and the Apollo Theater. There was no difference. It was, 'Here we go. Here's the stage. Let's rock it.' I remember we went up to the dressing room, and everyone started crying, and that's a beautiful story, but that wasn't my experience. I don't know if it's because I was fifteen or because I just loved to perform, and it didn't matter where it was." This is not to say, though, that the importance of the occasion was lost on him. "The Apollo is hallowed ground," he says.

It's nights like the Apollo that Jordan believes are a true testament to the intangible element that sets NKOTB apart from the pack and truly lies at the root of their success. "Five white kids in the middle of Harlem. Do we sing the best? No. Do we dance the best? No. But what is it about us? *Why?* We were in the toughest venue for a musical act to be well received. People get booed off the stage there. I was a little freaked out to play there, but I knew even then that it's more than the singing and the dancing. I think the crowd saw our love for what we did, and they saw the respect that we were giving them in our wanting to perform well and please them."

As exciting as the Apollo was, the guys knew there was much more work to be done. Donnie says, "We were excited to be at the Apollo, but it wasn't enough. We were still happy to hear 'Please Don't Go Girl' on the radio, everything meant a lot to us, but it was different. The first time was over. We were excited but concerned. We wanted results, and the results weren't quite coming the way we wanted."

Despite all of their efforts, the single and video for "Please Don't Go Girl" failed to make big waves on black radio. Joe says, "I remember knowing we were on the black charts. And then opening up *Billboard* and seeing we were at number fifty-five." But then, he says, "We dropped off. That was it." After three weeks on the chart, by May 7, 1988, the single had topped off on *Billboard*'s R&B/Hip-Hop charts.

At this time, Jordan says, " 'Please Don't Go Girl' was headed down the wrong path," following the same trajectory as the singles from their debut album. "Again," he says, "we marketed it to black radio and debuted the video on BET. I think those were Maurice's connections, and Maurice was hustling." Which is not to say that it completely fell flat. Jordan continues, "It wasn't catching on, but it was getting a little buzz. Especially in Boston, it had a buzz." Jordan remembers that the DJ at his high school prom played "Please Don't Go Girl" and "The Right Stuff." Similarly, Donnie says, "Our friends at school would say, 'Hey, I saw your video on BET.' Our black friends knew."

This wasn't enough, though. The New Kids were in grave danger of being dropped from their label once and for all. Looking back on this quickly tanking marketing strategy in retrospect, Jordan shakes his head in disbelief. "It made no sense. Obviously we weren't going to do incredible when we're pushed on black radio. Back then it was like, 'We'll start out on black radio and then cross over.' But that is the stupidest thing I've ever heard. *Hello?* Hopefully we can cross over to *black* radio once we're on pop stations— now, *that* would be a dream. Not the other way around. But that's the backward frame of mind we were in."

That crossover (if you can call it that) came quite accidentally when Randy Kabrich, a DJ at Tampa, Florida's popular contemporary hits station Q105-FM, got his hands on "Please Don't Go Girl" and decided to give it a whirl. It turned out that the station's young white demographic liked the track so much that it became the station's number one most requested song. Had Kabrich not discovered this single, the New Kids' history might well have stopped right here. "Oh, we were done," Donnie says adamantly. Joe concurs, "It was a miracle."

Of the significant tactical shift that followed, Donnie says, "It wasn't until we stopped being an R&B group—which happened once that radio station started playing us—that the machine kicked in. The record company realized, 'Oh, we got something with these cute little white kids. We're looking in the wrong direction; we're marketing to black radio, and we need to be marketing to pop radio.'"

With this, the single began to slowly spread across more mainstream pop stations. Preteen and teenage girls nationwide discovered the single, and from there, NKOTB. Fan Amber Jones reminisces, "I will never forget hearing Joe McIntyre's beautiful soprano voice for the first time. We were riding down the road in my mother's burgundy Safari minivan. I knew instantly that I just *had* to get that cassette single!"

All of a sudden things were heating up. Jordan remembers, "We got a call saying 'Please Don't Go Girl' was taking off in Tampa and that the record label wanted to do another video for it because the first one was bad. So that's when it was like, 'This thing is going. We're on a rocket ship now.' When we got that call, it was full guns blazing. Now we have stylists. Now we have a great video. Now we're taking planes to New York City instead of driving. Everything was just bigger. You could just tell, there's money getting put behind this thing."

For the second "Please Don't Go Girl" music video, NKOTB teamed up with director Doug Nichol, who would go on to direct the next three New Kids videos as well: "The Right Stuff," "I'll Be Loving You (Forever)," and "Hangin' Tough." Looking back, Joe says, "Those first four videos were beautiful. They were a big part of branding us. They're gorgeous." The redone version of "Please Don't Go Girl" was a much sleeker production, which featured the five guys singing on a stage in an empty room, mixed in with montages of them goofing around with girls and on amusement park rides on Brooklyn's Coney Island. Joe says, "I remember that me, Jon, and Donnie somehow were picked or decided we would go on that spinning ride, where you stick to the wall and the floor drops out. It's in the video, and we were all sick to our stomachs. It just captures our youth and us having fun so beautifully."

Though this was the band's second music video, it was NKOTB's first widespread release, receiving mainstream play on platforms such as MTV and the syndicated *Friday Night Videos*. Fan Courtnay McKeal remembers, "It's 1988, I'm fourteen, and I keep hearing 'Please Don't Go Girl' on the radio. It became an instant favorite. I pictured in my mind what I thought these guys looked like, but it wasn't until I saw the video for the first time that the vision became a reality. I instantly fell in love. I had many celebrity crushes up until that point, but this feeling was different."

As "Please Don't Go Girl" was gaining more of a foothold, NKOTB found themselves at yet another spur-of-the-moment turning point: in pop singer Tiffany's dressing room at the West-bury Music Fair on Long Island, New York. At the time, Tiffany was enjoying her position as America's sweetheart, with her eponymous debut album at the top of the charts on the credit of number one hits such as "I Think We're Alone Now" and "Could've Been." Jerry Ade, a booking agent whom Maurice knew, had been in the process of trying to get the New Kids on the road. In early May 1988, Jordan remembers, "Jerry Ade hooked it up so we could say hello to Tiffany and her manager and try to get us on the show. So we went to the dressing room to say hello. Jerry introduced us, and then Maurice was like, 'Okay. You guys ready?' We pressed Play and performed for Tiffany, her friend, and her producer as they were eating dinner. Her manager was like, 'That song "The Right Stuff" is a hit.'" Having won over Tiffany and her producer, NKOTB were given the green light to open her show that very night.

Onstage later that evening, Jordan says, "We killed it. The girls went crazy. It was the perfect crowd for us." Donnie remembers, "We broke all the rules. Tiffany's production manager was like,

'Don't go out there. Don't step on this. Don't do that.' First song, I was running up the aisles, stepping on all the equipment he said not to step on. It was awesome. That theater was in the round, so we were going crazy."

Of his propensity to break the rules, Donnie says, "At that age, if there was a sign that said, 'Don't step on this,' I was gonna step on it, for sure. But it was also, 'What is it gonna take to get this crowd? Let's engage them, let's take this on.' Maybe if I could sit there and sing a virtuoso number like Jordan, I might've. But, for me, I don't want to just have the crowd looking at us; I want them to be a *part of this* with us. Some nights it was just a means of survival: this crowd's gonna kill us if we don't connect with them somehow."

It worked. In the audience that night to see Tiffany, like almost everyone else, Robyn Paganucci and her girlfriends had no idea who this last-minute opening act was. She remembers, "When NKOTB came out, everyone was like, 'Who are they?' I don't remember if we heard any music on the radio or anything before, but it was kinda like, 'Is this gonna suck?'" The audience's concerns were quickly alleviated. Robyn says, "After a couple songs, everyone was really into them. All the girls thought all five of them were cute."

NKOTB maximized the intimate theater-in-the-round setup to win over as many fans as possible. Robyn says, "I remember one of the New Kids running in the crowd. I don't know if maybe there were two. They were definitely, definitely doing what they could to engage the crowd. Looking back on it now, they definitely wanted to make a statement and for every person in the crowd that night to leave being a fan. And they were going to do whatever it took to do that." After the show that night, she says, "A lot of girls left the concert talking about them. I think everyone started to wonder who was who, because there's five of them. I think everyone at that point picked out which New Kid they thought was the cutest and was intrigued to find out what his name was, who he was. After that concert, you started hearing some of the music on the radio and were like, 'Wow, I saw them before they were even heard on the radio.'"

A couple of months later, on the evening of July 19, 1988, the five guys (along with a slim road crew) gathered outside Maurice's house, getting ready to board their single bus and embark on their first national tour as Tiffany's opening act. While Jordan and Donnie had recently finished high school, Joe was still only fifteen and in between his freshman and sophomore years.

As the guys boarded the bus, a small group of family, friends, and "fans" bid them farewell. Donnie remembers, "My mother came. My sorta-girlfriend came. A bunch of our friends came—like twenty people. It was so cool. We got on the bus, and we're on our way. Results. Progress. We were all really excited." Jordan says, "I was crying. I think it was mainly over my girlfriend. All our friends were there, and they were hugging us. We were going off on tour. There were three girls waving us off—they were fans-slash-friends-slash-neighborhood girls. They were almost kind of like fans."

According to Joe, Jordan wasn't the only one crying. "I wasn't crying, but everybody else was," he remembers. Again, Joe chalks this up to age. "That doesn't mean that I was tough," he explains. "I think it meant more to them because they were older and had more life. They were high school *seniors*. I was a freshman. There was a big difference."

Tom McIntyre remembers seeing off his son and the other New Kids: "They left in a bus that would be lucky to get to Copley Square"—an area of Boston less than a mile away from Maurice's—"let alone wherever they were going." He chuckles. As Tom recalls, his parting advice was, "I always tell Joe, 'Knock 'em on their ass.'"

Marlene Putman recalls that night as a moment of realization that big things were afoot. She recalls, "The boys went on the tour bus with care packages from the parents. We were there to say good-bye, and the bus rode off. Off they went to become famous. They were going off, as far as we were concerned, to be an opening act for Tiffany. Wasn't this great? But that was really their first big bus ride off into stardom."

Love in Action

Bobbette Miller, a Donnie girl since day one, discovered NKOTB when she was six years old. The New Kids' music went on to help Bobbette through difficult times in her young life, including the loss of her mother. "Their music is medicine to me," she says. This sentiment took a very literal turn in December 2010.

Following a series of health problems, Bobbette was informed that her kidneys were functioning at less than 10 percent, and she would need a transplant—quickly. Her best friend and fellow Blockhead, Abbie Vicknair, took to the blogosphere in an attempt to locate a living donor. The link zoomed through Twitter, ultimately making its way to Donnie. Donnie retweeted the link, with a simple plea: "Save Bobbette!"

Vanderbilt University Medical Center, in Nashville, "could not keep up," Abbie remembers. "People were calling to see if they could get tested, and they were getting the busy signal. In less than a day, we already had people getting tested." On Easter weekend Bobbette received one of the best phone calls of her life: a donor had been located!

In June 2011 Bobbette had the opportunity to meet NKOTB in person. She says, "The love and support I felt from those guys was like we had known each other for years." When Bobbette thanked Donnie, he greeted her happily and shrugged off his role. Bobbette remembers, "He said, 'I didn't do anything.' But he did. That's what I like about those guys: they don't have to have all attention on them. They're just five genuinely nice guys." As Donnie sees it, "I didn't donate my kidney. A thousand people called the hospital to donate theirs. Someone *did*."

Not only was Bobbette's transplant completed successfully in June 2011, but, as an offshoot, multiple blood, bone marrow, plasma, and organ donations were made, ultimately benefitting many other patients. When Bobbette talks about all of this, she's careful to point out that it's not her story but a collective one. "This is *our* story," she says, referring to how the Blockhead community rallied in her time of need. "Love is an action, and when it's put into action, you can move mountains, and great things happen. We *are* a family. When push comes to shove and someone needs something, we band together, and we help."

chapter

05

Five Guys, One Bus

All that stuff we never experienced in college, we experienced on the road, just the five of us.

—Jon

Getting on that rickety bus marked the dawn of a new era. As they set out for their first trip from Roxbury to Davenport, Iowa, little did the guys know they wouldn't be getting off a bus again for quite some time. For as many hours as they had logged together over the past couple of years, they now found themselves adapting to the new circumstance of living in extremely close proximity 24/7.

Donnie remembers, "We're at the age where we're just getting out of high school or just getting at the age of our senior years in high school—the years where you start to find a job and move out on your own. Joe's younger and not only the baby of the group but also the baby of a family of nine. So he's young—*a lot* younger than the rest of us. He's being forced to go through that process before it's probably time for him. It's sort of all for one and one for all. We bickered and we fought, and we didn't always get along. But we were just starting out. And it was sort of the world against us, so we *did* band together. But we also didn't have any choice: there was no option for five separate tour busses at that time."

Space on the bus was tight. Jordan remembers, "Our first bus driver, his feet were awful. They smelled so bad that our manager had to have a talk with him. That first bus was mental—it was all five of us on that same bus along with a couple bodyguards. It was jam-packed." Jordan laughs, remembering the shenanigans that sometimes ensued. "One time I was in my bunk, and I heard some rustling outside, and I poked my head out the window, and Donnie was strangling Joe. I was like, 'Oh boy, we need a new bus.' It's tough living in those close quarters, man. Good God."

Despite the fact that they weren't exactly traveling in luxury, it was still exciting to get out and see the world. Jon reminisces, "It was amazing just to be gone, leaving home. We had to have legal chaperones because we were young. As kids, me and Jordan would go to Canada with my parents, and occasionally we'd go to Florida, but that was basically all I'd ever seen. New Kids was the first time I went to New York and LA."

Although there was some money behind NKOTB by this point, they were still operating on a slim budget and had to make do as best they could. Case in point, Donnie says that on that first venture out on the road, "We didn't have a wardrobe. We got a bunch of stuff from Reebok: literally, spandex pants. We wore the best of the Reebok on opening night. Then it got bad real quick. All we had left was the spandex and stuff. Jordan and Danny liked the spandex, I think. But I had skinny legs, and I can't even imagine."

Their first show with Tiffany was in Davenport on July 21, 1988. Donnie remembers, "The truth is, as it gets close to showtime, we're like, 'What are we doing here? These people don't know any of our songs.' But we showed up, and the crowd went *bananas.* That show is a cornerstone. The crowd was insane. *Huge.* They were ready for us. Before they even announced us, it was pandemonium . . . The audience screamed like it was Beatlemania. And we were like, 'This is gonna be so great. It's gonna be like this every night.'" Donnie also quickly points out that the reason nights like this are so special is because you can't expect them. "It ended the next night, because in the next town, no one knew who we were. They sat on their hands the whole night. It was like crickets. Some nights we would win the crowd over, some nights they knew who we were, some nights a few people knew who we were, some nights everyone knew who we were. It was a potluck."

Shortly after watching the bus pull away from Maurice's, Tom McIntyre went to check out the scene on the road for himself and was pleased with what he saw. "It was right after they left Boston," he remembers. "I wanted to go see what the lay of the land was because I had no idea. You have a vision of drugs and all that kind of stuff." But instead of debauchery, Tom found a red carpet laid out for the band. "Like, catering: I never thought there would be catering and that sort of stuff. Or their own personal protection, bodyguards—you know, things like that. I just stayed for a day and came back. It was very refreshing. Tiffany was a delightful kid. She was a very, very nice lady." As impressed as Tom was, the reality of NKOTB's general accommodations was not always so first-class. On that tour, Donnie remembers, "We'd have the bad dressing room on the tour with Tiffany. They used to put four cans of soda in the sink just to bust our balls."

The guys soon came to realize that their reception in one venue versus another usually had to do with whether or not "Please Don't Go Girl" had found its way to local radio stations yet. While the guys toured, the record began ascending the *Billboard* charts, only this time it was the more mainstream Hot 100 chart. For the week of July 30, 1988, it made a big jump from number 62 to number 46, officially pushing NKOTB over to the coveted left-hand column of the chart for the first time. As the summer wore on, the single continued to climb slowly.

Despite differences in reception from place to place, generally speaking, NKOTB had finally found their niche in front of Tiffany's young, primarily female crowd. Of the typical audience on that tour, Jon says, "We're five young guys, and these girls are like, 'Oh my God! You're so cute.' It just built and built during our first tour. That was just incredible." According to Jon, it still "took awhile" from that point, but females across the nation were definitely paying attention to the five cute, energetic guys playing catchy tunes before Tiffany came onstage every night. Jon remembers, "We were relatively unknown then, but after the show, we'd walk around the venue and have people be like, 'Oh, can I get your autograph?' Those early stages, it feels good: you're like, 'Oh my God, I'm famous!'"

Jordan describes it as an electric time: "We'd done some shows where the crowd went wild before, but this was another level. This was the perfect crowd for us: young girls. And we were nutty back then. We were just balls of energy. We were ready to explode—and we did when we hit the stage. Whether it was pretty or not, we went for it. Now we're smoother and more refined, but back then we just let it *all* hang out. We were nuts, but the audience loved it."

All these years later, fan Jasmin Queen remembers clearly her accidental introduction to NKOTB at a Tiffany concert at Starwood Amphitheatre in Nashville. "I was around ten or eleven years old," she says, "and my mom took me to my first concert: Tiffany. I remember hearing that New Kids on the Block were opening for her, and I had never heard of them. When those five guys took the stage, I was in love! I remember seeing Joey's big, blue eyes. I loved their dance moves and wanted to know more about them. I don't even remember Tiffany coming out onstage, but I do remember how the five boys from Boston made me feel."

Their sometimes unpolished, boyish antics also appealed to the audience of young girls. Then eleven years old, Michele Alberts remembers seeing them play the Montgomery County Fair in Dayton, Ohio. "It was a small stage in the blazing heat. It was love at first sight! I was so taken by those five guys, listening to them sing and watching them have so much fun together. I remember Donnie and Joe sitting on the stage making farting noises into the microphones and cracking up."

It was a happy time for the band both onstage and off. Jon says, "I think that was the best—the early days, all five of us on the bus, teenagers, our first time leaving Boston. We'd get to go and play in a lot of amusement parks and stay in hotels. I think that was the equivalent of us going to college. That must be what going to college is like: getting drunk and stupid and sex. All that stuff we never experienced in college, we experienced on the road, just the five of us." Jordan has great memories of this period also. He says, "We were kids in a candy store; life was a bowl of cherries. It's just like, 'The world is ours!' It was very new and exciting. We just had a lot of fun. I remember going on the rides after the shows, sometimes walking through the park discreetly before the shows."

Donnie remembers, "A lot of Tiffany's shows were in amusement parks and I'm a roller coaster freak, so we'd perform, then go into the park and hustle our way onto the rides with our passes. We'd slip into the back and ride roller coasters all night while she was performing. It was awesome."

These amusement parks were a great venue for attendees too: the combination of rides during the afternoon followed by a performance by five cute guys and a pop sensation made for the perfect adolescent cocktail. Fan Laura Brown remembers one such afternoon at the Hershey Lake Compounce in Bristol, Connecticut. "It was my first concert ever. My parents, sister, and I spent the day in the amusement park on the rides and eating tons of food. You could feel the excitement all over the park; we were all there for the same reason, and that reason was five of the cutest boys I had ever seen! We bought general admission tickets, and I was happy as a clam just to know that I would see them. Well, I did see the concert, but I watched it from the top of a garbage can, holding on to a pole to keep me steady. In spite of having a pretty bad view of the concert, it was one of the most exciting times of my life. I floated around on a cloud for quite a while after."

In some places, there was still a shock factor too. Fan Mara Ventura remembers that her local Fresno, California, radio station had "Please Don't Go Girl" in heavy rotation that summer. "I loved the song, and every time I heard it, I would run to play it full blast and sing along. B-95 announced that the New Kids on the Block would be coming to Fresno to perform a free concert at the Fulton Mall. We did not know who they were or what they looked like; all we knew was that we loved the song and wanted to see the group. When we finally arrived, there was a crowd of people awaiting their arrival. Some people in the crowd were surprised that they were not African American; I must admit that we were also surprised. I was kind of pushed toward the area in front of Jonathan and Joe. I loved every minute of it. My favorite part was when they sang 'Please Don't Go Girl,' especially because I was right in front of Joe when he was singing. After the performance, I left wanting to see them more. It's hard to explain, but I knew from that day that they were going to be my favorite music group."

Of all the excitement at that time, Jordan says simply, "A lot happened quick." Marlene remembers hearing about all of the developments in her sons' lives from afar. "I got a phone call from the two of them. They said, 'Mom! They love us! You should hear them screaming for us.' Then they let me hear on the phone all the girls screaming for them. Holy smokes! They *do* love them. Jordan and Jon said, 'They're waiting for us. At the fairs—they're waiting for us.' That was the first time when I knew they were being successfully received out of Boston."

In October, "Please Don't Go Girl" hit number 10; all told, the single ultimately spent twenty-eight weeks on the chart. Although big things were beginning to happen for the New Kids, Danny says they remained pragmatic about their growing success. After all, he says, "It took about twenty-two weeks for 'Please Don't Go Girl' to get in the Top Ten. It was a long process. So we were excited, but we were like, 'Okay, what work do we have to do next?' And, honestly, it didn't surprise me. I loved that record—I *still* love that record."

Hangin' Tough was released on September 6, 1988, on the heels of Tiffany's tour. While the album was still firmly within the confines of the pop genre, it was much more mature than the first and better reflected the group's tastes. The album contained a mix of ballads such as "Please Don't Go Girl," "I'll Be Loving You (Forever)," and "I Remember When," and upbeat pop tunes that defied audiences not to get up and move, such as "The Right Stuff," "Cover Girl," "My Favorite Girl," and the title track. Having long since abandoned the matching outfits and cheesy Cliff Huxtable sweaters, the black-and-white cover of *Hangin' Tough* featured five guys who looked like normal teenagers riding a subway. This time, the image represented who the guys actually were, complete with casual hoodies, and jean and leather jackets. *These* were guys who young girls could relate to.

When *Hangin' Tough* debuted, NKOTB made their third appearance at the Apollo, only this time it was nationally televised on *Showtime at the Apollo*. By this point, the guys felt secure in their ability to win over the Harlem crowd. Donnie says, "In our limited concept of the world, the Apollo was familiar with us. But also, now we get to do it on TV. In our minds we were like, 'We're gonna kill it. Now we get to show the world live on TV what happened last time.' The night we taped, Al B. Sure! was there. Guy was there with Teddy Riley. Pebbles was there. We killed it and got a standing ovation on TV."

Joe remembers how thrilling and surreal it was to mingle with the big artists of the day during that taping. He says, "We were walking in the basement of the Apollo, which is like the green room. Donnie was talking with Chuck D, his hero—there he is in the basement of the Apollo talking to Chuck D. And, for me, I was walking around, and Heavy D was there and Kool Moe Dee, and all these cool rap artists that I was listening to. I walked by Heavy D, and he was like, 'Now, this dude right here can sing.'"

With the release of *Hangin' Tough*, more mainstream airplay, and some coverage in teen magazines, word of mouth about NKOTB spread amongst the tween and teen set in a grassrootsy sort of way. Fan Tami Smith says, "I remember the day I first heard New Kids on the Block back in fall 1988; I was thirteen years old. I was on the pom-pom squad at school, and we were trying to find a song for our new routine. One girl brought in this new song called 'The Right Stuff' by this new group, New Kids on the Block. At that time, I was very much into hair bands. At first I was like, 'Nooooo way—I want some Def Leppard!' But we ended up with 'The Right Stuff' as our new song. After listening to it with an open mind, it started to grow on me. Then I received my new *Bop* magazine in the mail with a picture of this new group in it. I thought, 'Hey, they're kinda cute.'"

A couple of months after *Hangin' Tough* hit stores, NKOTB released their second single, "You Got It (The Right Stuff)," on November 7, 1988, this time directly to pop and Top Forty stations. As had been the case with "Please Don't Go Girl," "The Right Stuff" was also a slow burn. It didn't hit the *Billboard* Top Forty until a couple of months later, on January 14, 1989, when it landed at number 37. It rose from there, peaking at number 3 on March 11, 1989.

With the single release came NKOTB's second wide-release music video, again directed by Doug Nichol. At that point in 1988, rock ruled the day, with bands like Guns n' Roses, Poison, Bon Jovi, and Def Leppard dominating the charts. While there *was* a pop scene, it consisted of musicians like Madonna and George Michael (with the notable exceptions of Tiffany and Debbie Gibson). Though huge acts, they weren't necessarily relatable to young teen and adolescent girls.

The high-energy black-and-white video featured the New Kids performing a tightly choreographed dance routine, interspersed with scenes of them goofing off, driving around town in a jalopy convertible, and picking up girls, ultimately culminating in a game of hide-and-seek in a New Orleans cemetery. Though the video was PG, the setting and the band members themselves had a certain urban vibe, which added a bit of edge to the catchy pop tune. Plus, the New Kids looked like they were having *fun*. And indeed they were. Joe remembers the period around the filming of this video as one of his favorite NKOTB eras. "It was just good times. We were in our prime. The lights weren't too bright. We were having fun, we had been touring for a while. Not that long, we were still in the wonder of it all. We were still singing for our supper, unabashedly," he explains.

To this day, Rhea Udtujan-Serran still remembers the moment "The Right Stuff" video appeared on the late-night television show *Friday Night Videos*. "I was like, 'Who are these guys?' The video really caught my eye. It was different than whatever else I was listening to at that time. I was into a lot of late-eighties rock, but for whatever reason, I was mesmerized by this music video of NKOTB in a cemetery, chasing these girls." For Rhea, NKOTB were the first band she felt like she could really relate to. "They were fresh and something different. I liked hard rock, but I wasn't attracted to the guys. So, of course, when I saw Jordan Knight, I was like, '*Who is this?*' I would just stare at the video. The *feeling* was different. NKOTB was more relatable to me than Whitesnake or Skid Row."

Danny looks back on the filming of "The Right Stuff" as a time of novelty and discovery for the group. "Making that video, we were very innocent. We were coming off of just having our first Top Ten record with 'Please Don't Go Girl.' We were kind of still living that life of not a lot of budget for the video, not a lot of money for styling."

Thousands of other girls like Rhea were watching that same music video over and over again, teaching themselves what would go on to become the iconic "Right Stuff" choreography. Danny says, "I had a great time shooting the video, but you never think it's gonna become this kind of iconic moment or dance. You just don't think things like that are ever gonna become this big *moment*. We were innocent kids in the music business and just really trying to have a good time and make a good video, never knowing what it was going to become."

The guys continued touring on their own that fall to support *Hangin' Tough*. Rather than singing to backing tracks, this time they took a band of musicians out on the road and did club dates, small theaters, and miscellaneous venues. Joe remembers how zoned in NKOTB were throughout that period. "When *Hangin' Tough* came out, we would get going. We were serious about it: choreographers would come in, other performers would come in and pep us up and give us motivation, and we'd be into it. We'd be focused and sharp, and it was everything to us. We were very invested at that time."

Donnie remembers that period of rehearsal as a time of excitement and happiness. "Now life was kinda fun because I'd come home from rehearsal to my little apartment with my mom and her husband, and MTV would be on. We had cable by now, and 'The Right Stuff' video would be on. Our first song was a Top Ten hit, this one's flying up the charts, the video's coming on every hour— I used to see Michael Jackson coming on every hour, now *we're* coming on every hour."

Although they put a lot of preparation into the tour and were getting a lot of buzz, NKOTB still weren't exactly sure what to expect on the road. Donnie says, "Going on that tour was uncertain, because it was just us. It could be just us and a bunch of crickets." Their fears were unfounded. From the minute their tour kicked off at a roller skating rink in Allentown, Pennsylvania, excitement followed the New Kids. Donnie says, "That first gig, it was cold, late fall, and the line was just snaking around this roller rink forever. We couldn't believe it. It was insanity."

Some shows were more insane than others. NKOTB's October 23, 1988, show at the Wilson Theater in Fresno was particularly indicative of what was to come. Fan Mara Ventura, who procured one of the $6.50 tickets, remembers the mania. "We planned on arriving early because the concert was general admission. However, when we arrived, there was already a long line of girls. We learned that some of the girls had been waiting since the morning. When the doors opened, I remember the crowd of girls rushing to the stage. During the concert, there was a lot of screaming and pushing. I remember being pushed around from side to side. I couldn't believe the madness of the girls. Still, I loved every minute of watching the guys perform."

For as crazy as it got during the show, it was even crazier after. Jordan remembers that night in Fresno as a turning point. "People always ask me, 'When did you know you were famous?' And I always say 'Fresno.' We did a theater gig there, and our bus was in the alleyway. After the show, we were on the bus, and all the fans came out and swarmed it. We couldn't go anywhere because fans were all around and rocking the bus." For Jordan, being in the rollicking bus was exciting. "It's fun," he says, "because all they want to do is hug and kiss you; it's not like they're trying to stab you or anything."

Jordan laughs. "We used to have this inside joke when we first started getting famous, and there were moments that really showed how famous we were getting. We would look at each other and say 'the Beatles?' It was like an inside joke with each other as a way of saying, 'We're getting huge.' So anytime someone said 'the Beatles?' that was a moment a thousand people were outside our bus, rocking it back and forth, or when we were trying to get through an airport, and we just couldn't because there were so many people there. Fresno might've been where that whole Beatles thing started." Things continued in that vein from there. Donnie says, "Pretty much every show on that tour was great. Some were bigger than others, but they were all packed. They were all insane. Every next thing was another moment. That's what we wanted."

Even as things around them were going crazy, the guys were tongue in cheek and able to keep it all in perspective. Jordan remembers the fun they would have during interviews and when filling out standardized questionnaire forms for teen magazines. Jordan laughs about his stock answer for the inevitable "Describe your perfect date" section. " 'Long walks on the beach.' That was my line. 'I like long, romantic walks on the beach.'"

Across the nation, newly indoctrinated fans were falling hard and fast. NKOTB seemed to have some sort of alchemical quality that generated frenzied excitement amongst adolescent and teenage girls. Fan Nanci Workman remembers her first accidental run-in with the group outside of the small Bombay Bicycle Club in Memphis with her sister, Angie, and best friend, Karen. "We saw a tour bus off the side of the road, and Angie said, 'Look, someone famous is in that club!' Me and Karen, young and clueless, had never met anyone famous. I didn't even know what a tour bus was, but I knew if my sister thought it was cool, then it *was* cool!"

Of the night, Nanci remembers, "It was cold and rainy. My sister parked the car, and we ran with our umbrella across the street up to the club. I remember thinking, 'This is so *bad!*' I was absolutely scared to death—I thought we were going to go to jail because we were thirteen, and clubs were forbidden. But I was with my sister and my best friend, and if they were going, I was going too. We got to the door, and the biggest guy I had ever seen in my life was blocking the way. We knew we were too young to get in, so we stood there, huddled together under one umbrella, and waited to see who the 'famous people' were. Very quickly, the bus door opened, and about ten guys came out and ran to the door. They were all covered up by tarps and ponchos and umbrellas. We couldn't see them at all, but as they ran by, one peeked out from the tarp and smiled at us. In all honesty, I don't know who it was, it was so dark and raining so hard.

"They went inside the club, and we could hear the music from outside," Nanci continues. "We didn't care about the rain; we just wanted to know who those guys were. It seemed like we stood outside that club getting soaked for hours, listening to the music and loving what we heard. Then the back door opened, the tarps and ponchos went back up, and the 'famous people' came running out. This time not only did they peek at us, but they stopped and said hello. I remember thinking they looked like my brother's friends, except they were so *cute*. At the time, I had no idea I was actually talking to Jordan Knight. I'll never forget him telling me how much they appreciated us standing in the rain. The butterflies in my stomach made me feel queasy and weak because a cute boy was talking to me. They told us who they were: the New Kids on the Block."

Across the nation girls began to relate these five New Kids—innocent and cute with a bit of a mischievous edge and an apparent good dose of goofiness—to guys they wanted to date. And the best part of all? There was a guy for everyone. The New Kids were broken down into archetypes. Donnie was the crazy, outgoing "bad boy." Jon was the sweet "shy one." Danny was the athletic guy next door. Jordan, the cool one with the moves. And Joe was the cute little guy. Although this collection of archetypes would come to be seen as the general "pattern" for all future boy bands, in this case, the personalities were organic happenstance.

No one embraced their personalities more than the New Kids themselves. Although they spent a lot of time learning, rehearsing, and bettering their performance skills, they received no media training whatsoever. When cameras rolled for interviews, what you saw was what you got—and that was usually five very energetic kids who liked to goof around, ham it up, and maybe even flirt a little. In fact, Jordan believes this was a large part of their appeal. "I really believe that when people watched us for the first time and saw us together hanging out like normal kids and could see that we were just having so much fun, people could be like, '*I wanna hang out with them too!* I want to be a part of that. That looks so fun!' Enthusiasm is infectious."

As the New Kids' media reach grew, more and more girls began catching on. Fan Shannon Thorne remembers discovering NKOTB while watching Nickelodeon in 1988. "I was flipping through the channels when I spotted a group of young men performing on a show called *Don't Just Sit There*. A pair of beautiful blue eyes stopped me from turning to the next channel. I was hooked. I didn't yet know who these boys were, but it wasn't long before they had taken the world by storm."

For some girls, NKOTB represented more than just five cute guys on the screen—they offered an escape and a "safe place" from childhood traumas, big and small. Fan Anna Alexander is one of those girls who found solace in the New Kids. She remembers, "Growing up in a predominantly white neighborhood and going to a Catholic school as a minority was difficult for me. I remember being made fun of, feeling like an outcast, and days when kids would crank call my home and talk nonsense. Kids were mean growing up, and I dreaded going to school every day. There is one thing that I would look forward to every day after school, and it was NKOTB. I would come home after classes and watch my VHS tape of Jon, Joey, Danny, Donnie, and Jordan in concert. I would watch the cassettes until they broke. I would dream that I was a backup singer for them and would sing and dance my sadness away."

Although the band was now playing more targeted audiences than it had a couple years before, NKOTB still sometimes found themselves battling to win over crowds. Donnie says, "I remember the guys had a meeting with me one time because we would go to these sort of hostile environments. Like, we did a car show in LA in 1988, and it was all gangbangers and us. We should've never been there. But we're there, and the crowd's just indifferent. They're not booing us, but they're not clapping for us. They're just like, 'What the hell is this?' Eventually we always would do 'Hangin' Tough,' which was written as an ode to the Boston Celtics. We're about to sing it, and I just said, 'Hey, we're the New Kids on the Block from Boston, home of the Celtics.' And I *knew* the Lakers fans would get mad. They started booing us. But I would always tee us up to get booed during the speech to get applause, then come back with a punch line that would endear us to the crowd, and we could win them back over. They would stop being indifferent, and they would remember us."

On the Wednesday before Thanksgiving 1988, fan Kristin St. John of Cape Cod, Massachusetts, got a dose of NKOTB playing to one of their more receptive crowds up close and personal. That night, the New Kids were slated to play a show in the auditorium of Barnstable High School. Kristin, then a fourteen-year-old freshman, was delighted to land an interview with the band for her on-air debut on Barnstable High School's televised news program. Kristin remembers, "I'm dying on the inside because not only is this my first time on the camera, but I'm interviewing *these guys*."

She says, "During the interview, I was trying to be so serious, and they pretty much just ran right over me. I had my notes all written out, asking them how they felt about being compared to New Edition, the Jackson 5—trying to do my best impression of Barbara Walters. And it was complete and utter chaos. They were all over the place, playing with each other. But they were sweet. Someone came up and tried to interrupt us in the middle of the interview, and I remember Donnie told them, 'Come on! She's talking to us. We'll catch you later.' Jordan was wearing some stupid clip-on hoop earring, which he got from some random chick. He was off in his own little world, not really paying attention. Joe was a peanut; he was just this adorable, itty-bitty little thing. Donnie, like he always does, was answering most of the questions. As nervous as I was, I could tell that Donnie, especially, was trying to get me to focus on him so I would calm down. Most professional reporters even now would probably get overwhelmed interviewing five people. Looking at it today, I'm impressed with how Donnie helped me out. He really brought me down so I wasn't so nervous or running around in circles. They were the nicest guys, even to a fourteen-year-old doofus like me."

In retrospect, Jordan thinks that early interviews like this one are a big part of what so endeared New Kids to audiences. "To me, that was the *beauty* of it," he says. "That's the difference between us and the groups you see on Nickelodeon and Disney. Their clothes are all pretty and beautifully matched; we were rag-tag. Back then, we were polished and wise, but we had some kind of thing in us where we knew when we could mess around and be us, and we knew when to turn it on and be a little more polished. That's how seasoned we were even then. We knew. To me, the groups that are polished now, they may be polished, but they don't have a clue at the same time."

Joe agrees with Jordan's assessment of the role their personalities and lack of pretense played in appealing to fans. "How could millions of people *not* fall in love with those guys? I mean, *really*! And I say that humbly. That's what it's about. Say what you will about our music, but the fact that we could sing even a little bit, be that personable, and that open, and that sharing, *and* sing *and* dance? That's what makes us special. Every band has their thing. But our thing was that thing that you *can't* manufacture. You can't manufacture personality, you can't manufacture dynamic, you can't manufacture openness and honesty. And that's what we had. That's magic."

The New Kids would soon have a lot more opportunities to let audiences see their antics. Things were going well as 1988 drew to a close—but it was only the tip of the iceberg.

Baby Momma Bus

In the summer of 2010, a group of eleven fans embarked on what they called the "Baby Momma Bus" (a play on Danny and Donnie's shared tour bus, which was affectionately dubbed the "Baby Daddy Bus") for a few shows of the NKOT-BSB tour. Fan Celeste Daugherty explains, "Like any group of close friends in New Kids world, we wanted to see several shows together. We love the guys, but what makes the concerts even more fun is sharing them with our friends."

En route to the Tulsa, Oklahoma, show, Donnie hopped aboard the fans' bus in the wee hours of the morning and proceeded to chat with them as they rolled down the highway. Also on the bus, Chanda King says, "He sat there and talked about pretty much anything we wanted to know. He's like an open book and very honest. A lot of people wouldn't want to sit there with nine people gawking at you like you're in a fishbowl."

Before arriving in Tulsa, the bus pulled over at a Waffle House, where Donnie treated his fellow road warriors to breakfast. Chanda says with a laugh, "Donnie was eating everyone's bacon—literally, he's eating it off of everyone's plates." Marveling at her road trip with the New Kid, Celeste says, "*Who does that?* Donnie Wahlberg does. It was a short trip in a traveling hotel, but we made such amazing memories and had such one-of-a-kind experiences. I wouldn't trade it for the world."

First Time Was a Great Time

It was the loudest, craziest screaming I had ever heard in my life.

—Katy Cole, fan

By the dawn of 1989, things were beginning to take on a life of their own. "The Right Stuff" made it to number 3 on the *Billboard* Hot 100; by March 29, the single was certified gold. On the same day, *Hangin' Tough*—which was still climbing the charts—was certified platinum. Throughout all of this, the boys remained on the road, continuing to do press, signings, and shows—only now their scope was expanding rapidly.

NKOTB made their first foray outside of North America, trekking overseas to Japan shortly after CBS was acquired by Sony (headquartered in Japan). Jordan remembers those first experiences of international travel at such a young age as "amazing. The food was a little weird, but it was just all brand-new. I was only eighteen, and being successful and famous in another country just seemed so unreal." For Joe, all of this travel required tutoring on the road, since traditional high school was impossible with the

New Kids' jammed schedule. After finishing ninth grade with As and Bs, from sophomore year on, he says, "It was more like I was going to college."

With more visibility as each day went by, fans multiplied exponentially. For a while, the New Kids' parents gathered at the Woods' home to handle correspondence with fans in an unstructured roundtable sort of way. Marlene remembers, "When the fan letters started coming, the mothers got together and would try to answer them. Then it got to the point where we'd have to send out copied letters." This correspondence happened *despite* warnings from some members of the New Kids' management team. Alma remembers, "One day [the New Kids' then manager] Dick Scott said, 'Don't answer the mail.' But you have to answer when you get these letters, right? Dick said, 'They keep writing: they're not happy just with one letter.'"

This personal correspondence—even from the parents—made a huge impact on fans. All these years later, fan Tammy Neutts remembers, "When I was thirteen, I loved Donnie so much that I wanted to send him a gift for his birthday. I wrapped it, and off it went! About three weeks later, I received a beautiful handwritten card from his mom, Alma, thanking me for the bear and rose I sent and for caring for her son so much. That made my thirteen-year-old life! To this day, I am still so touched that she took the time out to send that to me. That is why I still love Donnie and NKOTB so much: they really do love their crazy Blockheads!"

It soon became clear that a more structured fan club was necessary. According to Alma, the official fan club originated with a phone call from Danny's dad, Dan Wood, a mailman at the time. She says, "Dan called all of us and said, 'You need to come to our house and get your mail.' When we went, I was like, 'Oh my God!' It was trays and trays and trays and trays. I looked at the stacks, and almost all of them had money in them to join the fan club. I was like, 'What the heck are we gonna do? This is *out of our control*!' So we parents had a meeting and decided we would start a fan club. It got bigger and bigger and bigger, and we had to rent out an office space in Fields Corner and then hired some of our kids to run it."

As their parents held things down on the home front, NKOTB rolled on, releasing their third single, "I'll Be Loving You (Forever)," on April 10, 1989. The third consecutive video filmed by Doug Nichol, it once again featured a montage of images, including the guys singing before a hyped-up crowd in a high school gym, hanging out with a group of girls, playing a pickup ball game, and walking across New York's Williamsburg Bridge. By this point, whether they were in Manhattan or Missoula, NKOTB were causing a stir in their wake. So when they filmed a scene that featured the five of them walking across the bridge, it's no surprise that Jordan says, "I remember a lot of fans being on there with us."

This video also holds the distinction of, as Jordan puts it, "launching the Batman craze, oh God." It turns out that the "I'll Be Loving You" video would demonstrate just *how* dedicated and detail oriented NKOTB fans were becoming. Jordan opted to wear a Batman T-shirt for the performance piece of the video, for no other reason than this: "The stylist brought it, and I just gravitated toward that shirt. I liked the colors, it was cool and young, and so I wore it." From there, Jordan remembers, "*Boom!* After I wore the Batman shirt in that video, I would just get Batman shirt after Batman shirt after Batman shirt from fans. I was eighteen, and I wasn't a big shopper—I wasn't even really into fashion or anything like that. I was on the road, and people would send me Batman shirts, and I would just wake up and throw one on because I had a thousand of them. So it kind of fed off itself and became this thing. Honestly, when the *Batman* movie came out, I actually fell asleep in the theater because I didn't like it. I wasn't even really that into Batman." Batman fan or not, a hefty percentage of the images of Jordan from that period show him wearing Batman paraphernalia as a result of this innocuous wardrobe choice. Plenty of people had the opportunity to see Jordan in this T-shirt because "I'll Be Loving You" provided NKOTB with their first number one song, hitting the top of the *Billboard* Hot 100 on June 17, 1989, and spending twenty-one weeks on the chart.

NKOTB were beginning to receive other accolades as well. April 24, 1989, was deemed New Kids on the Block Day in Massachusetts. Then, in front of a screaming hometown crowd, two days later the New Kids received their first trophies, fittingly at the Boston Music Awards. That night they were awarded the Outstanding Video and R&B Song of the Year awards, both for "The Right Stuff." These awards put them in the league of fellow local high-profile award winners such as Tracy Chapman, Bobby Brown, and Aerosmith. They also went home with an endorsement from then Boston mayor Raymond Flynn, who described them as "role models for the youth of Boston."

Across the nation, NKOTB were earning a reputation as the music industry's "nice guys" because of their positive messages about equality, staying in school, and saying no to drugs. For parents, it was a relief to see their young girls latching on to role models who enforced such sound principles. Carol Carpinella, the mother of a young NKOTB fan, says, "I saw them as such a good influence at that point in her life. There were a lot of other kids getting into bad stuff at her age: drugs and other kinds of music and different things. New Kids were such a positive influence. I loved it." Of the impact this had on kids at such an impressionable age, Aimee Nadeau says, "I remember Donnie did an interview once where he said he got in a fight with this young black kid at school. He said his mom came and picked them both up, kissed him, kissed the black kid, and told them both to make up. I'll always remember that story. It stuck with me and really made an impression on me about how all people were equal. I think that's one theme people got really early on from the New Kids. And then, also, the whole positivity thing and saying no to drugs. I seriously never tried drugs. I got through my teenage years because that message was driven home. I know a lot of my friends had that same experience because Donnie was such a role model in our lives. I don't want to say more so than our parents were, but the thing is, he was someone we loved and adored and looked up to so much that we wanted to be just like him. All the positive things he was doing with his life, we adopted into our own lives. I look at Donnie almost like a father figure in my life—a big brother kind of thing, I guess."

With *Hangin' Tough* and a series of consecutive singles burning up the charts, summertime came around, and it was time to hit the road with Tiffany once again, this time in arenas. As with the previous summer, some tickets for this tour were initially sold citing New Kids as the opener and Tiffany as the headlining act. However, before the tour even commenced, it became apparent that the vast majority of concertgoers considered NKOTB to be the main event. It was decided that it was in everyone's best interest to flip the bill, with Tiffany opening for the New Kids (although the tour was officially deemed "coheadlining").

Joe vividly remembers getting a "smackdown" from Dick Scott in the course of that bill-swap conversation. He says, "We were all in a limo on the way to Jersey from New York City, I think. The topic of how the bill would be swapped came up. It was inevitable, but Dick lightly threw out the idea that Tiffany would go on and do her set, then we do a song *with* her, and then do our set. It was never gonna happen that way because we demanded a much more explosive, exciting opening of our own. Nonetheless, I shot it down as only a sixteen-year-old (slightly) loudmouth kid would: 'That's whack, Dick! We can't do that.' Well, I caught him at the wrong time—he was managing the biggest pop group in the world, and it was only the beginning. So he laid into me. 'You don't have a clue, boy. You don't know shit.' He knocked me down to size pretty good. That episode has been repeated so much between us.

It was harsh, but Dick apologized later. He was a gentle man, and, although I was a good kid, I wasn't very good at saying, 'Oh, that's something I never thought about . . . maybe.'"

Of his take on the reversal, Jon says, "Tiffany was a good sport, but it was awkward for us because she didn't have to have us on her tour but graciously said she'd love to have us open up for her. I guess business is business, and she knew it. If Tiffany wanted to keep going, that's what had to happen, and she knew it."

Fan Kristin St. John, who had seen NKOTB play her high school auditorium just a few months before, remembers the difference six months made during that period when the group was ascending rapidly. She remembers the tone of the crowd when the show came to the Cape Cod Melody Tent that summer. According to Kristin, "Half of the female population was there. It was absolute insanity, almost like parents dropping their kids off at the mall. They pulled up, you got out with your big hair, your scrunchie, and your jean jacket, and you went inside and lost your mind. I *loved* Tiffany, and she blew it out of the box. Everyone was cool with Tiffany, but it was like, 'Come on, let's wrap this up and get to New Kids.' They came out, and all hell broke loose. I mean, obviously, they weren't playing Wembley, but it was Beatles-style crazy. It was a big thing."

The craziness mounted as the New Kids made their way around the country. Vanessa Liedtka remembers the pandemonium that greeted the group when it played Six Flags Great Adventure in Jackson, New Jersey. "Security was insane. They never experienced a crowd like this before. We were walked in groups of twenty, with guards in front of us, with locked arms, and guards at the end of the line, locking arms with each other. There was a downpour, and NKOTB were two hours late. My mom asked if I wanted to leave. I said, 'No way!' Finally, after over two hours of waiting in the pouring rain, NKOTB came on. I can't even begin to describe how excited I was and didn't care that I was probably catching pneumonia. They were soaked from head to toe but put on an amazing show."

In addition to their dates with Tiffany, NKOTB also played some music festivals that summer. Fan Jamie Farkas caught one such stop at KMEL-FM's Summer Jam at Shoreline Amphitheatre, located just outside of San Francisco. She remembers, "They were one of the last acts to perform, so they were big enough to be at the end of the show, not the beginning. There was Paula Abdul, Run-DMC, Milli Vanilli—just a lot of artists that were really hot at that point in time were there." As the New Kids performed, "You could just feel the energy in the crowd," says Jamie. "It was nighttime, the crowd was loud. We had general admission lawn seats, so we went out to the amphitheatre and stood all the way back. It was far away, but you could see Donnie climb on top of the speaker, and the crowd was going crazy. It just left you hungry for more."

That summer, Donnie says, "It wasn't a *huge* tour, it wasn't a long tour. But it was crazy. We were killing it. We were savvy, but we weren't really thinking about the lighting and this, that, and the other—the production guys did it. We were just trying to adapt our show to an arena. We really weren't aware of all that was going into it. We just took our club tour and went."

At each show, the crowd went crazy when the guys played "Hangin' Tough." At that point of every performance, Donnie says, "The building would shake. Every hand was up in the air, side to side. The way it looks now is the way it looked then, but maybe crazier." With this in mind, as their record label was trying to determine which track to release as the fourth single, Donnie felt "Hangin' Tough" was the obvious choice. He explains, "I was out to lunch with Dick Scott, and he said, 'The label's fighting over what should be the next single.' I just happened to be there for that conversation; he didn't really consult us, he was just talking to me at lunch. I told him, '"Hangin' Tough."' He was like, '*Really?* They're thinking about "Cover Girl."' I said, '"Hangin' Tough" is the biggest song we have. The fans go crazy for it. It'll be a smash.'"

So it was that on July 3, 1989, "Hangin' Tough" was released as NKOTB's fourth single. This went on to earn the group its second number one hit and pushed album sales up even further, with *Hangin' Tough* reaching quadruple platinum by September. The single also nudged *Hangin' Tough* to the number one position once and for all, after a whopping fifty-five weeks on the charts. New Kids on the Block were officially the first teen group ever to have the top pop single and pop album simultaneously.

The guys began making more and more high-profile national television appearances on programs like *Good Morning America* and *Dance Party USA*. Fan Sarah Iseler says, "The moment I saw those five boys from Boston come on my TV screen, my heart stopped, and it was hard to breathe. I was hooked instantly. I played their tapes over and over. If they were on a TV show, my specially marked tape went into the VCR so I could record them. I'm surprised that tape still works, considering how many times I watched it."

Amongst these heavily watched television performances was a nationally aired Fourth of July Disney special. Katy Cole, there for the taping at Disney World, says, "The guys performed 'Hangin' Tough' and 'The Right Stuff.' We had to get there really early to ensure we would get a good spot to stand. It was raining much of the time, so they filmed off and on, from what I recall. The crowd was filled with preteen girls screaming nonstop. It was the loudest, craziest screaming I had ever heard in my life. They performed the songs several times to get the best takes for the show, which was a little weird because they would start and stop and sing the same songs over and over. But on the other hand, it was great, since they were there for a long time, and I got to hear my favorite songs all day. They were lip-syncing, which was kind of lame, but pretty common for shows at that time to use tracks.

"My favorite part was watching the guys interact with each other as they were standing around between takes. I can still picture Jordan standing off to the side of the stage taking a drink of water and Joey and Donnie goofing off wrestling around. Those moments of seeing them as real people were so cool. They were in the iconic wardrobe of Donnie's coat with the eyes on the back, Jordan in the black-and-gold-checkered vest, Danny and Jon both in collared button-down print shirts, and Joey in a puffy jacket. I was almost as excited about being in the same place with the clothes as I was about the guys being there!"

Indeed, the New Kids had many "iconic" items of eighties-era clothing, some of which fans would come to emulate. At the top of this list was a black hat with the top cut out, worn by Joe on several occasions, but most notably at the taping of the *Hangin' Tough Live* video. This Grammy-nominated live concert recording featured the New Kids' full set, taped at the Mayan Theater in Los Angeles. Of this hat, Joe says, "I wish I had a cool story of how I took my jackknife out one day during some downtime in the studio and created a piece of pop couture, but, alas, some stylist handed it to me, and I thought it was cool." Although *Hangin' Tough Live* would go on to become twelve times platinum (and, to this day, remains one of the best-selling long-form music videos of all time), Donnie's remembrance of the affair doesn't extend much beyond his wardrobe choice and the exhaustion that was already settling in. "It was annoying, is what it was. We were promised two weeks off, and it was like, 'Oh, the record company wants you to come to LA and shoot a concert video.' It was always something. Really what stays with me about it is I didn't know what to wear. I waited until the last second, and I put on that 'Homeboy' shirt and the ripped jeans and stuff. I didn't wanna wear it; I didn't mind the 'Homeboy' shirt, I guess, but I didn't like the leather jacket and shoes. Not that I was full of swag back then, but I wanted a little more swagger, and that outfit didn't have it."

Due to their fans' young ages and subsequent lack of independent financial resources, for many, this video was a precious commodity. Kelley Kent remembers, "The closest we got to the group was in our imagination as we watched the VHS tape of the *Hangin' Tough* concert. My friend was in love with Joe, I was in love with Jon, my other friend was in love with Donnie, and another with Danny. We were so convinced we were going to someday become Mrs. Wahlberg or Mrs. McIntyre."

But even watching the New Kids on VHS was an event. Fan Carrie Johnson says, "Each weekend, my best friends and I would have a slumber party. We'd cook frozen pizza, drink Mountain Dew, pull out the sofa bed, and the three of us would watch NKOTB videos the *entire* weekend. We'd take turns telling each other who we'd marry and why and how we totally deserved to be in the 'Please Don't Go Girl' video instead of those 'other' girls."

As the New Kids continued their ascent, being a fan became somewhat of an exercise in diplomacy. Fan Melissa Seiler remembers, "On the first day of eighth grade, my best friend instructed me that Jonathan was my favorite. 'He's more your type and the only one not taken.' Before we closed our lockers, she handed me the laws of being a New Kids fan: if your best friend likes Jordan, you have to choose another." For Joe, these sorts of political dynamics back then demonstrate exactly how emotionally connected fans felt to the group. He says, "I mean, girls would argue about who their favorite New Kid was. Girls would fight on the street about if she wanted to be a Jordan girl and *she* wanted to be a Jordan girl, they were gonna fight it out: 'No, *I'm* the Jordan girl, and you gotta be something else.' How can you be any more connected to something than that?"

With New Kids pandemonium settling in, Columbia was now at full attention. In August 1989 the label released "Didn't I (Blow Your Mind)" from NKOTB's previously dead-on-arrival debut album. Thanks to this single (which cracked the Top Ten), *New*

Kids on the Block was suddenly a hot album three years after its release. It reached platinum status by November 1989 and ultimately went on to become a triple-platinum seller.

Quickly on the heels of that, the New Kids dropped their third album, *Merry, Merry Christmas*, on September 19. The holiday LP, a mix of classic Christmas songs and high-energy pop and rap tunes such as "Last Night I Saw Santa Clause" and "Funky, Funky, Xmas," was recorded while the guys were on tour with Tiffany. Nonetheless, Donnie remembers it as a fulfilling, creative process. "Recording was quick, but we put a lot of effort into it. Maurice did most of the writing, but I wrote 'Funky, Funky, Xmas' and recorded it in the hotel room. Maurice wasn't even there; he set up the studio, but he left. So I cut the vocals with the guys. We all had input on it and were working out our parts. I wrote a rap for each of the guys, and they would come down, and we'd work it out together. Like, I would produce Jordan's rap, and Danny would engineer. It was so much fun." In conjunction with *Merry, Merry Christmas*, the single "This One's for the Children" was released in August 1989.

One month later, "Cover Girl" was released as the fifth and final single from *Hangin' Tough*. Not surprisingly by this point, the track made it to number 2 on the *Billboard* charts. With "Didn't I (Blow Your Mind)" and "This One's for the Children" still on the chart, NKOTB had three songs from three different albums in the Hot 100 simultaneously. Not only that, but they were the first teen act to achieve five Top Ten hits from a single album. All from a group that was virtually obsolete a little more than a year before.

As thrilling as the lightning-speed trajectory of all this was, the nonstop pace could also be tiring and stressful. The tempo actually caused Joe to miss a couple of shows due to bouts of asthma. He explains, "For me, asthma is triggered by a lack of sleep and stress, which is kind of the same thing. But I wanted to do it all. We played a show at the Melody Tent in Hyannis at Cape Cod, which was like our hometown. I was stressed out. I got down there and had to call the doctors because I had an asthma attack. I'm sixteen and exhausted. I ended up missing the show."

Maurice was far less present during this wild ride than he had been previously. Donnie says, "After that second Tiffany tour, we were kind of on our own. Maurice was gone: he was back in Boston building his record empire, being the general, and developing his next act or whatever. We sort of envied him a little because he got to be in Boston and live it up. We were heroes in our hometown, but we never got to be there. We didn't have to harass girls anymore—we could get any girls we wanted—but we couldn't be there to do it! So in some ways, we were envious of him. We wanted to see what it felt like to pick up the Boston newspaper on a random day and see our faces on the front page, but we couldn't do it."

There was always something to do—and the New Kids had more ground to cover as each day passed. Around the end of their second tour with Tiffany, manager Dick Scott encouraged the group to take part in the televised *Smash Hits* awards ceremony in Europe. The guys asked Dick why they should do the show (hosted by the magazine of the same name), seeing as how they were still an unknown commodity across the pond. Donnie remembers, "Dick said, 'Because if you have a career in Europe, you can have a career forever.' We were like, 'Okay, whatever. We got three Top Ten records in the US, Dick; what are you talking about?'"

In the end, NKOTB followed their manager's advice and performed at the awards show. Once there, Donnie says, "Backstage before the show, we're sitting there, and we're nervous. We're aware that literally millions of people are watching this. So there's nervousness, but we hide that with bravado and cockiness. We performed 'The Right Stuff,' and it was over. We walked onstage and were totally unknown; by the time we left, the whole big arena was totally turned upside down, and we were the biggest stars in

Europe." Speculating on why exactly they created such a stir, Donnie elaborates, "We were like a wave. People would see us, and it was something new, and it would just turn stuff upside down."

For Donnie, the instantaneous success in Europe is indicative of how fast and furious the ride was at that point. He says, "Literally, we went from being totally unknown to playing arenas in Europe. I know there's a lot of legwork by the record company and our management and promoters; it wasn't an overnight success for them. But that *literally* was an overnight success for us; we went from completely unknown to *ba-boom*! That *Smash Hits* awards experience is the absolute living out of the phrase 'We came, we saw, we conquered.' It's an awesome feeling."

Europe offered some relief from the pressure building back in the States. Donnie explains, "In Europe, we're free. We're across the sea. Now we can talk the way we want to talk, we can be the way we want to be. We can say 'fuck' in interviews, and no one cares. Because that's how it was over there, so we felt free to be that way. The levels of freedom were different, and we indulged in it. Nothing big, just silliness. We would just talk more openly, we would just be more candid, more crazy, more fun. We had *such* good times over there. Europe was such a revelation. And the rest of the world became that for us too. It's almost like 'What happens in Vegas stays in Vegas.' Whatever happens outside the US stays outside the US. It was all good."

Jordan agrees with Donnie that there was a bit more room to breathe in Europe, simply because of the general cultural differences between there and America. He explains, "There's something about Europe as a whole that is more liberal and open minded than America, so you can just be freer in what you say and do. My recollection of going to England for the first time is that people were more raunchy. You could say stuff like, 'Oh, I'd like to give her a good shagging,' and they'd laugh and say, 'Ah! Let's have a pint.' You didn't have to watch yourself, or so it seemed to me."

Every now and then, there were rare little windows of opportunity for the guys to go home and take a breather. Donnie remembers a particularly poignant moment when they had the chance to hang out at home and enjoy some of their success. Each of the guys had recently been provided with his own Suzuki Sidekick SUV to use for a few months in return for an in-store autograph session they'd done at a Massachusetts car dealership. Donnie smiles, remembering the night that he, Danny, Joe, and Jordan took them out for a spin together. "We went to the movies one night, the four Sidekicks on the highway. I'm standing through the roof on mine, driving like a maniac. We were maniacs."

Joyrides aside, some of the guys just craved a little taste of homegrown simplicity. But even at home, things weren't exactly the same anymore. Joe remembers one trip he made to his dad's house in 1989. "I wanted to go by my dad's house, and there were, like, sixty girls outside the house. We never drove up the driveway behind the house, but I did that day because it was the only way. I could've run people over: I wasn't going fast, but they were all *over* me. And people in my house were like, 'What are you doing here? Why did you even show up?' I only spent about five minutes there and had to go home. I'm backing out of my driveway, which can barely fit a car, and I'm driving over the sidewalk to get away."

Joe says, "I would just wanna go home and hang out with my buddies on the corner, that's it. And I had cash, you know? I'd go to the ATM and take out three hundred bucks, and take my friends to pizza or Chinese food or whatever." The cash was a revelation, too—especially for band members who'd grown up with little money to spare. Donnie says, "We would get five hundred dollars a week in our ATM account. We didn't even have time to use it. I remember one time I came home, and my ATM account had forty thousand dollars in it, and I was like, 'I'm rich!'"

In the time between the Tiffany tour and the domestic Hangin' Tough arena tour that followed, Donnie remembers receiving the first significant disbursement of cash—enough to alleviate some of the financial strain that had plagued his family for so long. He says, "Our financial manager, John Dukakis, met with me and my mom and said that we were getting $125,000. We were like, 'We need a house.' We still lived in our triple-decker apartment in Dorchester that I hated. So, me, my mother, and my brother Mark started looking for houses. My mother fell in love with this one house that was $400,000, and we only had $125,000. So I asked John Dukakis, 'Can we buy a house with this much?' Even though we were getting ready to play a sold-out arena tour, he was like, 'Nah, you don't wanna put yourself that much in debt.'"

Still, Donnie and his family were enamored. He says, "We loved this one house. It was everything we'd ever dreamed of. I didn't know what I was gonna do. Me and Mark went up in the master bedroom and walked out on the balcony and looked down on the pool. I said, 'What do you think?' He was like, 'Man, can't you see us having a party, and everyone'll be down in the pool, and we'll be like—' and then he started dancing. And I said, 'I know, but listen: if I don't make another penny, you gotta get a job, I gotta get a job, Mom's gotta get a job, and her husband's gotta keep his job. We gotta keep this house. We gotta make it work because I can't really afford it yet.' Mark said, 'Okay. Deal!' I said, 'All right. I'm gonna buy it.' And we started jumping up and down and hugging on the balcony."

Knowing that his family was taken care of, Donnie and the rest of the guys set out on their first official headlining arena tour sans Tiffany. By this point, they had enough experience under their belts to assume responsibility for production of the entire show. When it came to selecting the opening acts, Donnie says, "We just wanted every girl group on earth. We had Sweet Sensation, Cover Girls, and then this group called the Good Girls. We were like, 'More girl groups! More girl groups!'"

For many of the guys, this arena tour was the highlight of the heyday experience. It was around this time that Danny remembers beginning to feel like NKOTB had finally made it. "I just remember being in this hotel suite with our agent and our manager, and they told us it sold out in five minutes. This was like Nassau Coliseum, Boston Garden. That was a big moment." Joe remembers that era as a whirlwind of "riding scooters around, doing goofy interviews—interview after interview, but having the energy for it." For Donnie, there was very much a feeling of being on top of the world. He says, "We didn't always get along; it wasn't always perfect. But it was a *great* tour. We were selling out arenas night after night after night. It was winter, it was cold, but we'd go out to restaurants. It was an exciting time. It was our tour, and we were learning a lot more."

Best of all, though, they were all sharing the extraordinary experience. As Jordan puts it, "While we were getting famous, there was someone in the next bunk going through the same thing, and you can talk about it and let it out, bounce it back and forth. I think that's what really helped us. I think just us having each other kept our egos and insecurities from getting crazy."

Though the Hangin' Tough arena tour was much like the tour NKOTB had done with Tiffany the summer before, there were some extra elements. Donnie says, "We did a Christmas segment in the show. It was awesome. It was *so fun*. We did a bunch of Christmas songs, these blow-up things came, and it snowed onstage. That tour was so great, man." Also featured in this Christmas segment was a funny bit that included Jordan donning a Santa suit and Danny in a woman's blonde wig. From start to finish, there was a lot of high-energy fun and goofing around onstage, which was infectious for sold-out audiences across the nation.

The audience had just as much energy and good humor as the band. Fan Jen Spiliakos remembers the insane atmosphere when she saw the New Kids play Worcester Centrum in Massachusetts. "NKOTB took that stage, and it was madness all around us. My friend and I were standing on the tops of the backs of the chairs to see better, right alongside other girls our age—and a surprising amount of moms, who sang along to every word. Security tried hard to get us all to stop standing on the chairs, but have you ever witnessed the power of thousands of screaming girls? Yeah, we didn't listen. And those boys? They encouraged it, reveled in it, adored the worship—and *worship* is the only word for it. The show itself was so good, too short, and over before I could catch my breath. When it was done, I sat down in my chair, and as the crowd cleared, deaf from too-loud speakers and buzzing on this amazing energy that hung in that arena, I cried—not during the show like a lot (if not most) of the girls, but when it was over, in part from it being over and in part just from the incredible emotion and adrenaline left running through my body."

The celebration rolled on as the guys packed in a one-two punch on Thanksgiving Day, playing the annual Macy's Thanksgiving Day parade, followed up by a show at Madison Square Garden that evening. Winding through the streets of Manhattan that morning, Donnie remembers, "The parade was awful—it was freezing cold. We were lip-syncing 'This One's for the Children' on a float, but no one could move their mouth." Donnie's mom, Alma, remembers seeing the guys on the float as a very surreal experience. She says, "Again, it's that feeling—looking around, and you feel like it's in a dream." Similarly, Tom McIntyre says, "Everybody watches the Macy's Thanksgiving Day parade all their lives. And then, to be sitting in the stands at the end of the whole business, it's just unbelievable. It was grand."

The best part of it all for Donnie, though, was the huge Thanksgiving feast between the two events. He remembers, "We had a great Thanksgiving together. All our families came together for Thanksgiving in New York." Joe agrees, "It was wonderful. It was in the function room of our hotel. Right outside, in this foyer, was a grand piano. Jordan sat down at the piano, and *all* of us—

like, forty people—all the family gathered around the piano and sang songs. Probably Stylistics songs, because Jordan always played that, and we sang 'This One's for the Children,' we sang Christmas songs. Just one more cherry on the top, but that was a really special moment that I'll never forget."

For most concertgoers, that Thanksgiving Day performance at Madison Square Garden required a lot of "negotiation" with parents who had to be convinced to let their daughters partake in a somewhat untraditional holiday celebration. Fan Heather Schulze Sciacca remembers, "I had begged and begged and begged to be able to go. It was obviously a family holiday, and I wanted to drag my parents into the city on Thanksgiving. NKOTB were little dots onstage, they were so far away. I've always been a little dramatic, so when they came out, I said to my mother, 'We're breathing the same air!'"

During that show, Donnie leaned down from the stage and hugged and kissed his dad, who was watching from the pit. Little did he know that this gesture would make an indelible impression on his father. Years later, Donnie's dad suffered a series of strokes, which caused his memory to fade. Donnie explains, "He just had this weird, selective memory. I remember going to see him, and he wouldn't know which brother I was, but once he figured it out, he only remembered certain things about each one of us. After his strokes, the only thing he would say to me—it was like a loop—he'd say, 'Do you remember the time you kissed me in front of all those people?' That was his one memory that he could really dial into."

It wasn't just the New Kids' parents who were getting a taste of all the excitement. Because of fans' young ages, many were attending shows with their parents in tow. Fan Dawn L. Jones remembers, "The news that NKOTB were coming to Oakland, California, in December of 1989 for the Hangin' Tough tour was the most exciting thing a thirteen-year-old could hear. I'll never fully understand why, but my mom decided it would be a good outing for the entire family, including my father and eleven-year-old brother. The night of the concert arrived, and the whole family went to the arena. I honestly don't remember much from the show except for seeing a giant inflatable snowman onstage as they performed some of the songs from the *Merry, Merry Christmas* album. Somehow we had seats on the floor. That was good news for me, but that also meant that we were at the center of all the teenage/prepubescent screaming. My parents discovered firsthand that young girls scream at a pitch like no other. After the opening act, an usher took pity on my parents and handed them earplugs. To this day, my mom talks about how that kind usher saved their ears that night. She conveniently found another mother to take me to future NKOTB shows after that experience."

With the holiday spirit still running high, just a few days before Christmas, NKOTB were slated to make their second appearance on the hugely popular *Arsenio Hall Show.* For the guys, this was an important performance, since their first appearance on his stage the previous year had been a disappointment. Donnie explains the debacle simply: "We sucked." Though the guys were singing live that night, background vocals were programmed into the keyboard to support them. Embarrassingly, then music director Greg McPherson misprogrammed these vocals so that they weren't in sync with the music.

With this previous failure in mind, the guys were invigorated for their follow-up performance and felt they had something to prove. That night, they decided to play "Funky, Funky, Xmas" and requested that Arsenio himself take part by contributing a rap as his "Chunky A" alter ego. Donnie says, "Even though we were doing a rap song, and it was a little different, we still were like, 'Let's go have fun, let's not be tight, let's make up for last time and smash this.' We did. And Arsenio rapped with us. We were just *so* on a high. Everything was going great. We were headlining this great tour; the tour was going to continue after the New Year and keep going endlessly. Our songs were all exploding. The Christmas album was a Top Ten album, *Hangin' Tough* was still a Top Ten album, the first album sold three million copies. We were so excited and proud, and it was still new and fun."

The evening was perfect—*almost*. For the first time, Jon skipped a performance. Though they didn't know it then, looking back, Donnie says, "This was the first sign of real trouble for Jon that he couldn't get up for *Arsenio*." Of his absence that night, Jon explains, "It was definitely anxiety. I don't know what caused it. I think a lot of times when we do things—be it dance steps or TV shows—that aren't planned out and I don't know what to expect, it just gets me *really* nervous. I was just a nervous wreck. It's funny because I was actually at Tiffany's house, and I think I made an excuse, like, I was stuck in traffic or something and couldn't make it."

Shortly after their *Arsenio* appearance, while in the dressing room preparing for a show at the Gibson Amphitheatre (then called Universal Amphitheatre) at Universal Studios, each of the guys was presented with a check for $1 million. "We went *craaaaaazy*," Donnie says. "We went *crazy*." Joe laughs and says, "I remember Danny did one of his way-over-the-top-but-he-means-every-ounce-of-it celebrations. He ran out of the room, and we're all jumping up and down, because we make the most out of those situations, *always*. Whether it was a million dollars or new outfits for a show, it didn't matter. We got excited. Danny was always the catalyst for that. And then we would all go crazy."

Later that night, Donnie approached John Dukakis, the financial manager who had informed him funds were too slim to purchase a new house just a few months before. "John," he asked, "we need a car really bad. Can I buy a car?" This time, the answer was a definitive yes. Taking Donnie's cue, the other five got cars as well (many of which were actually purchased for family members). So it was that when the New Kids arrived home for Christmas, five brand-new cars were waiting for them outside of their lawyer's office.

That night, Donnie took his family's new car and drove it to their new home. Remembering that memorable Christmas, he says, "I set foot in that house for the first time, and it was beautiful. My mother had the fireplace going and Christmas music on. I just was *grateful*. My mother opened the door, and I saw how happy she was written all over her face. She was home. She *loved* that house. She'd been there for a week, and it felt like we'd been there forever. Mark was there, and he was safe. He was happy. He was like a little kid. I gave him the keys to the new car, and to see the light in his face was so great. I was taking care of my little brother too. It was very, very special." In that moment, Donnie had pretty much everything he had ever wanted for himself and his family. He says, "I just loved giving tours of the house. Jordan came over and I was like, 'Dude! Look at my house! Look at my house!' I was so excited and so proud. And it *was* enough for me. I never needed more house than that."

In the wake of this disbursement, things changed in the Knight household as well. Marlene remembers, "I got retired by Jordan. He called me one day and said, 'Mom, I don't want you to work anymore.' I said, 'Okay, but I have to look after myself.' He said, 'No, no you don't.' So I gave the agency notice, and my last working day was in February 1990."

As 1989 ended, all was right in the world. All of the boys' hard work had paid off. They were successful beyond their wildest dreams, adored by millions of girls across the world, tightly bonded, and, best of all, able to provide for their families in ways they had never dreamed of. Of their journey to that point, Donnie says, "It's simple and clean, and it adds up. It all makes sense up to that point: tons of hard work, a lot of luck, commitment. But there was still a calm about it. I remember the *calm* I felt in that house. I was home for my little Christmas break. It was so peaceful. Nobody knew I lived there yet, so no one was outside. In 1989, in the winter going into New Year, everything was in perfect harmony. Everything was magical."

Though Donnie didn't know it at the time, that Christmas was a demarcation point for the band. Looking back, he muses, "I think that was the end of the innocence there. I think as the clock ticked over and turned to 1990, the world changed for us."

The Art of Translation

Though born in Japan, Orie Montrose moved to America when she was just two years old, living in California through her sophomore year of high school. That year, her father got a promotion, which moved Orie and her family back to Japan. Having just discovered NKOTB at the time, Orie went in search of a Japanese fan club for the group but came up empty. Finally, she decided she was going to start her own. She got in contact with a professional fan club manager, and the two began working together. A few days every week, Orie would go to the fan club and translate NKOTB articles from English to Japanese.

Then one day in 1991, she got the exciting news that NKOTB were coming to Japan. But that wasn't all. Orie remembers, "Their management company contacted our fan club to arrange meet and greets and help with travel plans throughout Japan. They also informed us that Marlene, Dan [Wood, Danny's father], and Betty would also be coming on tour." Orie was elated when her boss asked her if she would take on this task.

Orie took the next week off from school and traveled with

the band to Tokyo, Nagoya, and Osaka. She spent her days taking the New Kids' parents shopping and sightseeing. At night, she says, "I was backstage with the group eating meals at catering with them, translating at meet and greets, and collecting gifts for the guys from the fans."

Twenty years later, Orie went on the NKOTB cruise and took her album of photos from that week in Japan with her. She says, "The first day on the cruise, I saw Jon in the hallway, so I stopped to ask if he had a moment. I told him I had something to show him. He said, 'Sure, go get it!' I ran back to the room and got the pictures. He and I sat right outside his door and looked at the album together. That same night, I ran into Danny's father, Dan Wood. This time, I had my album with me. I showed it to him, and he said, 'You know, to this day I don't eat sushi?' We looked through the pictures together, and I was able to tell him how wonderful and sweet Betty was."

Remember When We Traveled 'Round the World?

People used to ask me, "How do you stand all those people?" I was like, "Are you kidding me? They made my kid rich and famous, for Christ sake."

—Tom McIntyre, Joe's father

Fittingly, NKOTB ushered in 1990 (and Joe's seventeenth birthday) onstage, playing a New Year's Eve show at Worcester Centrum. Holiday or not, they would spend the vast majority of the next two years on stages around the world. As Donnie puts it, "We were on tour, working three hundred sixty-nine days a year." The insatiable desire for NKOTB had become a worldwide affliction. Donnie's mom, Alma, remembers a conversation she had with a priest at the time, which put the mind-boggling scope of NKOTB's fame into perspective for her. He told her, "I was a missionary and I went to Africa. We pull into this village, and a little boy comes running up to the Jeep, and he's got a NKOTB T-shirt on."

The year began on a celebratory note, with a performance and double victory at the American Music Awards. Jon was notably absent from this first award acceptance, again due to nervousness. When NKOTB won their second award of the evening for Favorite Pop/Rock Band, Duo, or Group, all five New Kids took the stage and were greeted by a mixture of high-pitched screams of enthusiasm and more baritone booing.

This negative reaction was indicative of the polarization that had quickly settled around the group; because adolescent girls were so gaga over NKOTB, the boys hated them automatically. Though lighthearted about it, Joe and Donnie gave a nod to this mixed reaction during their award acceptance. Pointing up toward the noisy balcony, Joe said, "I know we're making you guys real mad up there, booing up there, but I'm sorry! We're doing it for the girls up there." Donnie added, "All you girls up there who are screaming, it may not be music to some people's ears, but you can scream *all* you want because we *love* it."

Looking back, Donnie says, "We shouldn't have acknowledged it, but we didn't know. Eighty percent of the crowd was screaming, then you could hear twenty percent of the guys up top booing, and we fed into it. Stupid. But it was youth. And pride. I mean, I'm proud we told them to go screw themselves." NKOTB also took the stage that evening, performing a tight but bubblegummy medley of their hits, cobbled together by Maurice. Donnie says with a shrug, "It was safe."

Adolescent boys were correct that they had met their match in the New Kids; the majority of girls around them were captivated. Fan Mandy Hale remembers how intoxicating the New Kids' Chattanooga, Tennessee, stop was. Lucky enough to be in the front row with her sister and cousins that night, she says, "I just remember being so wide eyed. At ages eleven through fourteen, we just knew that these guys were going to fall madly in love with us. There was no question it was gonna happen. We just had to be close enough for them to catch a glimpse of us."

In preparation for her date with destiny, Mandy remembers, "I sported this black leather suit: a black vest and black pants. I look back on the pictures now, and it's so hideous and such a fashion monstrosity. But I remember just thinking at the time I was eleven that Donnie wouldn't be able to resist pulling me or my cousin, Emily, up onstage for 'Cover Girl.' Leading up to the concert, we were arguing about how 'If he pulls me up onstage, you can't get mad,' and vice versa. Unfortunately, he pulled someone else up. It's so funny, that little-girl spirit that we just knew our dreams were going to come true. That he was going to pull us up onstage and fall madly in love with us, even though he was seven or eight years older, and we were just a hot mess of black leather and bad hair."

Even though Mandy and her cousin weren't pulled up onstage that night, the evening still made an indelible impression. She says, "Jordan literally laid on the stage and sang an entire verse of 'Didn't I (Blow Your Mind)' to my sister. Joe was my favorite, and he grabbed my hand and sang three words of 'Treat Me Right.' I don't think I washed my hand for a week or so afterward."

With adulation comes backlash. Soon NKOTB became a media target. With the knowledge that ardent fans would gleefully scoop up anything associated with NKOTB—clothing, bedding, buttons, trading cards, lunch boxes, marbles (even dolls and a Saturday morning cartoon before the year was over)—their management and label were determined to capitalize on what they saw as a limited window of financial opportunity. Fan Nicole Frisby remembers, "My birthday parties were NKOTB themed, the walls of my room and ceiling were covered in NKOTB posters, I had sheets, a comforter, shoelaces, dolls, a shirt for every day of the week, a lunch box, and the list could go on."

A virtual merchandise empire rose around the New Kids; before they knew it, there wasn't much their faces *weren't* on until it got to the point where they had little control over their own brand. Jon remembers, "Things were happening so fast that we'd have these five-minute impromptu photo shoots to get images for merchandise or promotional stuff. It was just done so quick and so bad that I think a lot of products were inferior. A lot of us five say they despise the merchandise, and it's too much. I often wonder if we had that today and had more control over the images and product and quality if they'd feel the same way." Before long, the merchandising and phenomenon of it all became the focal point of media reports about the band, with the music and performance serving as afterthoughts.

Another pervasive allegation launched against NKOTB by the press was that they were a "manufactured" group whose success had far more to do with Maurice's aptitude and savvy than it did with the guys' own talent and efforts. As the story went, NKOTB were cleverly designed to fill a gap in the white tween market. The fact that the group was initially marketed to black audiences and paid its dues playing tough urban crowds was already largely lost; for better or for worse, the New Kids were perceived widely as a targeted "overnight sensation." It didn't help that the *Hangin' Tough* credits didn't reflect the amount of work the guys had put into the album. Their positive messages were whitewashed into somewhat of a goodie-goodie reputation that didn't necessarily acknowledge these lessons were hard earned from urban childhoods rather than produced with the goal of parent-friendly packaging. This perception was particularly exasperating for a group that had not only put years of hard work into the success of this endeavor but also had strong opinions to boot. Joe says, "That was frustrating when the press would say, 'Oh, they're manufactured and blah, blah, blah.' You spend two days with us, and you tell us who's telling us what to say. No one's gonna tell *us* what to say."

Disproving these stories became more and more difficult as time went on. Maurice adored the spotlight and, after a while, wore a military general's uniform at New Kids events and in interviews. This enhanced the notion that he was "in charge" and pulling the NKOTB puppet strings behind the scenes. With Maurice's newly adopted persona in alignment with the image the media was painting, it became increasingly difficult to establish a clear case for the credibility they'd worked so hard to attain. Jon says, "Maurice was becoming more and more delusional and cocky— doing interviews that put us in a bad light."

Unfortunately, the burgeoning issues with Maurice didn't stop there. Perhaps most problematic was the fact that his songwriting seemed to be heading in a downward spiral as well. Because of the constant velocity, the guys recorded their next album, *Step by Step*, on the road. Jon says recording consisted of "taking the hotel mattresses off the bed and putting them around the microphone to soundproof the microphone so you don't get the background noise. It was very low budget. It's just weird that we're a recording act, yet we didn't have time to actually record because we were so busy on the road."

In contrast to the growth NKOTB demonstrated between their debut album and *Hangin' Tough*, *Step by Step* was a reversal. Looking back on the production process, Donnie says, "It should've grown to be more of a compromise between us and Maurice. Instead it was even *less* input. That doesn't make the *Step by Step* album bad, it just means we didn't get to put our fingerprints on it the way we wanted to."

The tracks Maurice wrote for *Step by Step* were *out* of step with some of the guys' tastes. Donnie says, "It's just sort of an album of circumstance. We had to get it done however we could. There was a detachment, I think—at least for me. There was just so much else going on that it was hard to zero in on the album. Quite frankly, Maurice did a good job on *Step by Step*. From a fan's point of view, it *was* the next logical album for the New Kids on the Block; it was better than *Hangin' Tough*. But from the artists' point of view, it wasn't quite right. Emotionally, it just wasn't the next logical album. It needed just a little more grit. That would've helped us."

Aside from the musical direction of the album, the recording process itself didn't allow the guys the sort of creative outlet that presumably would have bonded them together and been a great release in the midst of all the madness. Had it all gone down differently, Donnie says, "It would've probably saved us some drama amongst ourselves. It would've allowed us to be more artistic, and some of us that wanted to get it off our chest would've got it off our chest. I think we had different creative ideas, but we couldn't really implement them. I wanted to make a different album than that. I just wanted to say more stuff than I could."

Jordan agrees that had circumstances allowed them to be more hands-on with the production, "I think we would've took *Step by Step* in kind of a different direction." As he sees it, the biggest problem was that "You could tell Maurice was overly confident, relying on a lot of his old tricks. To me, *Step by Step* definitely wasn't the album that *Hangin' Tough* was, although it did have some great songs. 'Step by Step' and 'Tonight' were great productions. Some of the other songs were just lacking."

Aside from just the music, Donnie felt the general trajectory of the group was veering off course from his personal tastes. At the time, he remembers trying to convince Dick Scott to let the New Kids bring rap groups like Kid 'N Play and Heavy D on the road as opening acts. He also pushed to have a guest rapper on their record.

Donnie says, "The crossover music that everyone does today, I wanted that back then." Dick was opposed to the idea. He told Donnie, "Boy, their fans won't come to the show. Them white girls will get all the tickets before they can even get one of them. There's twenty million black people in America and two hundred million white people. Which audience would you rather have?" Donnie told Dick he wanted *both* audiences. "It don't work that way," Dick responded. "You better take the two hundred million white people."

Of Dick's stance on the demographic that NKOTB should cater to, Donnie says, "I get it from his sense, the life experience he had. But that bothered me. I wanted to try to do things with music. I wanted to expand. I guess, in some ways, I wanted to make a rap record. But I didn't *really* want to make a rap record—I just wanted to cross it up."

Though cross-genre collaborations are common today, such was not the case then, with rare exceptions like the partnership between rappers Run-DMC and rockers Steven Tyler and Joe Perry (Aerosmith) on the 1986 rap remake of Aerosmith's 1975 hit "Walk This Way." Donnie says, "At the time, it was forward thinking, but I didn't think it was forward thinking. And Jordan and Danny wouldn't have thought it was forward thinking. At that point, the storms were too rough to try to pull it together anyway."

While there was a cross section of music on *Step by Step*, it all remained firmly within the pop genre. In addition to "Step by Step" and "Tonight," the album featured a number of ballads, including "Baby, I Believe in You," "Let's Try It Again," and "Where Do I Go from Here." The furthest the album ventured out of the box was the reggae-inspired "Stay with Me Baby" and the rap-infused "Games." Again, each member had at least one lead, with Jordan featured as the prominent voice.

Regardless of any reservations NKOTB may have had about *Step by Step*, their loyal fans immersed themselves in it. Spanish-speaking Ruth Guerra Mendoza, at the time a recent immigrant to America, loved the New Kids and the album so much that it actually played a large role in helping her assimilate to her new country. She says, "I honestly believe that I learned English by listening to the New Kids. I would spend many hours listening to their music and following the lyrics that my cousin wrote out for each song. Then the *Step by Step* album was released, and I did the same thing: listened to the music and read the lyrics that came with the cassette. I looked up words in the dictionary. Little by little, I would recognize and match the words that were in the lyrics to the words in textbooks. Within six months, I was able to have a conversation in English.

"One day at school, it was announced that there would be tryouts for the school choir. I knew I wanted to do it, but I was too shy to sing in front of people in a language that wasn't mine. I practiced 'Where Do I Go from Here,' sung by Joey, for many hours in front of a mirror, but I still was too scared to sing in English. When the day of the tryouts came, I was so nervous and scared, but something told me to do it. I walked into the room, and the teacher told me that I could do it in Spanish if I didn't feel comfortable singing in English. I told her I would do it in English. I held the album lyrics in my hand and started singing. I pretended that the only person in the room was Joey, singing next to me. I didn't look up; I *couldn't* look up. The magic would be gone if I did. When I finished singing, I looked up, and everyone was staring at me. Everyone in the room started to clap. The teacher liked my voice, but more importantly, she liked the courage that I had to do it. I think that motivation came from thinking that Joey would want me to sing—as a twelve-year-old, we imagine the world in a different way. So I made the choir."

The lead single, "Step by Step," was the group's highest-selling track of all time and one of the smash hits of the year, with six and a half million copies sold worldwide. The *Step by Step* album was released a few weeks after the single, on June 5. It debuted at number one and spent forty-nine weeks on the chart, going triple platinum in the United States and selling twenty million copies worldwide.

To support *Step by Step*, NKOTB launched the one-hundred-date domestic Magic Summer tour in June 1990. Hitting stadiums across the nation, it was a razzle-dazzle show with a lot of effects designed to mimic magic tricks. Although the tour was a success (at the time, the second-highest-grossing tour ever in North America, behind only the Rolling Stones' Steel Wheels tour), the guys pretty much unanimously hated it. As Donnie puts it, "There was no magic about that tour.

"It was too big," he elaborates. "We weren't right anymore. It was *all* so magical before, but by summer—just six short months later—it was all different. It was dirty. It stopped being fun. Guys weren't getting along." Joe agrees that the demise from fun times to the depths of Magic Summer was quick. He explains, "It's amazing how fast it happened, because less than a year after the Hangin' Tough tour, everybody was like, 'Fuck this.' You look back and go, 'Wow! It changed *that* fast?'" Some of this change in mind-set was likely caused by increasing demands on the guys as their fame escalated. Joe explains, "Before 1990, everything was going at a fun pace. We still had the energy, and the demands hadn't caved in on us. It was just a natural flow, and, therefore, we could enjoy it and we could embrace it more."

The discontent on the Magic Summer tour was brought on by a number of factors. First of all, the venues, which included behemoths like Giants and Dodgers Stadiums, were just too big, making it difficult for the guys to connect with audiences. Second, most of the group's members weren't fans of the cheesy magic tricks and stunts the highly produced show required. Third, they were tired from the pace and the pressure. And, finally, all of this contributed to one of the biggest downers of all: big rifts were appearing in this band that had once been bonded so tightly. Although they now traveled on three separate busses (one with Donnie and Danny, another with the Knight brothers, and a third with Joe) because their budget allowed for it, to a degree, it also reflected the state of the New Kids' union at that point: they were all traveling down the same road separately.

Looking back, Joe says he's astonished that the guys allowed the spectacle that was Magic Summer to go down the way it did. "In 1990 I guess it was cool to be flying around the stage on wires, but I'm surprised Donnie agreed to be flying around. I'm surprised we agreed to bring big playing cards up and do a disappearing act." But, like so many other things at the time, because of the sheer volume of travel and responsibilities, the guys simply didn't have the option to take a hands-on approach. Joe explains, "We weren't in Magic Summer rehearsals for long. We were busy traveling around the world. We were touring, we were doing press, we were doing video shoots, we were doing album shoots, we were doing a tour already, planning the other tour. It wasn't like we had setup time. We had one meeting. The buck stops with us, but it's like, What the hell?"

Generally speaking, it was hard to wrangle anything back under their control, whether it was music, merchandise, production, or scheduling. Donnie says, "We stopped being part of the process. We were part of the entity, but we weren't part of the process. In the early, early days, we were part of the process. When we did the shows, we had input, we had thoughts, we had ideas, we had strategies. Performing for Tiffany that first time in her dressing room, we were all about it. Playing at the Apollo, it meant something to us. It was a challenge, and it was *us*. It was us and Maurice—there was nobody else there. We were *doing* it. We were in this battle. Then it became this huge thing."

Fans, on the other hand, prepared for the tour months and months in advance, counting down the days until NKOTB rolled into their town. Of the buildup, fan Kelly Stammel remembers, "There was so much anticipation for this concert; I received the tickets for my Christmas present. For an eight-year-old, having to wait six months seemed like six years, with such an exciting event to look forward to." In those days before the Internet, getting a ticket to one of these shows took a lot of patience and dedication. Fan Yvette Madrid remembers, "My *awesome* mom spent the night on the sidewalk outside of Ticketmaster to buy us tickets. When she came home with tickets in hand, my sister and I were so excited we could hardly stand it! I couldn't believe I was going to be in the presence of the five boys who I loved more than life itself."

At an early stop of the tour at the Saratoga Raceway in Saratoga Springs, New York, Donnie jumped off the drum riser and landed directly on a stage trapdoor, which gave way. He fell through and sliced himself up badly enough to land in the local hospital and miss the next few shows. At the concert that night,

Kelly Stammel says, "I remember being so upset that Donnie was hurt and not knowing if he was okay. One minute he was onstage, and the next minute he was gone."

Alma received a scary phone call at two in the morning informing her of her son's injury. A car was sent to pick her up in Boston a couple of hours later, and she traveled to Saratoga Springs. Alma remembers, "When I pull up to the hospital, the driver says, 'We better go around the back way.' The whole thing was roped off, and there were fans *all* the way around the whole front of that hospital, with their candles and lighters. I'm like, 'What *is* this?'" Alma made her way into the hospital to collect her son. As they were leaving, she tried to convince him to sneak out quietly through the back, but Donnie wasn't having it. Alma remembers that even though there were hundreds of people out there by that point, he said, "Oh no, Mom. I gotta go out the front way. They've been there all night."

As Donnie went out to thank the gathered fans, Alma waited for him out back by the car. As she waited, a man approached her with a letter for Donnie. He told Alma the letter was to thank Donnie for what he'd done for his daughter that night. Curious, she inquired about what had transpired. She remembers the story as he told it:

"They were on the way to the show that night, and they had a car accident. His daughter ended up breaking her arm, and it needed to be operated on. Instead of going to the show, they went right to the hospital. He said, 'I came down to see your son and asked if maybe he could just say something to my daughter. Your son got out of that bed and walked down to her hospital room and went in and *sat* with her. I can't tell you what that meant to me.' The guy's eyes were all filled with tears, and he says, 'She was so heartbroken that she missed the show. But then she said, "My God! Donnie was holding my hand!"'" As soon as this girl was released from the hospital, Donnie had her family flown to attend another show on the Magic Summer tour. This was an illuminating moment for Alma. She says, "Little by little, I was learning about Donnie. That's probably why I put up with all his craziness."

The tour rolled on, and, despite the fact that things may not have been perfect amongst the guys, they were still adored by millions of girls and got to go out onstage and perform every night. However, even as they were in the midst of being the biggest act in the world, Donnie began to sniff trouble. He remembers, "In 1990 we played in Denver, and a CBS promotional field guy said, 'Oh, my daughter had a New Kids–themed birthday, and she loves you guys.' The next time we came back about six months later, he said, 'My daughter's having another party, and she doesn't want me to play your music. The boys don't think it's cool.'"

This seemingly innocuous comment had a profound impact on Donnie. He remembers, "That stuck with me and drove me crazy. I knew the tide was turning on us. Rather than do constructive and proactive things, I would go onstage and make a speech every night about freedom of choice. It was a contradictory ramble, but it was all in the spirit of, 'Guys, everything the record label said about the life span of a teen heartthrob being short is true.' That's why there was so much merchandising and everyone was trying to capitalize. Because *they* knew from experience our time was short, and when it closes, it's *gone*. I sensed it happening, and I was fighting it. I didn't think the other guys were aware of it. Rather than be constructive and communicate that to them, I just went off on my own little mission to fight it myself. Maybe I didn't want them to know I was *afraid* it was turning. I didn't want the tide to turn. I did *not* want to become Leif Garrett or Bay City Rollers or whoever they compared us to."

It began to dawn on Donnie that he was embroiled in a situation he had never anticipated. "I didn't ever really think it possible for us to be as famous as we were. I didn't imagine that, so I didn't want *that*—we're talking about comparable to Michael Jackson fame levels for a while. I enjoyed it, but I knew up at those levels that . . . if we fall, we've got a *long* way down. It was scary. It wasn't constant. I still had fun and stuff, but I sensed the beginning of the end *way* before anyone else did."

For now, though, the New Kids remained the biggest act in the world, and fans adored them. At the Toronto show on August 3, fan Laura Shrader says, "What I remember most about the concert was that it was in this huge stadium. This was my first time being in a concert venue this large. I can still hear it: 'Are you ready? F-f-f-f-o-r the New Kids onnnnn the Block!' Our seats were way up high, and the guys looked like little ants onstage. But it didn't matter. We were in our glory. The concert was so loud. And we screamed as loud as we could, singing along the whole time too. It was everything my fourteen-year-old self ached to see. I remember at the end of the concert, leaving the venue in tears. It was overwhelming and amazing all at once. I loved the New Kids on the Block so much it hurt."

The experience was so powerful for then twelve-year-old Sue-Ann Lambert that she took great care to document the entire experience the day after her August 5, 1990, show at Civic Center Stadium in Ottawa. Following is an excerpted firsthand account of exactly what seeing NKOTB onstage was like at that point, told through the lens of an adolescent girl:

A group of five boxes put together to make a sign that said "New Kids on the Block" started slowly coming down from high up onstage. All of a sudden the boxes opened, and the New Kids came out of them. They froze for a few minutes, then started dancing . . . Donnie was on this sort of swing thing attached to rope or chains, and he was going through the air over the stage and doing flips . . . Once, I was looking through my cousin's binoculars, and it looked like Joe was looking over at me! . . . I have never seen the New Kids looking so perfect ever before. Their hair was done so perfectly and their clothes were dope!!! . . .

[Donnie] told us that if a nonbeliever tries to make us take drugs or do something bad, to tell the guy that Donnie Wahlberg told us to say, "Shut up!" . . . Then later Joe came on and picked up a bra that a fan had thrown onstage. His face turned

pure red, too! During the first song, Jordan slipped on the stage because it was wet and slippery, but luckily caught his balance. During the whole concert they were sliding, but on purpose . . . Jordan said that it was pretty wet and his voice was going. He continued, though, and when it came to his high part in "Step by Step" it sounded more like a shriek than "It's just you and me." On the screen you could see him grab his throat and stick out his tongue as if to say, "That was awful!" The show was great, though, and at the end there was a great big bang and flashes. I waved frantically to Joe when he waved towards us. Then he ripped his shirt a bit, and Danny went up to him and ripped it wide open! Then he finally took it off and threw it into the audience. Donnie took off his shoes, and he was about to throw them when a bodyguard came after him and dragged him offstage. He came back on, though, and threw them. Jordan, I think, picked up Joe and started to carry him offstage, but he put him down again. Joe also crawled between one of the bodyguard's legs.

For the New Kids, it was sometimes difficult to step outside of their own bubble and understand exactly *why* fans loved them so much. Joe remembers receiving some insight into the fans' perspective during the Magic Summer tour. "I was on my own bus, and right at the beginning of that tour, I started an immense, *immense* crush on Madonna. I would sit at the front of my tour bus with Earl [a bodyguard] and listen to *Like a Prayer* over and over and over again." Joe laughs, remembering, "I was seventeen, and Madonna was thirty-one. I knew very specifically how far we were apart. In fact, it was fourteen years. I went to Worcester Centrum, and I was right in the front row, and she looked at me and winked at me. It sounds clichéd, but right at that moment, I was like, 'Oh my God. We do that every night when we look at someone.' For the first time, I knew what our fans felt when we looked at them from the stage—and forget about if we winked or pointed." When

Joe had the opportunity to meet Madonna at an after-party shortly thereafter, he remembers, "I was like a little girl. But I danced with her, and she was sweet as hell."

Unlike Joe, not every New Kids fan had the opportunity to get up close and personal with her celebrity crush. With this in mind, NKOTB's parents came on the road during the Magic Summer tour and hosted autograph signings at JCPenney. Alma remembers being staggered by the turnout at these appearances. "I wondered, 'Do you really think anyone's gonna come see their mothers and fathers? Come on!' Anyway, we're sitting at the long desk, just chitchatting, and the security guard said, 'Oh, boy! The line is out the door, down the street, around the corner, across the parking lot. You're gonna be here for a while.' I had figured maybe a hundred people would come. I just kept wondering, 'What is this about?' I couldn't even comprehend it. It was too big." Fans lined up in droves just to meet the moms and dads. More than twenty years later, Jennifer Yantes still remembers meeting the New Kids' parents as a special experience. "The day after attending my first New Kids concert, I met their moms at a local mall. I especially remember the conversation that I had with Danny's mom, Betty. Even though the conversation was brief and there was a long line of fans behind me, she really made me feel special. She thanked me for being a fan and supporting her son. She was so sweet to me, and I've never forgotten that. Of all my New Kids experiences and memories, meeting their moms is definitely one of my favorites!"

Although the guys didn't come home often, when they did, fans were anxiously awaiting their arrival. Jon remembers that sometimes they would have to sneak out of their houses. "My older brothers would put me and Jordan in the trunk of the car and pull down our driveway and take us down the street because fans would just follow the car. There was so many things you couldn't do, like just hanging out." Sometimes it got plain old out of hand. Jordan and Jon's mom, Marlene, remembers one incident where "I came downstairs one morning, and there's a mother, a father, and a little girl standing right there in my kitchen! The father was insisting that I go get my sons and let them know his daughter's there because she wants to meet them." But even on a more mundane, day-to-day basis, she says, "They'd come and look in the windows. Honest to gosh, the cops would have to come to clear the road because they're across the road, just all over the place. It was hard to get in and out of our house." The cops were working overtime at the other New Kids' houses as well. Alma says, "The neighbors didn't like us at all. Not *at all*. We had to have a twenty-four-hour police detail. Used to sit in front of the house all day, all night, seven days a week."

Donnie remembers this part of fame as impossible to become accustomed to. "It's tricky," he says. "It's tricky when I just want to walk through the house in my underwear, and I forget and go by the window, and someone's there. There are moments when I wanted to explode. But I would suck it up." Having witnessed Donnie contend with the frenzy outside of his house on a first-hand basis when her daughter waited for him as a child, Carol Carpinella says, "I was amazed he would come out. There were the eleven- and twelve-year-olds screaming, and I could tell he probably just wanted to be anywhere else *but* there, but he *always* stopped, he would *always* sign autographs and take pictures. He was always, always wonderful with the fans. There was hundreds and hundreds of girls on the streets back then with their moms."

While there were certainly a lot of perks to having such successful children, for some of the parents, it was difficult to adjust to the entire scenario. Alma explains, "Even when Donnie came home, he'd never come home alone. He had to have a bodyguard. Then he had to have a couple of his friends, a couple of his dancers. I'd look out the window, there'd be a hundred, two hundred kids outside.

"I didn't know what to do with it," she continues. "And then one day I said to Donnie, 'I can't take all this.' And he said, 'I think maybe you need to go talk to someone.' Best thing I ever did. I also learned, it's not about *me*. I said to him, 'Why does it feel to me, the bigger it gets, the worse I feel inside?' And it all came to the fact I didn't think I deserved any of that. Why is all the good stuff happening? I was used to the crisis, the bad; you got nine kids, there's always something. This was a whole new thing to me. I just kept saying, 'Well, it'll be gone tomorrow.' But it wasn't—it was bigger tomorrow. All I had to do was say to myself, 'I'm just his *mother*.' He's still just Donnie. Not the Donnie *they* know, the Donnie *I* know."

For his part, Tom McIntyre embraced the fans. He says, "I was always grateful. People used to ask me, 'How do you stand all those people?' I was like, 'Are you kidding me? They made my kid rich and famous, for Christ sake. What's better than that?' There were never any hassles or anything—the fans were just grand. I'd go home and there'd be people from all over the world there: Spain, Germany, Canada, Japan, Austria."

For all of the families, there were great moments of connection with fans. Alma remembers one time, "They were all standing out across the street in front of my house. I saw them, and I was trying to get in my car in the garage—I just wanted to *go to the store*. I thought, 'Maybe they'll be gone when I come back.' I come back, and they're still there. I had no idea who they were, where they were from, or anything. So I pull the car in, and I get out in the driveway instead of getting out in the garage. I said, 'Donnie's not home. He's on tour.' Only one of them spoke English, and she said, 'We came all the way from Argentina, and we just wanted to see him and see where he lived.' I was like, 'Would you like to come in?' They all came in and sat, and the girl translated for me when we were talking. It was *fabulous*. They were lovely."

In worst-case scenarios, the New Kids' houses were flocked by media as well. Marlene remembers, "One morning, Jordan had an appointment, so I went up to his room to get him. He said, 'Mom, I can't get up. Look out my window.' Of course, there were all kinds of fans out there, but there's a truck from a TV station in

Boston and a great, big, huge camera right on the house. He says, 'I can't get up! They're gonna see me.' So I went outside and said, 'Do you have permission to be here taking pictures of us?' And the media people's attitude was, well, you should expect this. And I did expect it. I probably shouldn't have gone out with the attitude I did. But, I didn't like that my son felt he couldn't get out of bed."

Jordan remembers the feeling of wanting to walk around freely, even for just a little bit, and trying to find those little moments. Sometimes when they were at hotels, he says, "It was too much. It was too wild. You get cooped up, you get cabin fever. Sometimes I would find an emergency exit and just walk. Just so I could feel normal, I would just walk somewhere by myself. I would try to do that as much as I could, but it was very hard. Anytime we went to a mall, it was hard. It was pandemonium. Just within a matter of ten or fifteen minutes, it seemed like the whole mall would be following you. For me, it was fun but stressful at the same time. I don't want to sound like I don't appreciate it, but it was a hassle. I think a lot of times it was hard to trust anybody or anything because everybody wanted a piece of you."

For the fans who loved them so much, the chance to meet the guys—even for a few seconds—was priceless. Even without the benefit of the Internet or social media, fans were masterful at figuring out where to locate NKOTB when they rolled into town; the adventure of it all was a big part of the fun of being a fan. Jennifer Isaacson explains, "One of my favorite things about being an old-school New Kids fan is how hard we had to work for every bit of NKOTB love we got. These were the days before cell phones, Facebook, Twitter, Craigslist, and eBay. If you wanted good tickets, you either slept outside on the street to be the first in line or got the newspaper and called every ticket broker, hoping to snag the tickets before someone else got them. If you wanted to find the New Kids when they were in town, good luck to you. You had to make friends with all the other girls who got to the venue at the crack of dawn hoping for a glimpse of them coming or going from the busses or hoping for some inside info. We would pile into cars with strangers and drive all over town looking for busses, vans, or limos in hotel parking lots. In all my years of searching, the closest I got to the guys outside the venue was a quick rush-by at a hotel, and Joey McIntyre watching from his hotel window while a group of about fifty fans sang 'Please Don't Go Girl' to him from the street below."

Fan Mandy Hale had a bit more luck at the Ritz-Carlton in Atlanta, Georgia, where her parents took her and her sister in hopes of catching a glimpse of the guys. She remembers, "We knew they were going to be there and were determined to wait it out and see them. But it just got too late, and we were little girls, ready to call it a night. We trudged upstairs to use the bathroom, trying to drag out the night for as long as we could so maybe they would show up. Literally within a couple seconds of us going into the restroom, my dad barges in, guns blazing, not even thinking twice about the fact that he's this grown man going into the women's restroom."

Laughing at the memory, Mandy continues, "We're literally pulling up our pants, throwing water on our hands, flying out of the restroom. To this day, all these years later, I can remember the feeling of running down that staircase, busting through the big door, and literally just stopping dead in my tracks because Donnie was within two feet of me. We're just staring at Donnie and Danny like they're in a fishbowl, which I'm sure they were used to at the time. There were only three or four other fans there, so it was an up-close-and-personal opportunity to talk to them. But I remember being tongue tied. I'd had all these things planned out to say to them, but I just couldn't say anything. I don't know that I even said a word. My mom asked Donnie if he would marry her daughters, and he was so sweet and so gracious. They were so sweet, even though I'm sure they were exhausted and just wanted to get up to their rooms and go to sleep. They smiled and took pictures, gave us autographs, and hung in. They were everything we imagined they would be."

The New Kids had their own fun with celebrity encounters during this period. Donnie remembers the adventures he and Jordan would have, wandering around meeting people backstage at awards shows and other big events. Donnie says, "I would get in the mood for challenges and Jordan would always find me on the days of these events. He'd be like, 'What are you doing?' I'd tell him, 'I'm going on a mission. You wanna come?' I think we'd all be nervous in situations like the Grammys, but I wouldn't let my nervousness suppress me. I remember I met Vanessa Williams at the KISS concert and flirted with her in passing. Then I worked with her on *Boomtown* years later. She said, 'I'll never forget when I met you. You came right up to me and flirted with me. I said, "Who is this crazy kid?"' Jordan and I would always end up together at times like that because we would just click. We'd fly by the seat of our pants and meet people and mess with them backstage. I could've just as easily been back in the dressing room, crapping my pants."

No matter where NKOTB were, screaming followed. Fan Sarah Gordon remembers the pandemonium that ensued when the guys made an appearance on *Oprah* in November 1990. "The audience prep person came out and told us that we needed to be really excited and enthusiastic when the New Kids came out. Really? This was not going to be an issue. Turns out they would later regret those instructions.

"When they started introducing the guys to come out," Sarah continues, "I literally lost it. There were tears and screams, the likes of which had never come out of me before. I could not believe I was so close to them! During the taping of the show, it was very difficult for Oprah to ask anything because everyone was too loud. People would scream at anything the guys said. The instructions we were given at the beginning were coming back to bite them. Now we were too loud, and too enthusiastic, and too crazy. They were unable to calm us down. During the breaks, Oprah was very frustrated; we were told by Oprah and her producers to calm down. Nothing really worked. In fact, Joe even told us to not scream so much, and he could barely even get his statement out over the screams. Oprah then reiterated what Joe said. No one listened. I think it was pretty evident on camera how discouraged Oprah was with us. There was not much interaction during the commercial breaks with the guys. It was too chaotic. I can see how crazy those early years had to have been for the New Kids. I only experienced about an hour and a half of what it was like to be in a room with them, with people trying to be normal and get their jobs done and get a television show produced."

Indeed, it was a mad, mad time.

Banding Together

Over the past couple of years, Laura Barr (dubbed "LaLa" by Donnie) has come to be a liaison of sorts, pointing Donnie toward important information on Twitter. "Somewhere along the line, I turned into his 'Twitter 411,' as he calls it," Laura says. "He truly cares, but sometimes he gets so many tweets, he can't see all of them. So if it's something important, I'll pass it along."

One of the most important and heartbreaking examples of this was when Blockhead Jackie Hutchison passed away on July 19, 2009, the day after attending the last stop of the Full Service tour in Houston. When LaLa informed Donnie of Jackie's passing, "He asked me could I find out her family or a contact person."

After he learned about Jackie's passing, Donnie says,

"I asked around, tweeting and texting to find out what happened. I came to find out that Jackie was at my after-party. I lost it. I was worried that something happened there. Is this my fault? But the part that really drove me crazy was: Did I see her? As the information was coming, I started to remember. I saw Jackie and talked to her, and we took a picture. We shared a moment—I remembered it."

Upon finding out that he had the chance to see Jackie the night before her death, Donnie says, "Then it went from this terrific fear that I didn't get to her to this overwhelming gratitude that I did. I spoke to Chris, the girl Jackie was with, and she said it was the greatest night of Jackie's life. Jackie just kept saying how happy she was and how much that connection with me meant that night."

In the wake of Jackie's death, Laura says, "The New Kids actually sent flowers to her funeral, and Donnie set up a party in Texas, and the proceeds went to Jackie's family." Moreover, while editing the footage for the band's *Coming Home* documentary DVD a few months later, Donnie found Jackie in the crowd footage. He remembers, "We found her, and I said, 'Stop! The video's gonna end here, we're gonna fade to black and do a circle right around her.' That's the end of the *Coming Home* DVD. She was smiling. She died happy, and we made her happy. It's *unbelievable*."

For Laura, getting these up-close-and-personal glimpses of how Donnie and the other New Kids interact with fans has been a profound experience. She says, "It still amazes me that all of them go out of their way and care so much and that they're willing to interact with their fans as much as they do. That's what makes it so special. They always figure out something to just make a connection."

Hold On

We were all on our own island, and it was just a
bummer.

—Joe

Donnie likens fame to riding a ship over a wave. Up until 1990, he
says, NKOTB were sailing up the crest. As they rode, there were
different elements to contend with: finding autonomy within the
group, grappling with the public perception of NKOTB, dealing
with the media, and working with the record company and its
demands. And then, he says, "The fans are like a storm, brewing all
the while. You need those winds desperately to make the ship go,
but those winds can become so loud and violent. You're trying to
just stay steady on the ship: I just want to call my girlfriend, I just
want to hug my mother, I just want to walk down the street in my
old neighborhood. Or I just want the world to know who I really
am. I don't want to be the *thing*—the cartoon character."

In the midst of all of this, the guys had very little control—
particularly as time wore on. Donnie explains, "Meanwhile, it
doesn't matter what we say or do. We're going up this giant wave
anyway. The fans are blowing the winds in our sails. The ship is
going up this giant wave, and the press is exacerbating it all the
way. And guess what? There's only one way to go, man: down."

As 1990 wore on, storms began brewing. In November, pop duo Milli Vanilli confessed that they hadn't actually sung on their multiplatinum, Grammy-winning album, *Girl You Know It's True*. The scandalous story made headlines everywhere and resulted in the National Academy of Recording Arts and Sciences withdrawing Milli Vanilli's Grammy Award for Best New Artist, awarded just a few months earlier. Although this obviously didn't overtly involve NKOTB, an accusatory spotlight was also turned on other groups in the wake of the scandal. Because the New Kids were the biggest pop act in the world at the time, they were often mentioned in articles about the fiasco, for no other reason than that they dwelled in the same genre. For Jordan, these types of media-ignited firestorms made performing difficult. He says, "It was really awful the way the press just threw us in without even considering or giving us any benefit of the doubt. We just got thrown under the bus. The media was really bad to us. We got hammered. But what was worse was I had a tough time singing on TV—like, I would panic. I had bad stage fright. On certain shows, my voice would quiver because it just seemed like so much pressure to perform well. People didn't give us a break, we had to be perfect. So I put that pressure on myself, and it backfired all the time. It was a mental condition. I couldn't get over it."

After finishing up the American leg of the Magic Summer tour, the guys went on the road for another hundred shows, this time internationally. Then it was back to the United States for *another* arena tour at the beginning of 1991. From there over to Asia. One tour after another, with barely a pause in between. Though the magic tricks were stripped out after the original Magic Summer run, it was essentially the same tour, over and over and over again. The guys always loved performing, but this constant recycling took a toll. Donnie says, "After the Magic Summer tour, we rolled right into the continuation of it, which was basically just scaling it down to arenas—the same tour, but a different name. And that tour sucked; it just was the Magic Summer tour indoors. It was like, 'Guys, we're beating this show into the ground. Enough.'" Joe says, "We were doing new shows and new choreography, but it was all over the place and just lost its touch. I think you could've seen it from afar, but even if you didn't, it was easy to notice that *pfffttt*. I mean, we were all on our own island, and it was just a bummer."

At the beginning of 1991, *Forbes* magazine named NKOTB the highest-paid entertainers of the year, ranking them above huge acts such as Madonna and Michael Jackson. They broke viewership records with events like their subscription pay-per-view concerts, in March and December 1990. Their tour rolled on as they continued to sell out arenas around the world. However, even at this stage, there were signs that things were beginning to cool down. After nine consecutive Top Ten hits, "Let's Try It Again" (released in October 1990) received little traction, spending only eight weeks in the Hot 100 and topping off at number 53. There was a general backlash forming against the pop music that had dominated the scene for the past couple of years, with the tide turning to more alternative bands like Nirvana, Jesus Jones, and EMF.

In the midst of this, NKOTB's group dynamic continued to diminish due to constant pressure and sheer exhaustion. Things that the members once appreciated about one another now threatened to become liabilities. "At first you love everyone's different ways of doing things because it saves your life," Donnie explains of this evolution. "At first you're a hero for it. 'Thank God Jordan could sing so good tonight.' But eventually it's like, 'Why does Jordan get to sing so much?' Or, 'Thank God Donnie ran out in the crowd at our first show.' But then as everyone gets comfortable, it becomes, 'Why does he keep running in the crowd? He don't have to do that no more.' It gets funky. Every group has the same stuff. There's no real advice for it. Hire a therapist."

Every now and then issues like this would even boil up onstage. In the early nineties, Donnie used to give a speech onstage alone every night; when he finished, the entire group would join him to sing "Games." "Eventually," he recalls, "when I would finish, the guys would never be there. In their mind, I was probably talking too much—which I *was*. And in my mind, I was talking to the crowd with the goal of trying to save the group; to tell these fans, don't let negativity confuse you, and stick to your guns. What I wasn't really aware of was that I was really saying, 'Don't grow up and change.' The fans were gonna do it anyway, and there's nothing I could do to stop it, but I just didn't know. I couldn't go down without a fight. So I'd make these speeches at every show to rally the troops." One particular night, Donnie decided to cut the speech short. The rest of the group wasn't out by the time "Games" began playing, so Donnie sang it by himself until they arrived.

Joe explains, "We didn't come onstage late to prove a point, it's just that the speech was so long every night that you started to wander around backstage. This particular night, folks wandered a little too far, I guess." Since the guys weren't there, Donnie sang over Jordan's part. This rubbed Joe the wrong way, so he retaliated by singing into the microphone when Donnie's next part began. Donnie remembers, "That pissed me off because I didn't sing over Joe's part; I sang over Jordan's part." Volleying back, Donnie changed the lyrics of the song's rap from "Every time I look I find you, dissing a mission that's strictly righteous" to "Every time I look, I find *Joe* dissing a mission that's strictly righteous." Having had enough, Joe walked off the stage and into the dressing room, where he got in the shower, ready to call it a night—only the show wasn't finished. "So," Donnie says, "I finished the song, and I went back to get Joe—or to fight him. Whatever came first. I was open for whatever."

Back in the shower, "I was fine," Joe says. "Pissed off, but I felt vindicated. Then they said we had to finish the show, because apparently Donnie wasn't going back out there either. But they coaxed us into talking. It took awhile, as ten thousand people waited, not knowing what the hell was going on. I remember coming out of the showers—I forget who talked me back out, but Donnie was playing a video game, focused on the screen, not turning to me or looking my way as I walked up. And I said, 'Let's get out there and finish it.' I couldn't really get the words out because I was crying. But we finally did all go out there. It wasn't a pretty ending. There were no big hugs at the end, onstage or off."

"The next morning," Joe continues, "I woke up and heard Donnie talking on the other side of my hotel room wall; our rooms were next to each other. The walls were thin, so I could hear him pretty good—so good that I had to do the old ear-to-the-glass, glass-to-the-wall trick. Donnie didn't say anything that wasn't true. And I remember he didn't say anything really mean about me. It was what it was: the culmination of three solid years of touring without a break from each other."

Looking back, Joe says, "This incident epitomized the dynamic of the group *back then*. There's rumblings about stuff or people's behavior behind people's backs, and me and Donnie end up hashing it out as everyone else watches from the sidelines, while in reality, me and Donnie are arguably closer together on most viewpoints than others. But that's the kind of guys we were and the kind of families we came from. We are both intense people at times and have a grandiose sense of what is right and wrong. At times that is honorable, at others it can cause you a lot of pain." The only difference in their dynamic (as this incident following the "Games" debacle demonstrates) is that, as Joe puts it, "He had a lot of brothers and I had a lot of sisters, so he might have been tougher and I might have been more sensitive. But we were both acting out."

When incidents like this—or, even just the basic sense of separation that plagued the group back then—occurred, Donnie says, "It's terrible. But there's no safe time. The only safe time is when you're getting along. When you happen upon each other and rediscover that 'Hey! I like this guy! We don't even talk to each other anymore.' You're having a fun night, and then you say one wrong thing, and it's over. Jordan and I would click and speak for a few weeks, and then not speak for a few weeks. Me and Joe would speak for two days and not speak for two weeks. Me and Danny were together all the time. Jon and Jordan were together all the time. But everyone else would fight and fracture."

Offstage, the tone of things was changing too. Fan Nicki Giorgi remembers the vast difference in climate both inside and outside the venue between the time she saw the Magic Summer tour's Oakland Stadium stop in September 1990 and the New Kids' subsequent show at Cow Palace in San Francisco the following February. She says, "Looking at the ticket, I am actually shocked that it was only five months after the Magic Summer concert. The New Kids were maturing as rapidly as I was. We both looked completely different only a few short months later. The mood was already changing. I remember walking up to the Palace, and there were people 'protesting' across the street—the backlash was in full swing. They had picket signs, one saying New Kids Are Too Old. Another had a Donnie doll hanging from a noose. Really, who protests a concert attended by little girls?"

Although it was hard to seize control, there were still some victories amidst the chaos. A key moment came when NKOTB had the opportunity to go back and revisit *Step by Step* through the production of *No More Games*, released in February 1991. The project originally began as a Maurice production, when Columbia decided it wanted to release a remix album. Donnie remembers, "Maurice did his own remix album; he didn't even tell us. It was awful. The label heard it and was like, 'This is terrible.' Then I heard it and was like, 'Yo, can we do a real remix album?'" Columbia agreed, and Donnie seized the reigns. Jordan says, "I think the remix album was Donnie's coming-out party as a producer because he really took that by the horns and worked really closely with the record label and the producers, Cole and Clivillés, in orchestrating that whole thing." (David Cole and Robert Clivillés were better known as dance music duo C+C Music Factory.)

As the supervising producer for the album, Donnie hooked up with a team of producers and reimagined twelve songs from *Hangin' Tough* and *Step by Step*, including "Games," "Call It What You Want," and "Cover Girl." Donnie says the album "was important. It was growth. And I'm glad I learned some things even if it was too late. As long as I learned them, I didn't care. That remix album was very important for a lot of reasons. One of them is it sparked new life into the music. Jordan sang a lot of songs on *Step by Step*, and he's got this high-flying voice, and people have a certain perception of that. But Jordan likes hip-hop. He's a street kid. He fell in love with it. And Joe fell in love with it, or at least with elements of it. I smelled trouble and knew we needed to toughen up. They might've been more indulged in some of the songs that were a little syrupy, when we were already overdosed on syrup. We needed to change it a little bit. We got a chance to address that side of us that was not allowed to be creative with Maurice."

The remixed version of "Games" was released in February 1991. Although it failed to do much on the charts, it made a statement and signaled an evolution in NKOTB's image. The accompanying video, directed by Paris Barclay (who worked with L.L. Cool J on the video for his hit "Mama Said Knock You Out"), portrayed a clearly grown-up NKOTB. Featuring the guys at a Boston nightclub, it was gritty and had swagger. Five months later, the remixed version of "Call It What You Want" was released in much the same vein and met with the same lukewarm results. Nonetheless, making that video was a great creative process for Jordan and Donnie, who worked hand in hand with director Tamara Davis. By this point, seizing creative control was more valuable to the guys than chart statistics.

This new burst of creativity and control ended up affecting the

Back in the day.

NKOTB frenzy reached a fever pitch by 1989–90.

Katie White

Flavia Lacombe

Diana Levine

Donnie

"*Back in the day, I couldn't stand Donnie. We used to have fistfights. We loved each other, but we hated each other. . . . Now I would say I'm closest to him. We understand each other.*"—Jon

Sable Tidd

Andy Barron

Dove Shore

Danny

"Danny has a thing where he gets really excited. Like, when something fun happens, he gets overly excited, almost like a comedian. He's silly and fun like that."—Joe

Diana Levine

Brian Babineau

Jordan

"I laugh with Jordan more than anyone because he's such a straight man. I usually steal what he says. Like, he'll say stuff under his breath and then I'll tell that joke for a week."
—Joe

Jon

"We have a special relationship. I think I relate to him more than he probably ever thought I was capable of. There's an innocence about him in this whole process that sort of still makes it fun to watch."
—Donnie

(left and above) Meeno Peluce

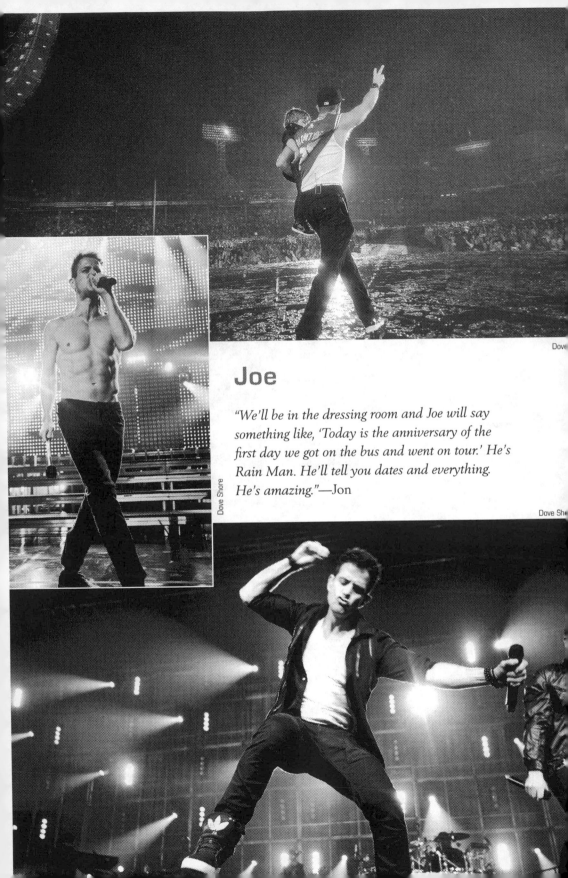

Joe

"We'll be in the dressing room and Joe will say something like, 'Today is the anniversary of the first day we got on the bus and went on tour.' He's Rain Man. He'll tell you dates and everything. He's amazing."—Jon

The annual cruise has become a highlight of the year for the fans—and the band.

The energy at NKOTB's live shows is explosive.

Dove Shore

Brian Babineau

Sheila Van Noy

Kim Ellmyer

The band loves their fans . . . and the fans give that love right back.

Fan Michelle Ball (above) blings out jerseys for the band—just in time for the NKOTBSB tour opener.

Chanda King

Dove Shore

Since the reunion began in 2008, it's been a wild, unpredictable ride full of special moments.

Dove Shore

Meeno Peluce

Fenway Park, June 11, 2011.

Melissa Kellog

Stronger Than Ever

state of NKOTB for the better. Donnie says, "We got to do a funky version of 'Step by Step' that sounded like 'Vogue' by Madonna; it was sick. We put that right in the show. We put the new version of 'Call It What You Want' into the show. We put the new version of 'Games' into the show. Suddenly there was new life. Suddenly, when we were on our last legs of being able to tolerate each other, we had a new spirit."

Another victorious moment was the group's American Music Awards performance in 1991. Unwilling to stage a repeat of the "safe" performance that Maurice had put together the previous year, Donnie and Jordan rallied together to spearhead an act that would truly reflect where the group was at. That night, NKOTB performed an in-your-face version of the remixed "Games" with a crew of backup dancers (including the then unknown Jennifer Lopez) and featuring a guest appearance by rapper Flava Flav of Public Enemy.

"That was definitely a big deal," Jordan says. "We were just very loose. We were able to use dancers behind us. It wasn't a Maurice production, it was a New Kids production. We were controlling the music, the choreography. It just *really* felt like us. Maurice didn't put the track together and tell us to throw a routine together. It was like, What do we want the track to be? Who do we want dancing? What goes here? What goes there? I did a dance duet with a kid that I used to dance with when I was twelve years old. This kid used to knock on my door and be like, 'Yo, let's dance,' and we'd break-dance wherever. So, I don't know how many years later, he's on the American Music Awards with me doing a dance me and him choreographed. That was really cool."

The performance from a noticeably edgier NKOTB was stunning to both live and televised audiences. Donnie says, "It was another 'We came, we saw, we conquered' moment. But this time, it was much more earned. It was a very focused attack. They showed us in the beginning in the opening monologue of the American

Music Awards because someone made a joke about us. A year before, it would've killed me that they made a joke, but I didn't even hear the joke in '91 because I knew we were gonna kill it. We won two awards in 1990, and nobody in the industry cared afterward. Then we went to the after-party in 1991, and everyone stopped us. L.L. Cool J grabbed me, NWA grabbed me. They were like, 'Yo, you crazy. That was dope.' Me and Dr. Dre were talking about the performance. Russell Simmons called me and asked me if I'd do an album with his label, Def Jam. It was a *totally* different thing."

Fan Shea Brock remembers the American Music Awards as a victorious moment for fans too. "It wasn't very popular at that time to like the New Kids. As a matter of fact, it was something we'd get teased about and ridiculed for on an almost daily basis. I remember walking into class the day after the American Music Awards when Flava Flav came onstage. We were so proud and held our heads a little higher."

Laughing, Donnie says it was an added bonus that the American Music Awards happened to air the night after NKOTB's scheduled Super Bowl XXV halftime show, which wound up being preempted due to the Gulf War crisis. The New Kids *did* perform the Disney-produced "A Small World Salute to 25 Years of the Super Bowl" halftime show in front of the 73,000-plus fans present in Tampa Stadium that day. However, the routine did not air during the game's live ABC television broadcast because of a special news report about the progress of Operation Desert Storm. A taped version of the halftime show was run on some ABC stations after the game was over, but not all ABC affiliates aired it, thus drastically decreasing viewership. "The American Music Awards became more important because the halftime performance the day before was [Walt Disney's] 'It's a Small World.' We're twenty-one years old, we're trying to be grown-ups, we're being criticized left and right for being cornballs, and we're holding little children's hands singing 'It's a Small World.' It's *okay* to do that, but when that's all people think you are, it's frustrating. That was a triumphant weekend. It all worked out because they didn't even show the halftime show. They showed President George Bush making a speech, so I was like, 'Phew!' No egg on my face. And then we went and did the American Music Awards and kicked ass."

Donnie refers to events like the remix album and the American Music Awards as "retying the knots" on the New Kids' ride back down the wave of success. He explains, "Our wave wasn't a superhard crash. It went slow, so we were able to fix things. And sometimes what happens is that you're on the wave back down, and you don't know. You're like, 'I can tie this knot so good now. Look how good I tie it!' And it's like, 'This is all gonna be so good from now on.' But the ship's going down. You're not at the bottom yet, but it's going down."

Even fans began to feel that things were changing. Mandy Hale remembers feeling more of a comedown than usual from the high of the last NKOTB show she saw in the nineties: a 1991 stop in Nashville. She recounts, "After this show, we all felt a little more let down than usual that it was over, as though we almost sensed that change was in the air. I was starting middle school and had a little boyfriend. It was a feeling of, Okay, these were our girlhood crushes, and this was so much fun, but now it's time to grow up and start dating actual boys and start experiencing teenage life outside of NKOTB. Plus, the guys were growing up. They were starting to really change, and there were starting to be news stories about trashed hotel rooms and that sort of stuff. They were just growing up themselves and branching out past that wholesome, good-guy image. I think it was just a mutual feeling from being at the show, which felt like a last hurrah. After that show, we started to slowly put our buttons and cassettes away. We kind of transitioned into a different season of life."

In June 1991 Joe finally finished up the requirements necessary for his high school diploma and had a small graduation ceremony in London, where NKOTB were playing a nine-night stand at Wembley Arena. When all was said and done, he had completed three of his four years of high school on the road. He remembers, "They surprised me and gave me my diploma and stuck a cap on me. There's this picture of me, and I'm literally white as a ghost, with these huge circles under my eyes. At the time, I had my first girlfriend. I would stay up until five or six in the morning because she lived in LA, and I'd be on the phone with her because I felt guilty if I didn't call her. So I would stay up instead of going, 'Hi, I miss you. I'm gonna go to bed.' No, I'd stay on the phone until five in the morning, wake up at three, go to the show, do the show, stay up all night. It was insane. That was my life." In the back of his mind, Joe says that he always knew how unnatural it was to be living this kind of life and enjoying such levels of success at such a young age. "I *got* that 'This ain't right, man. I'm a teenager, and this is not where a teenage guy should be.' That thought was always there: I should be working at a grocery store, and going to school, and dating girls, and hanging out with my buddies. That's what I *should* be doing."

Also in Europe, Tom McIntyre remembers witnessing a rowdy crowd at an Austria show. He says, "We're there early in the afternoon. Around the stage, they would put up these steel barriers so people couldn't get up. When we got there, they didn't do it—they said they would have security men standing there instead. Their tour manager said, 'No, you should get that steel, because as strong as you think those men are, they won't be able to stop the crowd.'" Nonetheless, the venue opted to go without stage barricades that evening. Tom remembers watching the crowd from an elevated position. He says, "The New Kids come out and are halfway through that first song. When you see a crowd fall, Jesus, it's amazing, because two people fall, then three people, then everybody. They stopped the show and [the New Kids] walked offstage. Then they decided to put the steel barricades up after all."

Around this time, Donnie remembers that the sense of free-dom the guys once felt while touring internationally was dwin-dling too. He says, "There was a riot at one of our concerts in Germany, and I called home, and everyone was like, 'Oh, what happened? Is everyone okay?' We realized we were making news at home while overseas. Now we could be in China, but they're still talking about us back home."

At the end of 1991, NKOTB released a greatest hits album, *H.I.T.S.*, to international audiences. One new song, "If You Go Away," was included in the package and released both internation-ally and in the States. A beautiful ballad written and produced sans Maurice, the song featured more sophisticated group harmoniza-tion than ever before. The single made it further up the Hot 100 chart than any of their recent releases but still topped off at num-ber 16. Jordan says philosophically, "If we would've put that song out in 1989, it would've been number one for two months. It's such a great, beautiful song. It would've been a smash. But that's what happens."

For as tight as the guys had once been with Maurice, time, separation, and all the events of the past few years had taken a toll. Come 1992, when they officially parted ways with him, it didn't even feel like much of a decision. Jordan says, "After *Step by Step*, it was over. We didn't need him anymore, plain and simple. We just grew apart. He was just saying weird things in the media, acting crazy in the general suit, his stuff was getting cheesier and cheesier. It was just all done. We weren't the unit that we used to be. Every-thing must change."

The actual split was low key. Jordan says, "We didn't make it a rivalry or animosity. Just behind closed doors, we kind of amicably parted ways. We didn't publicly trash him, ever." Donnie and Joe both agree that the separation probably happened a bit *too* late. Joe says the split came "when it didn't matter anymore. I mean, we were still touring the world, but we knew. We didn't have our cohesiveness. Everyone was on their own planet. It was sad, you know? You want that cohesiveness." Donnie agrees. "You learn the lessons," he says, "and sometimes you learn the lessons too late. Like, we should have bought Maurice out three years earlier. It was *sad* that day. But it was time."

Though their relationship with Maurice was at times complex and the dynamics shifted drastically over time, ultimately the New Kids have maintained a sense of gratitude and appreciation for all that he helped usher in. Donnie explains, "I believe there is a craziness in all of us. You have to sometimes tolerate it for that magic that each person possesses. Maurice *is* crazy, but he was crazy enough to believe he could do this with us. And so I have to tolerate some of his other craziness. I don't *understand* him at times, but he was crazy enough to believe in me." Even now, Jordan says, "For all of us, he was the big inspiration and teacher. He was a genius."

On January 29, 1992, the aftershocks of the Milli Vanilli scandal came back to haunt NKOTB once again when their former music director (from 1988 to 1990), Greg McPherson, alleged that not only did the New Kids lip-sync their concerts but also that Maurice and his brother Michael were responsible for 80 percent of the vocals on *Hangin' Tough*. At the time, McPherson had a pending breach-of-contract lawsuit against Maurice for funds he believed he was owed from *Hangin' Tough Live* revenue. Although McPherson's allegations against NKOTB were not part of this lawsuit, they certainly did call public and media attention to his plight. His claims against the New Kids took wing in the media.

NKOTB, in Melbourne, Australia, at the time the accusations came out, quickly changed their schedule to fly home and defend themselves on *Arsenio*, where they performed and talked at length, disputing the allegations. Fan Tina Allman made the trek from San Francisco to Hollywood to attend the *Arsenio* taping. "We could tell there was a certain level of frustration for the fact that they even had to answer the claims," she remembers, "but at the same time these were guys who grew up having to fight for everything they had. There was no way they were going to take this lying down." For fans who had witnessed New Kids performances, it was clear that McPherson's allegations were unfounded. Tina explains, "Anyone who has seen their show knows they're singing live; bad notes are hit, they forget lines, new ones are ad-libbed, and it's a spontaneous production. They ended *Arsenio* by performing 'If You Go Away.' As further proof of their side of the argument, some of the vocals were a bit pitchy, which was completely understandable, as they had just flown halfway around the world. But they ended the song with a beautiful section of harmonies; a perfect way to punctuate their appearance." Singing lead that night, Jordan remembers the occasion as a prime example of the pressure resulting in stage fright. He says, "That whole thing was so stressful on me. *So* stressful. I got through it, but it was terrifying. My fear and anxiety got the worst of me."

NKOTB filed a defamation suit against McPherson a couple of weeks later. In April he released the following statement: "The allegations that I made regarding New Kids on the Block lip-syncing were untrue. They did sing lead on their albums."

Less than a month after the lip-syncing debacle, on February 17, 1992, NKOTB played a show in Seoul, South Korea. It was pandemonium from the moment they arrived, with thousands of hysterical girls clamoring to break through security lines and get near the guys as they arrived at the airport. Traveling with the group at that time, Marlene Putman describes the venue itself as "huge. There was great concern amongst the New Kids' security that there wasn't enough safety at the venue." Even before the show began, everyone had a bad feeling. Marlene says that NKOTB's staff warned her to stay on the stage because "We'll get through the second song, and then it'll be all over." Looking back, she says, "They should never have started the concert in the first place, but a contract is a contract. And venue security is saying everything is fine, so who are you to really say it isn't, I suppose."

From the stage, Marlene watched the predicted madness ensue once the show began. She says, "I'm on the stage with the road manager, the Kids are performing, and, before you know it, there's a big surge forward to the stage. It was *total chaos*. They got the boys off the stage in a hurry. Boy, they got us off that stage mighty fast." Jon recalls, "It was open seating, it was just a mess. Our manager was like, 'You gotta get out of here. Somebody's gonna get hurt.'"

The guys left the stage and attempted to make a break for it. Marlene remembers NKOTB security shuffling them to the area underneath the building where their cars were waiting—only the drivers weren't there. She says, "I just remember the panicked look: Where are the drivers?" After a flurry of phone calls, transportation finally arrived. Back at the hotel, Jon says, "The promoters came back and were like, 'You're not leaving the country until you do the show.'" With the promise that the venue would bring in more security, the New Kids returned under armed military guard.

Once they returned, the atmosphere was tense. Jon recalls, "They shuttled us back to the arena, and I remember walking up the backstage hallway. It was like we were prisoners. Here's hundreds of military guys lining a hallway where *clearly* there's no fans. And they made us go back and do the show." When the terrifying concert was finally finished, Marlene says, "We all stayed together in a couple of rooms at the hotel that night. We all gave their tour manager our identification so she could keep it safe. We didn't want to be separated because we didn't know what was going to happen to anybody."

The guys found out later that in addition to the thirty fans who were injured that night, one young girl was trampled to death. Tearing up about the incident all these years later, Jon says, "We didn't find out about the girl dying until a couple days later when our manager told us. That was my worst memory because at that point I was like, 'This is *not* worth it.' I contemplated leaving the group. I was like, 'Somebody died to come see me.' Yeah, that was my worst memory. It was an awful time. An *awful* time. To be forced to go back and finish a concert when you knew there were injuries . . ."

Despite some of the weighty trials of 1992, Jordan looks back on that period as his favorite of all the NKOTB tours back in the day. "I just felt freer, looser, better. I was having more fun onstage. I just felt a lot more comfortable," he says. In the end, Donnie says, "We were into it. We were having *fun*. We were together again. We were a unit. It wasn't perfect, but it was real cool. That remix album reinvigorated us. We got to be individuals. We got to say a little bit, 'Yeah, we came from Dorchester and Jamaica Plain. We came from neighborhoods and we came from streets, and this isn't groundbreaking stuff, but this is where this group should've gone.'"

Of those crazy years as the biggest thing in the world, Donnie summarizes in a nutshell: "In 1989 it was all for one and one for all. In 1990 it was every man for himself; no love. And 1991 was even worse: we were like foreigners; we didn't even know each other anymore. In 1992 we found our way back to something cool." Part of this, Donnie believes, was a new maturity that led them to understand they were five separate people with distinct personalities and ways of doing things. He says, "In 1992 I remember the awareness of, 'Oh! Those guys don't necessarily want to hang out with me and be around me.' And it was like, 'Oh! Well, that's okay. Because I don't know if I necessarily want to be around all of them all the time *either*. So, okay! This doesn't have to be bad. It can actually be good.' You could almost feel it in the air. There was less fighting. You could almost feel the fact that most of the guys came to that point of 'We *are* different. And it *is* okay.'"

And it was in that state of mind that, finally—for the first time since opening for Tiffany all those years before—NKOTB were able to get off the road and take a deep breath.

Once in a Lifetime

Growing up in eastern Bosnia, war was a very real part of Elmira Redžić's childhood. With battles raging all around, her family kept their suitcases packed, ready to flee at a moment's notice. Fear was a part of life to the point where, Elmira remembers, "We were afraid to sleep at home. My family would go to our friend's cottage during the night and the next morning would go back home."

Every night, Elmira and her sister would drag these packed suitcases to their friend's house. Inside the suitcases were their most beloved possessions, including NKOTB posters, pictures, and cassettes. Finally, Elmira's dad told the girls that they had to stop bringing their suitcases; if they needed to flee, the luggage would slow them down.

In 1992 Elmira's village was attacked. Knowing that she would never again return to her childhood home, Elmira shoved what she could into her pockets, including a small stone from her garden and her *New Kids on the Block* cassette. A harrowing journey ensued as Elmira's family fled. They were separated from her father and grandfather as they made their way through the woods in the rain during the night. A bridge had to be improvised to allow them to cross a fast, deep river. Elmira remembers, "Halfway there, I remembered those things I was carrying in my pockets. I thought that I had probably lost the stone and that the cassette and the posters had been ruined. It made me feel so, so sad. I knew those things were not exactly the smartest things to worry about while bullets were flying over my head, but I could not help myself at the time. That small stone and that cassette and posters were the only things I owned then, my only possessions."

Somehow, Elmira's reminders of home survived the journey, as did she and her family. Over the next four years, as war continued to rage, Elmira says, "We were cut off from the rest of the world, still trying to figure out what was going on and how people you grew up with could take guns and drive you away from your home. One way of dealing with it was to actually try to escape from it, so I did the only thing I could: whenever there was electricity, I listened to that NKOTB cassette. I was also daydreaming about peace and those happy days that I had spent with my friends when we were making plans to go to a NKOTB concert one day."

After years of struggle, in the summer of 2011 Elmira decided to get away for a bit and visit her aunt and uncle in Canada. To her surprise, while there, she found out that NKOTBSB were playing a show in Hamilton, Ontario. Although she never would have thought it possible, Elmira suddenly found herself in the same room with those voices that had provided her comfort for all those years. She says, "I simply could not believe that I was actually there. Even when the concert started, and I got to see NKOTB live onstage for the first time after all those years, it still seemed so surreal. Watching them perform those old songs took me back to those happy days of my childhood before the war began, and reminded me of my friends who I do not get to see anymore thanks to that horrible war. I felt truly happy after many, many years. It honestly was a *once*-in-a-lifetime experience for me."

Face the Music

I just had a little cry by myself because I knew it
was coming to an end.

—Donnie

From the end of 1992 through 1993, the New Kids enjoyed a
commodity that had been in short supply for the past several
years: time. They got off the road and returned to Boston. While
they still came together for appearances and to record, the constant motion ceased for the first time since 1988. Jordan remembers it as a fun period of being able to enjoy all the fruits of their
labor. "I loved the time off. I got to enjoy normal living. I was a
young, famous kid with my own apartment and a lot of money. It
was awesome."

During this time, the New Kids recorded their next album,
Face the Music. Now off the road, they could take their time, and,
with Maurice out of the picture, they had complete creative control. They teamed up with a variety of producers and writers, including dynamo Teddy Riley, who had strong roots in hip-hop and
R&B and a resume that included acts such as Michael Jackson and
Bobby Brown. NKOTB, especially Danny, Donnie, and Jordan, also
played a large hand in writing and producing *Face the Music*.

The recording process was slow going. Donnie says, "We ventured out into new waters and relied on different people. There were different producers, and we had to work on their clock." In addition to working according to other people's schedules, NKOTB also needed the freedom to breathe. "It was slow," Donnie says. "I did a song with Jordan, and it took two weeks to do his vocal. We'd do a line a night, then play backgammon." Still, it was exciting to finally be able to create an album that reflected completely what they wanted to do as a group. Jordan says, "We all kind of had a vision of what we wanted, what should be done, how we should get it. It was kind of like shedding our skin. It was time to move on."

Face the Music featured a more pronounced hip-hop, R&B edge than anything NKOTB had done to date. The guys' gravitation away from easy-to-swallow pop was clear from the first second of the album, which opened with the sound of a match striking, followed by a sharp inhale. It included a healthy mix of sounds, including driving hip-hop beats on tracks such as "Dirty Dawg" and "You Got the Flavor," poppy harmonization ("Girls" and "Keep On Smiling"), and ballads ("Never Let You Go" and "Since You Walked into My Life"). On the album cover, the group for the first time opted to use the acronym NKOTB rather than the full New Kids on the Block.

At the end of 1993, NKOTB released "Dirty Dawg," their first new song and music video in nearly two years. The guys came out of the gate swinging with a video that made an unmistakable proclamation that this was a new iteration of NKOTB. The footage included a girl being chased through a field by a dog, alternating imagery of NKOTB singing with rap duo Nice & Smooth and hanging out at a club, "little" Joe being slapped in the face by a girl, and Jon getting a drink thrown in his face. The video was so unpalatable to some that it was actually banned from Canada's MuchMusic station for what it deemed violent and misogynistic imagery. The message was clear: these guys were not boxing themselves into the teen idol category anymore. But the question was: Was the public willing to accept this evolution?

Over the next few months, it became apparent that the answer was a fairly resounding no. "Dirty Dawg" made it no higher than number 66 on the Hot 100. When *Face the Music* was released a few weeks later, it topped off at number 37. For the most part, *Face the Music* fared better with critics than NKOTB's previous albums had. Of the track "Never Let You Go," the March 26, 1994, edition of *Billboard* said, "If people can get over their preconceived notions of NKOTB, they will discover this richly textured, wonderfully sung pop/R&B ballad—the likes of which would add sparkle to any station it graces. Jordan Knight has developed a worldly falsetto, and he is well served by Teddy Riley's astute production. Donnie Wahlberg's rap injection is fine window dressing. Programmers should listen without prejudice—and then add it." Though most critics liked the album, almost every review included an *if* or *but* of some variety, usually pertaining to NKOTB's image or the anticipated fallout from their previous success. It was nearly impossible to get through an article without some commentary about the guys' "new" image and usage of the acronym NKOTB. In an effort to turn the attention toward the music rather than the band, Columbia went so far as to release "Dirty Dawg" samplers to clubs and urban radio stations with the moniker "BONK-T."

All of this was exacerbated by the general climate of the music scene in 1994. The tide had turned away from pop; alternative rock (Beck and Smashing Pumpkins) and R&B and rap (Janet Jackson, R. Kelly, and Snoop Dogg) dominated the airwaves. Though *Face the Music* was actually somewhat in line with the latter category, ultimately it all came down to NKOTB's perceived image—and their image did not align with the music of the time. While the truth is that this was an R&B album created by guys who had been raised on R&B and hip-hop, the New Kids' previous teen idol reputation made it difficult for audiences to swallow.

As Jordan sees it, "Pop music was kind of on the decline; never mind the New Kids. All the radio stations were tired of us by that time. 'We've had enough of that. We've had four years of that.'"

There was also the fact that NKOTB's fans were maturing and turning their attention in different directions. Fan Kerry Mott says, "We were growing up, and they were growing up. Times changed. I went off to college, took my NKOTB posters off the wall, and that was that—it was time. I did buy *Face the Music* when it came out, and I remember thinking it was good music, but just not them. They were trying too hard. When I listen to it now, you can't hear any joy in their voices."

Despite public reticence, NKOTB soldiered on, quickly releasing their second single, the ballad "Never Let You Go." They also launched an international promotional tour of press and signings. Unlike previous album promotions, this time around appearances were more likely to feature two or three New Kids as opposed to the full group. Jamie Farkas remembers taking note of this when she attended a signing in Hayward, California. "You kind of knew this was the last hurrah. One thing that made it seem final was *just* Joe and Jordan did this signing at Southland Mall." Full band or not, most of the interviews from that period have a solemn edge, with the five goofy kids of yore nowhere to be found. They were right to be serious, though: the New Kids were faced with the task of finding their place in a market that had become difficult to crack.

For Jon, this was a particularly trying period. He remembers, "It's a bad memory: being overseas and promoting this album and really knowing it's not going anywhere." This lack of traction was exacerbated by the fact that Jon was tired—both generally speaking and from the pressure of hiding his sexuality and who he really was from the world. "I was so run down. I had just been in a couple relationships with guys, and nobody knew. I knew I didn't want to be confined anymore. I think I was dealing with my inner demons." Jon ultimately realized that it was time for him to part ways with NKOTB. As he remembers it, the actual discussion was quite straightforward: "I just came out and said, 'I want to leave the group,' because that's what was on my mind." It was after making this proclamation that Jon began to have doubts. He remembers, "Then it became a stewing process. And it became such a process that the guys were like, 'Just go. We don't want you back.' That was weird."

From a mother's perspective, Marlene remembers, "They were in Spain, and the crowds just weren't there—the interest had waned. Jordan called me and said Jon was talking about coming home. And Jordan was upset—*really, really* upset. He saw the writing on the wall, but he didn't think leaving the group was the way to deal with it. But Jon was determined. He said he was tired, it was useless. He said, 'I'm coming home.' So I told Jordan, 'I can't tell him to stay. All I can say is if you're going to leave, leave with integrity.' I think he did that."

The New Kids' then publicist decided that it was necessary to come up with a reason for Jon's absence on their impending tour. They floated a story that Jon had injured his back while riding a horse. Of this ridiculous spin, Marlene says, "A big story was concocted by their people that he had fallen off his horse. I don't know how that was concocted because his horse was in Massachusetts and he was in Spain." At a signing at the King of Prussia Mall in Pennsylvania shortly after Jon left the group, fan Christina Lepore remembers, "My sister and I noticed there were only four chairs at the table and began to question which New Kid was a no-show. Danny was the first New Kid I met, and he was sweet and sincere. I asked Danny about Jon, and he and Donnie began laughing. I wasn't quite sure what was so funny about my question, and Donnie told me Jon had fallen off a horse and hurt his back. Not knowing the truth at the time, I felt bad for Jon and was concerned for his health."

As a foursome, the band set off on a short domestic tour of clubs and small theaters in the spring of 1994. There was a certain full-circle quality to it all as they departed. Donnie muses, "Joe does a good job of explaining: it's one tour bus, then two tour busses, then five tour busses—until one day you end up back on one tour bus." Though Jon didn't get on the bus that day, he *was* there when NKOTB boarded the bus for the last time. "I actually took my car, drove downtown to where I knew the bus was picking them up, and I parked up the street and sat in the car and watched them leave. It was *crazy*. Crazy. I felt so bad. I felt like I let them down. I was always like, 'I'm gonna go to one of the shows'—but I never did."

Jamie Farkas remembers how thrilled she was to see the guys back on the scene after their extended absence, although this excitement was tempered with the knowledge that this might well be her final chance to see the band. With this in mind, she and her mom traveled several hours to Hollywood to see NKOTB's final appearance on *Arsenio*. Jamie remembers the vibe that day. "There were girls that came far for this show; I think we all kind of knew. That curtain came up, and they played 'You Got the Flavor.' It was the first time I'd seen them all together in three years, minus Jon. Me and my mom were so excited, jumping up and down. It was so refreshing, so great to see them all again. They looked different, they were sporting a new look, and had female dancers with them and different moves."

The day after the *Arsenio* performance, Jamie and her mom made the long trek back up to Northern California to see NKOTB play an out-of-the-way resort in Clear Lake. She managed to grab front row tickets for the cabaret show and had the previously unheard-of experience of witnessing an intimate NKOTB performance. Jamie says, "This was front row unlike any other front row. Usually there's a gap between the front row and the stage, but there was no gap here. They did all *Face the Music* songs. Jordan and Joe got on the shoulders of their bodyguards and walked through the audience. No one stood up because of the table setup, but I did when Donnie held my hand. As much as it was sad they didn't have the audience they once had, I liked the smaller venue. It provided an intimacy we'd never had."

Nicki Giorgi saw them play a theater in Ventura, California, that same week. She remembers having a clear understanding that change was in the air. "I was in high school now. Nirvana and Pearl Jam had come onto the scene, and, most importantly, New Kids were somewhat absent from the spotlight. They had a new album out, and I didn't even have it. What had happened to our love affair? There I was at the show in my baggy overalls, all of a sudden a little removed and a little too cool to get too excited. I remember that Jonathan wasn't there. They said that he was sick. I was steps away from them, but I didn't know the songs they were singing. The magic was sort of gone."

Within a few weeks, NKOTB decided to call it a day. The tour was officially over—and so was the band. Though *Face the Music* failed to make waves, in some ways, this last hurrah was still a victory. Donnie says, "We finished the Face the Music tour on one bus, and we got along fine. We were right back to square one. Jon wasn't there, but it was the four of us, we were all together, we were friends. Me and Joe used to go out to eat all the time on that tour. I'd go out and find soul food restaurants in every town, and he'd come with me." Despite public perception, Donnie says, "It was a *great* note to go out on. I remember one of the last shows, we were in Kansas. I just went out, and the sun was setting, and the fans were already in the building, and I just was alone. I was calm. I just had a little cry by myself because I knew it was coming to an end. I had given ten years of my life to this group."

For all the fanfare that had followed NKOTB for so many years, their breakup was a quiet one, with little media attention. Danny says, "There were more things we could've done, and some people didn't want to do it. There were tour offers to go to other places, and, in hindsight, I'm glad we didn't do it. We were gonna do a farewell tour, and we didn't. We just kind of went away, and no one knew why. It was just time. It was so hectic, and we got so big so fast. And then the merchandise was a bigger story than the group at some points. Also, I had my son at the time, so I was ready to just be Dad and get away from everybody."

In retrospect, Donnie is grateful that the breakup happened in 1994 rather than a few years earlier because he believes it ultimately left the door open. "I think if we had broken up a little earlier, we never would've gotten back together because it just would've been too ugly. It would've been a *bad* breakup. Instead, when we disbanded in 1994, it was like a healthy breakup. It was time. It wasn't a perfect breakup, but we sort of completed a journey and had closure. So when we decided to open it back up, we'd learned to respect each other. Had we broken up at the point of contentiousness, I don't know that we could've gotten back together. There would've been a lot of old scars."

Though the writing was on the wall, the New Kids' breakup was still devastating for fans who had stuck with them for the entire ride. All these years later, Lisa Hummel still remembers vividly how she learned they were disbanding: "I'll never forget. It was a normal, nondescript day in 1994. I had rushed home from high school to find a thick manila envelope on my kitchen table. The postmark was Boston, and the return mailing address was NKOTB. The adrenaline pumped through my veins. I didn't remember entering a contest, but I knew instantly: I must have won something! I carefully opened the package, excited to discover my prize. Inside was a letter and a black NKOTB T-shirt. Curious, I read the letter to see what contest I'd won. And that's when the tears started. It was a letter from the fan club. They thanked me for my membership. They said they appreciated me being a fan and they were sorry, but the fan club was disbanding. The T-shirt was in lieu of the remainder of my membership fees."

Lisa understood that this marked the end of an era. She says, "By that point, the 1990s had changed things for both of us, of course. I had entered high school and got distracted from NKOTB. The New Kids had to face new competition: grunge was in, and boy bands were out. But until that day, we had a good thing going, I thought. And then NKOTB quit me before I quit them. That day, I knew that saying good-bye was the end of an era . . . I was letting go of the New Kids on the Block, but I was also letting go of a certain sense of innocence."

For all parties involved, it seemed that it was time to let go of the innocence and enter adulthood. Looking back, Donnie says, "We *all* had to go away and grow up. The fans had to grow up, and we had to grow up. We had to grow up without the fans, and we had to grow up without each other. I *couldn't* be the person I was and be in this group anymore. I couldn't do it." And so it was that after living under the glare of the spotlight throughout their late teens and early twenties, the New Kids suddenly found themselves back in reality. For each of them, this experience of coming back down to earth was a journey.

Only twenty-five years old by the time this period of his life came to an end, Jon remembers struggling as he tried to figure out what came next. "After '94, I went into a deep, dark depression and wouldn't get out of bed because I didn't know what to do after doing so much," he reflects. Because much of Jon's family was living under his roof at the time, he remembers spending many of those long nights taking care of his nephews. "I was the insomniac babysitter for all of my nephews. I have such a bond with my nephews because I couldn't sleep. I'd hear my nephews cry, and I'd go into their room and pick them up. They'd stay up with me all night, just all snuggly on my chest." Being around the kids had an extremely positive impact on Jon during this period, bringing normalcy back into his life and serving as a reminder of what was really important.

For Jordan, the transition was easier. "It was exciting," he says. "A new chapter in my life. I really wanted to do a solo record, so I kind of just got into the swing of that. I just settled down. I fell in love with my wife at that time. She moved into my apartment, and we kind of set up house. It was just a new, fun time. I signed a record deal. It took a long time to get the record company to pull the trigger on that album." For Jordan, there were no regrets or feelings of having lost out on certain aspects of his personal life or youth while being part of the band. "We couldn't [go through normal rites of passage] publicly, but there was definitely time to do it privately. We were definitely young guys—we had fun. We didn't miss out. There's a ton of stuff that we got that if we weren't famous, we would've missed out on. The best thing about it is that we were together, so we could enjoy it together. We were in a shell, but we could be normal guys."

Danny immersed himself in fatherhood and also embarked on solo endeavors, both as a producer and a singer. He ultimately moved down to Miami, which he believes provided him with some necessary space to move forward. He says, "For me, if I would've stayed living in Boston, I probably still wouldn't have the best regular life because everyone knows everyone in Boston. But when I moved to Miami, it made a huge difference. I literally go about my day, and someone will say something to me once or twice. It's usually something like, 'Hey, you're that guy!' And that's it."

Joe, as the youngest member of the group, had a different experience than the others. Because he missed out on the traditional high school and college experiences altogether, Joe says that in some ways, the New Kids years were "lost time" for him. He explains, "That was time I couldn't be with my parents. It's time I couldn't be at my house. It's time I couldn't be in my hometown and hanging out with my friends on the corner. It's all good, but you had to make up for that time later. It costs, you know? It costs when you're a teenager in the biggest group in the world. I was *not* an adult."

As a testament to this, Joe says that when NKOTB disbanded, "I got drunk. I was doing what kids in college do. It's like a breakup—the relationship was four years, so I needed two years to unwind. Actually, I probably needed three or four. So from the ages of twenty to twenty-five, I sorta didn't want to do anything. I went out, I did a couple of creative things here and there, but at the height of it, I started going out every night. It wasn't fun. I'd go out, and everyone would be like, 'Oh, look who it is!' and there'd be the snickers and laughter or whatever. I'd have to have a couple drinks to take the edge off. And then I'd be the life of the party."

Though Joe contemplated going to college, he was nervous about how his "untraditional" high school education might set him behind his peers. "I could've gone to any college I wanted to with the right phone call. I had a meeting set up with the head of Boston College because I knew a woman who was very well connected there. But I didn't even have the wherewithal to grasp that. I was too fried to think, 'Oh, lemme go to college and figure it out.' That would've been a *brilliant* move."

Though older than Joe, Donnie also struggled with that feeling of being a kid dropped into an adult world. "When New Kids ended, I looked in the mirror one day. I was twenty-five, and I saw myself at eighteen and realized, 'I have not matured. The stuff I was afraid of at eighteen, I'm still deathly afraid of.' All that struggling for autonomy we had gone through was in a vacuum. I had learned to spread my wings as part of a band, but I hadn't learned how to spread my wings as a man. I remember looking in my eyes and seeing a scared kid. That made me even more scared. I went through a lot of that. I thought I was prepared for NKOTB to end. I had produced a number one record [*Music for the People*] for my brother Mark. I had total confidence that I could produce records and do other things outside of New Kids. But when we disbanded in 1994, it was hard. It was *very* hard for me."

As the years passed, each of the New Kids found his own path. Jon began a career in real estate, where he found success fixing up, renting out, and flipping houses. For him, the road to that point took awhile. "I think I was paralyzed due to fear of not living up to what it was I had done. So for *years*, I sat around and did nothing. And then I was like, 'Okay. I don't need to make a million dollars this year. Let me go make one hundred thousand.' And it wasn't until I went out and started my own company and made one hundred thousand dollars that I was like, 'Okay, that's good enough.'"

In 2001, with Jordan by his side, Jon made a brief foray back into the public eye with an appearance on an *Oprah* episode dealing with panic and anxiety. For years, he had quietly suffered from these issues while appearing onstage before thousands on a nightly basis. Though many people connected with him, Jon says the appearance portrayed him in a bit of a false light. While he *had* grappled with generalized anxiety for years, he did not suffer from actual panic attacks until appearing on that *Oprah* episode. Looking back, he says, "I'm actually kind of disappointed that I did that *Oprah* show the way it was done, because there's a difference between a panic attack and generalized anxiety. To me, panic attacks are freak-out moments. On *Oprah* I went into freak-out mode. I'd never had those modes—that was the first time. So I think people see that and think I'm freaking out at any moment, when it's not like that. But the anxiety, that's real. It is something I struggle with more on some days than other days. It's so stupid: I'll get worked up about five emails. All day I look at them and freak out, when all I have to do is call the person and put it behind me. I can just torture myself all day."

Nonetheless, people were touched by Jon's appearance, and some were even impacted positively because of it. Fan Jessica Jones says, "From about the time that I entered school onward, I had always been a nervous child and suffered from panic attacks, although nobody really understood what was going on, and I never saw a doctor about it. Everybody just thought it was in my head. I turned on *Oprah* to find that face from my childhood contorted in panic before the cameras and the audience on that stage. I sat riveted, having realized that I was looking in the mirror. It really had nothing to do with NKOTB at that moment, because I was simply seeing a man who was going through the same thing I endured throughout my life, except that day I understood that it was an actual medical condition. It is widely known in my family that Jonathan Knight was the reason why I sought help for my anxiety disorder, and although there will never be a cure for it, I have learned to keep much better control over it ten years into my recovery. I made a decision that day to not let it control my life, because Jon didn't let it control his life. If he could get up onstage in front of all the cameras and all those people and survive, then I could survive my life as well. That epiphany was one of the most important moments of my life."

Danny concentrated primarily on being a dad to his four children during NKOTB's off years, and also dove into a combination of business, creative, and philanthropy pursuits. After losing his mother to breast cancer, Danny dedicated himself to raising awareness about and generating funding for finding a cure through his Remember Betty charity, which directly benefits Susan G. Komen for the Cure.

In addition to starting a record label and producing music for other acts, Danny also released solo albums of his own. For him, these creative endeavors became a form of self-expression. Danny explains, "I was going through problems in my marriage and just needed an outlet, so I taught myself to play guitar and started writing and singing. There's not a lot of money in any one of us doing a solo record, so for me, anything I do is for charity and just to be creative. I just want people to hear my stuff and hope they like it. I don't want the pressure of dealing with a record company and trying to sell records. I just want to be creative and then give the money away."

Donnie originally intended to remove himself from the pressures of the limelight by working behind the scenes producing other musical acts. However, he soon found that he was uncomfortable hitching his horse to the unpredictable whims of other artists and record labels. Despite his initial fears, he delved into acting, at first in independent films and small roles. Of those early days as an actor, he says, "I always resented and was determined not to be 'that guy' that was famous at eighteen and then disappeared off the face of the earth and appeared on *Where Are They Now?* So I just kept working, even at times where I didn't know what I was doing. I just kept going to auditions, even though I didn't know how to act well. I wasn't ready to be an actor. I wasn't ready to do a lot of the things I was trying to do, but I didn't want to be a footnote, so I just kept pushing forward even when I was afraid. Even when I wanted to close the curtains. Even when I didn't want to go to that audition. I would leave with five minutes to go when I had to drive forty-five minutes to the audition. I'd call my agent on the way: 'Can I not do this? Can you just get me the part or tell them I don't want to come? Tell them I'm sick, and I'll do it in a few days?' I'd want to get out of it any way I could. But I kept driving."

On set—especially in his early acting days—Donnie was a far more quiet, subdued character than he had been with NKOTB. He explains, "When I showed up on movie sets, I would be nervous. I would be really prepared and quiet, and I would wait. I would listen—that's where my listening skills really developed, being an actor. I didn't listen in the early days of New Kids; I just talked a lot. I was the least experienced actor, and I was nervous. Eventually I got comfortable enough and paid enough attention and listened and didn't talk enough that the fun Donnie could come out. Knowing that balance, that's what acting is about for me now."

In 1999 Donnie had a breakthrough in a small but memorable role as Vincent Grey in the blockbuster movie *The Sixth Sense*, for which he transformed himself into an emaciated, almost unrecognizable visage. Over the years that followed, he built up an impressive resume on both the big and small screens that teamed him up with Hollywood heavy hitters and included critically acclaimed projects, such as *Ransom* (1996), *Band of Brothers* (2001), and *Boomtown* (2002). Donnie says, "Eventually I showed up enough times that I started getting good at what I was doing. My music career helped me as an actor. It gave me rhythm, it gave me timing, it gave me so many things. I started getting parts and knowing how to work in that environment and believing in myself again, because other people said, 'You *are* good. What you have is good enough.' It made me work harder. It made me want to get better."

Ironically, both Jordan and Joe made comebacks on the music scene as solo artists in 1999. By this point, music had come back around to pop again, with a whole new batch of boy bands (as they were now commonly known). Only this time around, there was room for more than one at a time, with groups such as Backstreet Boys, 'NSync, 98 Degrees, and Take That all finding success. Jordan observes, "When the New Kids were around, there was only a handful of outlets: local stations, MTV, *Dance Party USA*. There was no social media, nothing like that. I think there was only room for one group at a time, really. The one that stood out the most was gonna make it, and there was no room for anybody else. A lot of groups tried to come out, but they never really compared to New Kids—or if they did compare, they were considered rip-offs. But it seems like these days you *can* have more than one. What boggled my mind was Backstreet Boys and 'NSync—when one came out, and the next year the other came out, and they were both *humongous*."

The lineage of 'NSync and Backstreet Boys could be traced back directly to the New Kids. Lou Pearlman, the originator of both bands, was fascinated by New Kids and their success, and essentially modeled his groups after them. The big difference between the New Kids and their descendants was that whereas NKOTB had been organic, the members of these later bands were brought together from disparate locations through talent searches for the purpose of creating a blockbuster act. As Jordan sees it, that is the key discrepancy between New Kids and pop acts that followed, including not only boy bands but also the batch of pop stars who rose from the Disney empire and the slew of pop sensations who would emerge from reality competitions like *American Idol* a few years later. He says, "It does seem a little cookie cutter . . . With a lot of those groups, all those kids come from different areas and casting agents."

Though the climate was right for Joe and Jordan to reemerge in 1999, both of them had to work their way back onto the scene. For Joe, this involved recording his first album, *Stay the Same*, without the backing of a record label for promotional and financial support. He remembers pounding the pavement in search of a label. "I had my record already done. Everyone was having meetings with me, but everyone was saying, 'Yeah. Nice to meet you, but no thanks.' I couldn't even get a decent manager because of New Kids." Finally, Joe decided to take matters into his own hands. Joining the cyber age, he initially promoted and sold his album on his own website; simultaneously, he took the single of the same name straight to DJs, ultimately winning national airplay. Once the project proved successful, Joe was picked up by C2 Records, a Columbia Records subsidiary. The album ultimately went gold, charted at number 10 on *Billboard*, and garnered Joe a Boston Music Award for Single of the Year.

Between 1999 and 2008, Joe kept himself busy with an eclectic variety of performance and musical endeavors that included four diverse studio albums and television and movie roles, including a recurring character on the television show *Boston Public* and the lead in the movie versions of *The Fantasticks* and *Tony 'n' Tina's Wedding*. Additionally, Joe went back to his theater roots, performing everywhere from local theaters to off Broadway, to the Tony Award–winning Broadway production of *Wicked*.

Although Jordan signed a record deal with Interscope Records not long after NKOTB broke up, it took several years and a lot of back-and-forth for his eponymous debut solo album to hit shelves in 1999. His first single, the quirky, get-up-and-dance "Give It to You," made a big splash, due in large part to the quick-moving, riveting dance moves on display in its music video. The single went platinum and hit number 10 on *Billboard*; the album went gold and landed at number 29. He also received a lot of exposure on MTV and earned a nomination for Best Dance Video. Jordan remembers that period fondly, saying, "I had a sense of pride." From there he went on to tour as an opening act for 'NSync, as well as doing shows on his own. He says, "That album took me around the world. It took me to Asia, it took me to Europe, it took me to South America. It was *amazing*. To do things with the New Kids, you have to gear up a whole army. Solo, it's like a light infantry unit. You can slip in from behind enemy lines. It's a lot easier. Gear up and go."

In ensuing years, Jordan released two more solo albums. They failed to repeat the success of his debut, primarily because of personal struggles during that period. Jordan says, "I was a heavy drinker at one time, and I quit about six years ago," in 2006. "After 'Give It to You,' some of my solo career was just drunkenness. I sort of went down the drain through drinking. Thank God that got cleared up—it was the best achievement of my life. It was ruining me, but I loved the feeling of drinking so much that I would've kept drinking if the physical pain hadn't made me stop. It hurt— *bad*. I woke up and was seriously like, 'I'm gonna die.' It creeps up on you, and before you know it, you're in trouble. You don't see it coming. It's evil. It really is a disease. I was in Vegas, and I had an awful, *awful* hangover. I called my wife and said, 'I gotta go to the hospital. I gotta stop this.' So I just did. Honestly, I didn't really think I had a choice. But I *do* have to give myself credit for sustaining it. I'm very far removed from those days now. I go to Vegas now, and I'm in my room, there's a minibar, I'm all alone, and I don't drink. I just think of the hangover, and I don't want a hangover; even if it's a little one, I don't want it."

Although the New Kids were long gone, a small percentage of their fans remained loyal, even when there wasn't an active group to support anymore. As the 1990s drew to a close, the combination of the rising prominence of the Internet and attendance at New Kids solo events (most notably Jordan's and Joe's solo shows, and Donnie's filming in Toronto nonstop for three years) allowed fans to connect with one another and build relationships. Leslie Wharton remembers these solo years as some of her favorite. She explains, "I personally found this to be *the* best time of fandom. It was so much easier to see the guys. I met them numerous times over the years. I feel that these meetings seemed to be more personal, as you weren't just another face in the crowd, since there weren't many faces in those crowds. Once, while hanging out with Donnie on the set of *Saw II*, my sister, friend, and I were asked about a possible reunion and what our thoughts were. Honestly, we said it would be awesome, *but* we would miss the smaller crowds."

These newfound opportunities to meet the guys were only part of the fun. Fans who began to recognize one another from various shows built real friendships that started with NKOTB but grew from there. In addition to the shows, fans also began to gather online, first on Listservs and then on message boards as technology increased.

It was through one of these early Listserv groups that a New Kids on the Block convention was organized by fans. For two years in a row, in 2000 and 2001, a group of girls from disparate locations, from New England to New Zealand, decided to come together and hang out for a weekend. Of course, the obvious place to gather was Boston. The original intent was to convene for a relatively laid-back weekend at a hotel. Before the girls knew it, the event exploded. Members of the guys' families—whom fans had become acquainted with through attendance at solo shows—decided to participate, and, most exciting of all, Danny made an appearance, playing solo material, doing a Q&A session, and taking pictures with fans. Laurel Moffat, one of the primary forces in organizing the convention, remembers working with him prior to the event. "I'll never forget the first time I talked to Danny on the phone—I literally was gripping the edge of my desk because I could not believe it was happening. He was always completely down-to-earth, completely friendly, never any kind of ego or anything."

In addition to Danny's performance and Q&As with some of the New Kids' family members, the convention served primarily as a chance to connect. Nicki Henry remembers, "It was just supposed to be us having a good time together, reminiscing together. For us, it was more about the fans than the New Kids, but it did blow up a bit, I think, because of getting the families involved. We had articles coming out two days before, people announced it on the radio, people were trying to call and get in. But, really, it was just all about us. We'd go down to the hospitality room in our little comforters and just hang out. The families were hanging out all night long; girls were sitting around in an expanded bar showing them their old pictures. They really enjoyed it."

Of the draw for fans even without four-fifths of NKOTB around, Nicki explains, "It's just an amazing sisterhood. It *really* is. NKOTB meant a lot to us. They got us through all that teenage stuff. It's just a common bond, and it's amazing. People don't get it, but it's not about hanging out with NKOTB. It's not just about trying to get close to the guys. It's a sorority."

During these in-between years, there *were* attempts to get the band back together for one-off appearances. In 2003 MTV tried to get NKOTB to perform for its twentieth-anniversary Video Music Awards, to no avail. The next year, VH1 made its own televised pitch on the show *Bands Reunited*. It did not go well.

On *Bands Reunited*, host Aamer Haleem hunted down members of defunct bands one by one. The ultimate goal was to convince all the members to agree to a one-off concert for the show. Danny remembers the circumstances of his adamantly negative on-air reaction. "They were stalking me for two weeks," he says. "I was always on the motorcycle or with my kids. They couldn't get me alone. [The footage VH1 aired] was the one day I came back from the gym alone. They got a nice cursing out." Of these failed attempts, Danny says, "It's a very simple thing: we never got back together because it was on everyone else's agenda. The only way it was ever gonna happen was on our terms. It couldn't have been anyone else's idea. There were so many people throwing so many ideas out there, it was ridiculous. I was to the point where anyone who asked me, I was like, 'It's never gonna happen.' For fifteen years, my answer was 'It's never gonna happen.'"

Behind closed doors, the answer as to whether or not a reunion might ever happen depended upon which band member you asked at any given point. Although the subject came up every now and then, it was generally just between a couple of the guys in a casual way. For the most part, their contact with one another was rather sporadic, and in some cases, they didn't speak at all. Jon, for instance, says that besides his brother Jordan, "Between 1994 and 2007, I really didn't talk to any of them. I think I saw Donnie and Danny once. I went to one of Danny's shows and Danny's mom's funeral. That was it. There was really no contact."

Donnie says, "Whenever we would talk about getting back together over the years, if I was talking to my friends or one of the guys, we would inevitably come to a moment of, 'God, I hated it when this one did this. I hated it when that one did that. If we all get back together, they're still gonna do it. So, I don't want to get back together. I don't want to be around that. I'm acting now, I don't need to depend on anyone else. I got *me*.'"

Nevertheless, there were private moments when a little spark would ignite that just might foretell a glimmer of hope for some future incarnation of NKOTB. Donnie remembers one particularly poignant moment in 2005: "I was doing a television miniseries called *The Path to 9/11* in Morocco. We'd finished shooting and were on a Russian military helicopter, flying. I sat in the door of the helicopter with my legs hanging out, and the pilot's swerving as we're going over mountains and lakes in the desert. We're in Africa, the cradle of civilization, and I'm flying around thinking about the New Kids. I was thinking how fulfilled I was in that moment and that I wished and hoped that someday we could all feel that together. I was like, 'Wherever they are, I hope they're feeling what I feel right now.' I was proud. I was fulfilled. I felt *good*. I was doing what I wanted to do. And not only that, but I was having my career the way I wanted it, yet I could still hide in plain sight. I just wished that we could all feel that collectively. It was sort of unresolved with New Kids. The final chapter was never written."

A Knight Steps In

In 2007 then-twenty-one-year-old Frank Cicero of Staten Island, New York, appeared on an episode of MTV's show *True Life*, on which he shared his struggles with panic attacks and agoraphobia. After the show aired, Frank received a message from Jon on Twitter. Frank remembers, "He gave me great advice on how to conquer my fears and start to get better. Our friendship continued on Twitter, where he gave me a glimpse of life on the road."

Though Jon gave Frank tickets to a NKOTB show in 2009, he was ultimately unable to attend due to anxiety. After a lot of hard work, by the following year, Frank was doing much better. On Memorial Day weekend, he participated in a meet and greet with NKOTB, which was filmed for a follow-up episode of *True Life*.

Of that day, Frank says, "I was finally able to tell Jonathan Knight thank you in person. Donnie, Jon, Jordan, Danny, and Joe all appeared on that MTV episode with me. It is something that I will never forget: a guy who never met me reached out to help me, and after a three-year-long wait, we finally met in person. I was greeted with hugs from all the guys, and we chatted for a while. It was one of MTV's highest-rated episodes of the series. After my show aired, thousands of fans found me online to message me well wishes and thoughts. It showed me just how strong the New Kids' fan base is."

The Thought of You Still
Makes Me Crazy

We were all kind of floating. I've made plenty of records on my own, but to be back and know that I was making a New Kids song was *really*, really special.

—Joe

Depending on who you ask, the New Kids' reunion started with a friend of a friend, a T-shirt, or a divorce.

In 2005 Joe decided it was time to part ways with his manager and was in search of new representation. After the split, a friend of a friend told Joe's wife that music mogul Irving Azoff was a big fan of her husband's. The first time this news made it to Joe, he thought, "Huh. That's weird." Then it happened again. The second time, Joe decided to put in a cold call to Azoff's office. Looking back, Joe says, "I don't even know who this guy that clued me in is or where he exists, but he might be responsible for the NKOTB reunion."

Joe received a call back from Jared Paul, a manager at Azoff's office. Joe and Jared went out to lunch shortly afterward and struck up the beginnings of a friendship. This friendship deepened over the next couple of years, as Joe (who came in third place on season one of *Dancing with the Stars*) performed alongside other former contestants in the *Dancing with the Stars* tour that Jared was running. Based on both their personal and professional relationship, Joe came to realize Jared was, as he puts it, "the real deal."

Joe says, "Donnie and I would have this three-hour conversation about every six months: how a reunion would work or why it would work." After finishing the *Dancing with the Stars* tour and seeing a Duran Duran show at the Staples Center in Los Angeles, Joe realized, "We have to do this. We can do this." He encouraged Donnie to meet with Jared, thinking he might be just the person to facilitate a NKOTB reunion. But, Joe adds, "I wasn't gonna push it. I told Donnie, 'You're either gonna like this guy or not.' You can only lead the horse to water." In the spring of 2007, Joe, Donnie, and Jared casually kicked around the idea of a NKOTB reunion over a game of golf. "And then," Joe says, "Donnie didn't call Jared for eight months."

For Donnie, a NKOTB reconvergence was not much more than a blip on his radar. By this point, he was fully immersed in his acting career and, moreover, wasn't sold on the idea that there was a real market for NKOTB. After his initial discussion with Jared, Donnie says, "A month passed—I didn't stay in touch with Jared or Joe. Jared called and said, 'Hey, what are you thinking?' I was like, 'I don't know. See what's up in Europe. Map out a strategy for Europe, because I don't think it's gonna work in the US.'" Thinking little more of it, Donnie moved on to his next acting gig.

For Jordan, the NKOTB reunion began when the group was presented with an offer from the T-shirt company Junk Food to produce vintage NKOTB shirts for Hot Topic stores in 2007. Jordan remembers that by that point, "A lot of people were asking me more and more, 'What's up with the New Kids, man? Are you guys gonna get back together?' It was no longer taboo if we got back together—that's how it was coming across."

In the midst of group emails about the T-shirt deal, some members of NKOTB began an extremely casual, joking discussion about a potential reunion. Jordan recalls, "We were talking over email about the shirts, and I *think* I threw it out there, like, 'I'll see you all when we do our Vegas revue.' And then Joe wrote back, 'And if you're serious about that Vegas thing, blah, blah, blah.' So the tiny little conversation started with that, at least in my eyes. For me, that's where it started in 2007."

Jordan is quick to clarify that the reunion didn't begin with him or any other particular group member but rather was a stroke of luck, with everyone ready to revisit NKOTB at the same moment in time. "We *all* started it," he says. "I think we all felt the same thing." But for Jordan's part, he had certainly reached a point in life where he was ready to go back to the group that started it all. "The idea of it, for me, just seemed like something that the world was ready for again, and *I* was ready for again. I was newly sober. I was feeling good about myself. I thought it would be fun to do it with the other guys and have a brotherhood instead of doing something on my own. That really appealed to me. Enough time went by where it just felt right. And the T-shirt deal solidified it more for me. Just all these little things started adding up."

Jordan went out to Los Angeles and stayed at Joe's for a couple of days, where the two hung out and played pool, and Jordan had the chance to meet Jared for himself. "Jared gave me the pitch," Jordan says, "and I was like, 'I like it. I'm in. Let's do it.'"

But without Donnie—or any other one of the band members, for that matter—a reunion would not be possible. According to Jordan, after he and Joe met with Jared, "We were kind of waiting on Donnie because Donnie was acting, and, for him, it was probably like, 'Do I wanna go back with the New Kids, and is it gonna hurt my acting career? I'm getting a lot of credibility, and is this New Kids thing gonna hurt it?' I think that's what he was thinking—and rightfully so. He was kinda weighing it."

Of that period, Jon remembers, "I heard rumblings through my brother that Donnie was toying with the idea and that he was actually going around filming and interviewing people and testing the waters. Personally, I was shocked that Donnie wanted to come back."

The truth is, had Donnie's situation been different, he might *not* have come back—at least at that point in time. For him, the notion of a reunion "was *there*. The potential was always there to do it. It was just, was I really going to come to a point where I was willing to stop what I was doing? Be willing to sacrifice that and put it away?" But it just so happened that around this same time, Donnie's marriage was breaking up. With this, he found himself alone and depressed in Connecticut, filming the movie *Righteous Kill* with Al Pacino and Robert De Niro. Though he refers to being a part of this stellar cast as a "pinnacle" moment in his acting career, the experience was difficult nonetheless. Donnie explains, "I was playing a part that really didn't have any emotional stuff to do, and I was *suffering* so bad. It was just right in the middle of total emotional chaos. I couldn't do anything to help myself. Movies are slow, and the days are long, and they're boring. I had all this pent-up emotional energy, and I needed to go somewhere and let it out." On his off days, Donnie would stay with a friend in Boston. He remembers, "I would just lay on the couch and be depressed. We were riding Harley-Davidsons a lot at the time. Just sort of trying to breathe."

As luck would have it, Donnie stopped by the office of NKOTB's longtime music lawyer, Jamie Roberts, while in New York doing a wardrobe fitting for *Righteous Kill*. Jamie gave Donnie a CD of a couple of demos from a Canadian songwriter and recording artist known as Nasri, and told him to take a listen. It wasn't the first time this had happened, but in the past, Donnie hadn't actually listened. A few weeks passed. Then one day Donnie happened to run across the CD. "I heard 'Click Click Click' and was like, 'Wow. This song is kinda cool,'" he says. But it was another song on the CD that really caught Donnie's attention. He remembers running errands with his friend while listening to "You Got My Heart." By the time they arrived at the pharmacy, Donnie sent his friend in alone while he stayed behind, absorbing. "The song was getting to me," he explains. "I just broke down crying and was crying the whole time."

Despite his earlier reticence, Donnie was immediately spurred into action after hearing "You Got My Heart." "I called my lawyer and said, 'We gotta get these songs. Can you call this kid?'" Donnie's next call was to Jared Paul. "I called Jared and said, 'I found some songs.' He was excited: 'Great! I'll help arrange it.'" Within a few hours, the songs were purchased. Later that night, Donnie drove to Jordan's house to pick him up and play the newly acquired tracks. Jordan remembers, "He actually came by my house and was like, 'Listen to this song.'" Jordan's response was immediate: "I said, 'It's a great song. Let's record it. Let's do it!'" Donnie contacted Joe and Danny. After hearing "You Got My Heart" for the first time, Joe remembers, "I let my wife listen to it, and she got tears in her eyes—she loved it, she got chills." Danny says, "Donnie called me and said, 'I'm gonna send you this song.' And it was that simple."

Although NKOTB had ended as a foursome, it was important that all five members participate if there was to be a reunion. Donnie explains, "It doesn't work without all five of us. It *won't* work. Nobody's gonna come to see four of us. It *has* to be all five." Together Jordan and Donnie called Jon to give him the pitch. "One night Jordan called me, and he said, 'Someone wants to talk to you,'" Jon remembers. "It was Donnie on the other line. And he was like, 'What do you think? What do you think?' I thought it was a great idea because I remember watching the Spice Girls reunion and thinking, 'If they can do it, we can do it.'"

Music in hand, Donnie rented out a studio in Los Angeles, where Jordan and Joe hunkered down to begin testing the waters with "You Got My Heart." Remembering that first session, Joe says, "It was *really* exciting just to get back in the studio. It was really loose, it was really light. I think everybody was just happy to give it a shot and see what happened. So we were all kind of floating. I've made plenty of records on my own, but to be back and know that I was making a New Kids song was *really*, really special. It felt very youthful to me. There was just innocence and a *desire* that was not attached to anything rigid. As big as the New Kids getting back together was, it just felt like we were doing it for the love of the game." Of those initial moments in the studio, Jordan says, "It was very surreal. After the first two or three songs, I started getting more used to it. It was getting our feet wet. It was just me and Joe singing. Donnie didn't even know if he wanted to sing at that point."

In fact, Donnie wasn't even in the studio with Jordan and Joe as they recorded the majority of "You Got My Heart." By the time he arrived, the two had finished most of the vocals for the duet. From there Donnie and Nasri worked together on a big finish to complete the soulful love song. Though "You Got My Heart" was never released, Joe says, "It's a good performance, and I think you can feel the love in it. I had such fun and was so excited knowing that we all wanted to jump back in the foxhole. I was excited that these guys that I respect so much wanted to go for it again. Expectations weren't *huge*; I just think that we wanted to maintain our integrity. It was enough to go, 'All right, let's try this next one.' The vibe really kind of set the tone for the album."

It was in the course of recording the next song, "Click Click Click," that Donnie's mind-set changed. "I didn't think I was going to sing, I was just gonna rap," he says. "My whole thing was I wanted to stay behind the scenes on the music part of it. I'm gonna find the songs, and help write the songs, and finance the songs. Those two guys are gonna sing. Then I started singing on 'Click Click Click,' and that was it. I was hooked! We were *all* hooked."

In many ways, those first two songs were a bit of trial by fire. "It was still sort of a feeling-out process," Donnie explains. "If the recording process went terrible, we might've stopped. Jordan might've said, 'I'm not happy doing this,' or 'We don't have any chemistry, guys.' But it didn't. We clicked. It's when those first two recording sessions went so well, and me, Jordan, and Joe rediscovered the chemistry that we have, and we wanted to keep doing it."

After they finished "You Got My Heart," Jordan remembers, "I was like, 'We should do a whole album.' Donnie and I were on the same page as far as doing a whole album, because that's fun—that's the juice. If we go on tour, we want to sing dope new songs. Thank God we did. It really revived us and brought us to 2008. It wasn't *just* nostalgia. Even though seventy-five percent was nostalgia, to have that good block of new, fresh songs with all the best players in the game made us look good and made *us* feel good. There was way more motivation. It just upped our game."

Donnie agrees that, for him, new music was an essential part of reuniting. "I wasn't gonna do it any other way," he says. With the direction and scope of the project clarified, Danny and Jon joined the other three New Kids in the studio. "Talk about nerves, going to meet them all again for the first time after not seeing them for so many years," Jon remembers. "Just not knowing who these people are, what they're all about. It was awkward. But after ten minutes, it was like, 'All right. These are my guys.'"

There were still some growing pains as the guys learned how to work together again after fifteen years of independence. "For me," Jordan says, "it was an adjustment. It takes time for me to warm up, so maybe it was easier for other people than it was for me. We all kind of had to nudge each other a bit to figure out where we each fit in. 'No, this is my spot, remember? Get away!' We kinda had to fall into our old places again." There was also the matter of learning how to collaborate with a team in a way that allowed everyone's voice to be heard. Joe says, "All of a sudden you are back with four other bosses, and because we have so much history, we can't really tell each other what to do. Which is part of the challenge and exercise of this. It wasn't easy, but we obviously worked it out. I keep looking back at the time we got back together as very exciting, but also stressful, because I wanted it to be an inclusive, creative experience for everyone, with me having my ideas and voice heard. They were—but jumping back into the dynamic after fourteen years was tough sometimes."

On so many different levels, both creatively and interpersonally, compromise was imperative. Donnie and Joe, both strong willed and opinionated, especially put a lot of work into their relationship during those early days of the reunion, as some of the old stuff from the past reared its ugly head. Donnie reflects, "I think Joe came back with a lot of the old frustration of not really ever having his voice heard and respected. That was one of the struggles we had coming back together. At first it bumped, and it rubbed me wrong, and we had some blowups. But I had to learn to hear what he was saying and to respect his voice and the need for him to have his voice heard. He didn't always have to have his way, but he wanted to be heard. Looking back, after twenty years of not having my voice heard, I'd be feeling the same way. I'd be feeling *frustrated*."

After years of separation, the guys found themselves spending the vast majority of their time together once again. Eventually Jordan and Jon moved into Donnie's house, where they stayed for some of the recording process. Jordan says, "When we first started talking about the reunion, I would go out to Cali and stay in a hotel. Donnie eventually moved to a house in Sherman Oaks, and me and Jon just moved in with him and set up our own room. It wasn't even set up well; I just put up black sheets over the windows so I could sleep. I'd wake up, and Donnie would already be gone for the day and two or three Red Bulls in. I'd give him a call and ask, 'What's going on?' He'd be like, 'Nasri's coming in.' It felt the same as waking up at Maurice's house and playing the drum and keyboard. We definitely went back to the old days with that."

Also reminiscent of the old days was Ping-Pong. Donnie had a Ping-Pong table in his garage, where much of *The Block* was recorded, and twenty years later, the game became a focal point once again. "Me and Donnie were the nut bags," Jordan says. "Joe and Danny would jump in, but we were the crazy ones. We would just get everybody involved." Donnie agrees that he and Jordan ruled the Ping-Pong roost. "Me and Jordan would have epic battles *constantly*. Every game me and Jordan played would go into overtime. It would just be a battle for hours. Joe couldn't beat any of us. But what happens when you play the same people over and over is they start to learn. So eventually, the big moment at rehearsal one of those days was Joe beat Jordan for the first time."

For Donnie, the recording process was therapeutic. He buried himself in both the studio and business ends of the reunion as a way of getting through the emotional difficulty of his divorce. For as much as he was aware that in some ways he *had* to immerse himself in the reunion to get through his own personal crisis, he was also aware that the reunion was a financially and professionally risky endeavor with no guarantees. It potentially put at risk the reputation he had spent years building as an actor. He remembers, "I just stuck my head in the water and started swimming. I ignored my agent's phone calls. I didn't want them to make me aware that I might be doing something crazy. I knew I was possibly doing something crazy, but I had to do it. I didn't talk to my accountant, because I didn't want to hear, 'You know, you're spending a lot of money on this.' I really went underground. I wouldn't allow myself to think. For the first few months, I didn't know what to expect, but I had to do it, so I just dove in. There were so many factors saying don't do it—so many more factors than were saying do it. But I couldn't sleep at night, and I was depressed, and I wanted to do something different, so I just started to explore."

Aside from recording, the group also had the somewhat daunting task of finding a home for its work. Because no pop group had ever embarked on a reunion project of this scope before, NKOTB represented a gamble for record labels. Donnie remembers, "I was going into the offices of all these record companies and saying, 'This reunion's gonna work. We're gonna do it with or without you.' I wanted them to get on board and was basically lying. I mean, sooner or later we were gonna need some of these guys' money and belief in us."

In November 2007 Universal Music Group A&R rep Aimee Nadeau, a NKOTB fan, found out about the reunion by a fluke when a colleague and friend happened to have a meeting with a music scout who was pitching Nasri (then writing with NKOTB). Aimee was eventually pulled into the meeting by her colleague, based on her reputation as a longtime New Kids fan. She remembers being incredulous: "I was like, 'You mean Nasri's in the studio with Jordan Knight doing some solo stuff?'" The scout replied no, repeating that Nasri was working with the New Kids. Still thinking there must be some sort of misunderstanding, Aimee tried again: "You mean he's in with Joey McIntyre of New Kids on the Block?" "No," the scout repeated, "he's in with New Kids. All five New Kids." Soaking in this information, Aimee remembers, "I was like, '*What? Are you kidding me?*' I kind of freaked out—I grabbed a pillow off the couch and hugged it and was laughing."

Delighted to hear that NKOTB was reuniting and motivated to bring them on board at Universal, Aimee got to work. She connected with Jared and requested a meeting. At that point, Jared was still somewhat uncertain of the scope of the project but said he would discuss with the guys the potential of teaming up with

Universal. From that point, Aimee says, "I actually knew the harder task was getting my bosses interested in the New Kids. It had been so long since the New Kids had done something, and their last album in 1994 had fizzled. I spent days working so hard to put bullet points together for my boss and show her things that were going on: like, how successful the numbers on the Spice Girls reunion were; how Take That had just put together a tour in Europe and had major sales on it, even though they hadn't done anything in a really long time either. My boss is known for signing Korn and Third Eye Blind and rock bands; she's not what I would call a pop person." Nonetheless, Aimee got her boss's consent. After some internal meetings, Universal decided that its Interscope division would make the ideal home for NKOTB. In January 2008 a meeting was scheduled for Interscope president and founder Jimmy Iovine, Donnie, Jared, and Aimee.

Aimee, a New Hampshire native who grew up just an hour outside of Boston, had been a fan of NKOTB since she first saw them open for Tiffany in 1988. In the course of her many years of fandom, Aimee had struck up a friendship of sorts with Donnie, though the two had not been in contact for some time. Because Aimee's correspondence with the NKOTB camp was primarily with Jared up to this point, Donnie was unaware that Aimee's familiar face was behind the potential Interscope deal. Of this full-circle situation, Aimee says, "I would say that my experience with New Kids was kind of like a pay-it-forward thing and Donnie's old karma coming back at him. When I was a kid, I always used to go to their houses and sit outside with all my friends. Donnie was so nice to me; he always took a liking to me and my friend. When we were a little bit older and he was working with other groups and writing, he had a studio in his house, and he would actually invite us in. I remember being in the studio, sitting in the corner, watching everything that was going on. That was kind of what inspired me to get in the music industry. It was a whole three-hundred-sixty-degree thing, where it was his kindness and his taking me under his wing and letting me see the 'underside' of the industry that led me along my own career path, which ended up kind of playing a part in their comeback."

Walking into the conference room to meet with Jared and Donnie face-to-face for the first time at that January 2008 meeting, Aimee remembers, "Donnie and Jared were waiting in there. I walked in, and Donnie was like, 'Oh my God! It's you. I can't believe it!' And he was hugging me and laughing. 'I should have known.'" Aimee laughs, remembering Jared's confusion over the whole situation.

All coincidence aside, it was ultimately the music that sold Interscope on NKOTB. According to Aimee, "It wasn't the numbers or anything other than the fact that Donnie did the legwork, and he came in with five songs and played them for Jimmy Iovine. It was the music that made the difference. Had Donnie not done any of that legwork, had they not recorded anything, I don't think the deal would've happened. But the fact that he walked in with songs like 'Click Click Click,' 'Coming Home,' and 'You Got My Heart' did it."

NKOTB saw Interscope as the perfect partner as well. Aimee says, "I know when I talk to Donnie about it, he says, 'We were meant to be with Jimmy, so I know that no matter how the cards fell, we were meant to be at Interscope. But I'm glad that it was through you.'" And there certainly is no doubt that it seems fitting a fan would play a role in all of this. As Aimee puts it, "It was just this random thing that happened that was meant to be."

In 2007 the band acquired the domain www.NKOTB.com from the fan-based group Keep Keepin' On, which had been running an unaffiliated tribute site at that address for the past several years. Right before Christmas 2007, the soon-to-be-former site owner posted a message informing visitors that NKOTB's legal team had requested the group be allowed to assume the site for future projects. "Does this mean a reunion is just around the corner?" she wrote in a post dated December 25, 2007. "This might be the Christmas present we've been waiting years for!"

Throughout the recording process, Donnie had been working on a nostalgic video montage set to the tune of the newly recorded track "Close to You." Upon seeing the video, Jared recommended that it be used to launch the official NKOTB website. In early 2008, fans who happened upon the site were greeted by a flickering television set playing this video and inviting them to sign up for forthcoming information. The weekend of its quiet debut, the site received a million hits.

After fifteen years of complete radio silence, seeing even a hint of activity on the website was exhilarating for fans. Amber Lantz says, "I began to surf the Internet and went to NKOTB.com—like I had done several thousand times before—but this time it was different. I started making phone calls to my fellow Blockheads that had been in hibernation for the past couple of years. Every phone call I made was met with excitement and anticipation of what was to come. A few days later, I logged on to find new music. As the song began to play, I heard five familiar voices singing 'Close to You.' I cried like a baby! I cried for hours, as I kept replaying the song over and over. I had yearned to hear these voices all together again, and it was actually happening."

This first web posting was a sign of what was to come. Danny says, "We didn't have the Internet the first time around. Having the website go up in anticipation of us getting back together—Are they doing it? Are they not?—it added to everything. We got to grassroots the whole comeback. The impact of the comeback was huge because of the technology."

Initially, NKOTB were set to make their first public appearance as surprise guests on the *Today* show, where they would announce the program's summer concert series lineup. Of this plan, Donnie says, "About two weeks before the *Today* show, I started getting worried." He was concerned that if NKOTB made this surprise appearance without having fans in Rockefeller Plaza, outside the NBC studio, news of the reunion would have minimal impact in the media. Without fans present, Donnie says, "There's no hype. It's just us. And then we have to hope the press's spin is good. We're strictly relying on, 'Guess what? We're back.' Not 'We're back!' followed by screaming. New Kids has always been about instant reaction. The media was always fascinated by the hysteria and adoration of the fans." With these concerns in mind, Donnie called Jared to tell him he felt NKOTB might have to bow out of announcing the summer series.

In what turned out to be a stroke of luck, as Donnie was reconsidering NKOTB's reentry strategy, the *Today* show was informed that Miley Cyrus was willing to make the summer concert series announcement. As the biggest pop act on the scene at the time, *Today* felt compelled to book Miley in lieu of the New Kids. The show's producers did, however, offer NKOTB the opportunity to appear the day *after* the summer concert lineup announcement.

Donnie was relieved when Jared informed him of the change in plans. "I told Jared, 'This is good. But we can't go on the next day. Don't have her announce *us*—have her announce a reunited mystery group.' And then we'll leak out that it might be us, and we'll go on a week later. Let the *Today* show build up who the mystery group is and create a buzz so everyone's gonna want to know who it is—and we'll make sure our fans know. And they'll come."

Miley made the announcement and began the initial hype of the "mystery band," scheduled to appear the next week, as per Donnie's strategy. The *Today* show continued building suspense over the next several days. NKOTB were hard at work too. Donnie says with a grin, "We made sure everyone knew it was gonna be us. We did all the work we could do: we emailed and did everything we could do to create awareness that we were the surprise, but still no one knew officially."

Despite all of this strategizing, there was one factor that NKOTB and their camp could not account for: the weather. As luck would have it, the elements decided not to cooperate on the morning of the New Kids' debut appearance on April 4, 2008. Of the curveball, Donnie says, "It was freezing cold and pouring rain and just disgusting outside. So now, all the betting, all the chips that were pushed in the pot on the fact that we bought a week— all of that was called into question because of the weather. We banked on the fans, and it's freezing cold rain, which might stop them. Did I think there were gonna be fans there? I hoped so! I'm telling everyone else my stupid plan's gonna work, but I didn't know if it would work."

It was a nerve-wracking morning for the guys. Donnie recalls, "That morning, everyone had that look in their eyes like, 'What are we walking into today?' All we ever want is our fans to be there, screaming and going crazy. Because if they're there doing that, we're unstoppable. The fans are the sixth part of it. If the fans aren't there, we'll fight—we're from tough families, and we're street kids—we will show up and fight. But that's a street fight. With our fans, we're a force, and we know this. With our fans, it's more fun, it's more exciting. We'll sing better, we'll dance better, the mistakes will be laughable. The weather is nothing. But after fourteen years and with that weather, we weren't sure if the fans would still show up."

In the moments before the New Kids went live, the five guys were crowded into a tight box designed to enclose the "mystery group" until the announcement was official. "We kept hearing about that *box*," Joe remembers. "We're thinking it's gonna be this huge tarp that's gonna drop down, and there's gonna be some smoke and pyro, like *Oh my God!* And there we were in the middle of Rockefeller Center in this twelve-by-twelve box. We could barely fit in it, and with this velvet rope, it looked like a puppet show."

Fan Laura Barr, who made the trip to New York from Alabama just to be there for the announcement, remembers, "The guys were actually supposed to sneak out and hide behind the curtain for the big reveal. But Donnie, being the goof he is, couldn't sneak out. He riled us all up, gave us a thumbs-up on his way into the box. The most surreal moment for me was seeing the guys' feet poke out from under the curtain. That's kinda when it really hit me: this is really happening."

"That stupid *box*," Donnie remembers. "We're in the box, and Joe said, 'Well, there's no turning back now.'" Despite all of the concern and stress leading up to the big reveal, in the end, the announcement was met by thousands of shrieking fans crammed into Rockefeller Center's courtyard, pouring rain be damned. Of their reception upon exiting the box and stepping in front of the *Today* show's cameras, Donnie says, "I just was relieved. Thank God the fans showed up. Because if I walked out of this *box* and our fans weren't there, I don't know that I could've carried on with this endeavor. The fans made that silly box okay. The fans made everything okay. And the fans, in my estimation, made it a story. It was on *all* these shows, and everyone was talking about it. If the fans aren't there, I think it's a curiosity. But with the fans there, it's a force. It was like, 'Oh my God! All those fans came back in that awful weather after all these years? This is gonna be *huge!*' And it was." Despite their initial concern about the rain, in retrospect, Joe believes it was a blessing in disguise: "The story was that thousands of people showed up to see us *in the rain*. And thank God, because if it was a sunny day and any more light was shined upon that little *box*, there would've been trouble. Our fans are always helping us out."

Anticipating the announcement, screaming fans packed Rockefeller Center, rendering it nearly impossible to hear the guys announce that they would be staging their comeback national performance live on *Today* in six weeks' time. NKOTB also informed the ecstatic audience that a new album and tour would follow. Danny says, "I was shocked that people came out just to see us say, 'Hey, we're getting back together.'"

The *Today* show was the first time that manager Jared Paul witnessed the New Kids and their fans interact up close and personal. He says, "I think one of the things you just can't argue with is the power of the fan base and that loyalty. To see them show up in droves, and then, on top of that, to watch the guys spend the time—not blow past them. Take the hugs, take the pictures, and they know all the fans by name. That's the part that was like, '*Huh?* What multiplatinum, multimillionaire celebrity knows their fans like this?' There's nicknames for the fans, and they have stories, and the fans all come with their pictures from the time they met them in 1980-whatever. That, to me, was a blessing, and it was a bit overwhelming. But it was so beautiful to see because it was so obvious in that moment that the love had never gone away, and it had cemented the relationship. People may have sort of packed up that relationship emotionally in their life somewhere and put it in the closet, so to say, but this gave them the opportunity to pull the box back out and just relive. And it's going strong, obviously. Still to this day."

It was perhaps impossible for NKOTB to understand the impact their announcement had on their fans—even those of the more latent variety. Even Abbey Fisher, a huge fan all the way through 1994, had long since abandoned hope of a New Kids reunion and moved on. Upon seeing a link to the group's on-air announcement, she remembers, "I had to pinch myself because I could not believe what I was seeing. Instantly, I turned into a thirteen-year-old, and it was exactly what I needed. The best part was that they all looked so happy to be together—even Jon was smiling! I was so happy for him and for all of them. I was happy for all of us. We had all survived. And we were all back together again."

Fan Karen Alexander remembers, "When I first heard that the

guys were reuniting, I was driving, and I screamed so loud and got so excited that I literally nearly wrecked my car. I called my mom to tell her the wonderful news, and I just started bawling from pure joy. I knew the long wait was over and that regardless of what was to come, I'd at least have one more chance to see the band that shaped my childhood and brought me through some of the toughest days of my life growing up."

With that, the date was set, and it was game time. As Danny puts it, the New Kids were now tasked with "living up to the hype we created for ourselves." The guys spent the better part of the next several weeks perfecting their performance. It was an intense period, as they got their groove back both as a group and individually. Many of them had not danced in years, yet in just a little over a month, they would be performing live in front of millions of people. "Out of the entire comeback, that was the toughest time for me," Danny says. Jordan remembers, "At first it was like, 'We're doing this? Serious?' We all bought sneakers and sweatpants and appropriate workout and dance attire. Now, we just walk in with whatever we have on. It seemed like more of a daunting task when we first started rehearsing: Do we still have it? Can we *actually* do this? And then I think we got one chorus of one song, 'Summertime.' We looked in the mirror, and we're like, 'We've got it! We've got it!' We celebrated."

Aside from the sheer physical intensity of the rehearsals, there was also the fact that some of the New Kids now had kids and families of their own to take into consideration. "During that time, there was a six-week period I didn't get to see my kids," Danny remembers. "There were just a lot of times where I was missing my kids and really not knowing what the hell was going to happen and what I was doing. I was to the point where I was kinda feeling like, 'This better work out to be worth me missing all this time with my kids.' It's a big price, especially for me, because I'm divorced, and all four of my kids live with me. I'm a hands-on dad. I do everything with them. I take them to school, I pick them up, I cook dinner. I do the whole thing. I want to be home with my kids, and that's all I want to do."

But along with the sacrifices, there were also rewards. Joe remembers, "People were *excited*. This time it was guys too, because it wasn't like, 'Oh, you're stealing my girlfriend,' anymore. We're older now. So they would ask us, 'Is it true?' And we were like, 'Yeah, yeah, it's true.' And they'd be like, 'Nice!' and excited. There was a feeling that they were happy for us."

Just three days before their *Today* show debut, on May 13, 2008, NKOTB released their first single since 1994's "Never Let You Go." "Summertime" became NKOTB's first Top Forty hit since "If You Go Away" in 1992, peaking at number 24 on *Billboard*'s Pop 100. "I almost cried when I heard their new song," fan Julie Prestsater remembers. "It was like putting on your favorite pair of jeans, so familiar and cozy. It's funny how, after so much time, I could still pick out all their voices and was still so pissed when the video came out and they showed so little of Danny." Stacy Scales remembers being a bit taken aback by NKOTB's sudden resurgence. "We never really gave up hope for a reunion. I also must admit, I never really thought it would actually happen. It seems it all happened so fast, it didn't seem real. Maybe it isn't that it really did happen fast, but just that we had waited and hoped and prayed for so long, when it was truly becoming reality, it was hard to believe."

Though the *Today* show has gone down on record as the reunited NKOTB's debut group performance, there was actually one before it. Played before a small, select group of fans on May 13, 2008, at the House of Blues in Los Angeles, this initial performance served as a dress rehearsal before appearing in front of millions of viewers on national television.

Britta Geiogue, one of just a couple hundred fans in attendance, won her ticket through a lottery at NKOTB.com. For someone who had last seen the band play a stadium setting in the early 1990s, the House of Blues environment was staggering. "It was just five microphones on a little, tiny stage in a little, tiny room," she recalls. "We were like, 'You've gotta be kidding me!' I mean, no one had seen them together in fifteen years. Just seeing the five microphones together was exciting. At age thirty, it's ridiculous."

Even in the moment, Britta remembers that it was difficult to wrap her head around what was about to happen. "We just kept thinking they weren't gonna come out. No one had seen them together in so long, it just seemed unbelievable. I somehow kept thinking it was going to get canceled or something, because I couldn't believe I could get so lucky as to see this. They were running about forty-five minutes late, then all of a sudden they were right there on the stage in front of us."

It was like a time warp. "It was like being thirteen again," she continues. "I was reaching out for their hands and singing along. I kept wishing I could have given that experience to my twelve-year-old self, but I don't know that I would've been any more excited at twelve than I was at thirty. I started singing along to 'Tonight,' which I hadn't even heard in fifteen years, but I still knew all the words. The guys were reaching down and touching all our hands and stuff. You just kind of let it go and forget your age." In many ways, that House of Blues performance ignited many of the same feelings in Jon as it did in fans. He remembers, "Thank God we did that because it really knocked my nerves down *a lot*. It was amazing, it was magical, it was surreal."

As the guys were prepping for their debut performance, the streets surrounding Rockefeller Plaza were jammed with excited fans, some of whom had been lined up for five days prior to the performance. Fan Heather Schulze Sciacca was one of those waiting. "I camped out for about four days before the performance," she says. "A friend of mine who worked in Rockefeller Center told me there were girls in line much earlier in the week. I'd sat in the back row of Madison Square Garden back in the day; I saw them a bunch of times when I was a kid, but it was always in 'blue heaven.'"

Heather resolved not to be relegated to the back this time. Her dedication paid off before the performance even began. She says, "We knew it was going to be different this time around, because at three in the morning a couple of days before the show, Jonathan Knight came through and woke up the line. We were pretty much all asleep somewhere on the sidewalk, and he took the middle barricades and started banging them together. I'm in my thirties, but it was like fourteen-year-old me was woken up in the middle of the night by Jonathan Knight. He goes, 'What is wrong with you people? You're *crazy*!' We ran over, and he took pictures with us. He was like, 'You're nuts for being out here. I heard you were here, but I couldn't believe it.' It kind of set the tone for the whole experience. I was like, 'This is gonna be different.' Jon was always the one that seemed to be the shyest—the one who was maybe a little bit more hesitant than the others. And there he was, out there to see us. It was really something else."

By all accounts, the line and what happened in it were a sight to behold. Amber Lantz says, "I was amazed at the many friends I met, and just how far some of them had come just to be here to witness this historical event—from every state and other countries. I pulled out my video camera and began to interview all the girls in line. Some came from as far away as Japan, South Africa, and Italy, yet some had driven only a few miles to be here. It didn't matter; we were all sisters. By the time we were done filming, the line had wrapped all the way around the building twice, and they had to set up more blockades to make room for the girls who were still arriving. As the night passed and the morning came, I heard hundreds of stories of how NKOTB had touched so many lives and how we had all been waiting for this day to arrive. I made so many new friends and reconnected with lots of friends from my past."

The moment of truth arrived on the morning of May 16, 2008. Despite the fact that the rain was pouring down (again), the New Kids would be taking the stage to perform for the first time in fourteen years in front of an audience of thousands in the plaza and millions more watching the telecast. For those patient, drenched fans, the excitement began several hours before the actual performance. Amber Lantz says, "Suddenly, we heard a familiar voice on the microphone: 'Testing—one, two, three, testing.' '*Oh my God! It's Donnie!*' The guys were starting their sound check. Then I hear girls screaming, 'I saw them, I saw them!' A girl told us she could see NKOTB's reflection in the glass from the building behind them. I pulled out my video camera and zoomed in, and saw the most beautiful sight: all five members of NKOTB onstage together for the first time in over fourteen years. I passed the camera around and started to cry. Other fans started hugging each other and crying on each other's shoulders. It's hard for me to put the feeling I felt at that moment into words. It was like an *awakening*. I felt alive again, I felt love again, I felt like I belonged again, I felt young again, I felt like me again."

Fan Lindsay Yost says, "As the sun began to rise, we began to hear the New Kids rehearse their set list. From a distance, I could hear the melody of 'Hangin' Tough,' and I unexpectedly got goose bumps. As the line slowly advanced and we rounded the corner onto the street where rehearsals were under way, I heard Joe's voice belting out 'Please Don't Go Girl'—and suddenly and involuntarily, I reverted back to experiencing the feelings of the young teenager who had her walls covered with posters of his face."

Determined not to let the rain adversely affect them, Danny remembers, "The day of the performance became more about not busting your ass or anything. Everyone was talking about this and that, and I was like, 'Listen. The most important thing is that no one falls.' The falling thing now, it ends up on YouTube, everyone sees it, it's on everyone's website. The rain actually took the pressure off. When we *did* go to perform, it was kind of like 'Just don't fall, and have fun.'"

When the performance began, the rain didn't matter. Tracy Maccabee remembers, "Finally we saw the curtain come down with 'New Kids on the Block' written on it, and everybody went crazy. The rain was coming down hard by then, and the stage was full of water. The guys were slipping and sliding around and made the best of it." Even in the pouring rain, NKOTB's performance was just as tight and full of energy as it had ever been. Outfitted in matching suits, the New Kids launched into "Step by Step," then segued into a medley of classics, including "Hangin' Tough," "Please Don't Go Girl," and "The Right Stuff," woven together by a "Click Click Click" interlude. They also performed "Summertime" for the first time on television and finished off with an energetic performance of the apropos "Tonight." It was a party in Rockefeller Plaza as the guys let loose onstage and fans cheered them on. With a thrust stage that jutted out into the audience, by the end of the song, NKOTB were essentially out amongst the crowd. This proximity—which never could have happened during the band's initial run—was a good indication of one of the primary differences between the twentieth- and twenty-first-century versions of NKOTB.

"After they were done performing and finished up the short interview, we thought they were done," Tracy says. "The whole crowd started chanting, 'Come back here!' About an hour later, Joe and Jordan came out of nowhere and jumped onto the small stage. I went nuts seeing them only a few feet away. The rest of the guys joined them, and they did a small interview with Matt Lauer and Al Roker." It was on this platform in the midst of the crowd that Joe was able to really grasp the magnitude of the event. "The way the main stage is set up, you don't get the total sense of it," he explains. "But then we got up on this smaller staging, and that was the first time we got to see the crowd. *Oh my God!* This was serious stuff. The crowd went *way* back. These people didn't see our show *at all* because they couldn't see the stage from where they were, but they came. It went forever. There was a discrepancy as to whether Bruce Springsteen or we had a bigger crowd on the *Today* show. And one of the *Today* show crew guys gave us a wink because he didn't want to give it up that maybe we had a bigger crowd than Springsteen."

Amazed by their reception, Danny says, "When it started, and I looked out and saw the crowd, I just could not believe it. I could not believe that this many people were really interested in seeing us back out there doing it again. The look on the fans' faces, it was clear we took them back to their youth again. Then, on top of that, you go through that whole *Today* show experience that's so overwhelming and so amazing, and I'm just like, 'What's gonna happen from this?'"

What Danny and the other guys couldn't see were the millions of viewers glued to their televisions and computer screens. Fan Jennifer Rivera remembers, "I have to admit I was nervous to see how NKOTB would be after all these years. Could they still sing? Dance? Would people care? I didn't want a public backlash to tarnish my pristine childhood memories of the first boys I ever loved. Watching the *Today* show, I held my breath, but they were better dancers, they were better-looking, they sounded great! And the crowd—it was pouring rain, but it was still one of the biggest crowds the show had ever seen. I think I let out a squeal in front of my husband, who just doesn't understand."

For many fans, seeing the New Kids together again represented so much more than just a band reuniting. Jennifer Farris explains what that *Today* show meant to her: "NKOTB was a symbol—a representation of an entire era in our lives, an era that took place before we became worried about recessions, wars, and mortgages. All of a sudden we got the fever again. We wanted more New Kids. We wanted concerts, new music, and press coverage. Demand for the group was reborn."

Laurel Moffat remembers the feeling in the air of the plaza that morning. "It was an odd energy because everyone had been up all night. You were sleeping on the street. You were eating total crap if you were eating anything at all. And then it rained. We weren't hugging each other or crying. Everyone was having their *own* moment of disbelief and excitement and reminiscing. And getting rained on—there's a bit of hilarity in that. My friend calls it 'Drowned Rat Weekend.' It was gross outside, but nobody cared. It was all about seeing NKOTB and being there. I think that's been the overarching sentiment of all of this: just being there. It doesn't matter how far away you are—just so you can be there."

Although Jon didn't know exactly what to expect going into the reunion, the fans' response that day clarified a lot for him. "They reacted above and beyond what I expected. I didn't know that we would be so well embraced again. I think the *Today* show was a sign of things to come."

Indeed, the *Today* show was just a small taste.

Carpe Diem

As was the case with many fans the first time around, Maria Carpinella attended NKOTB shows with her mom. Between 1988 and 1994, NKOTB served as the basis for a lot of mother-daughter adventures. Looking back, Maria says, "I loved it. I had the cool mom, and everybody wanted to be doing what we were doing."

Between 2002 and 2006, Maria and her mother, Carol, suffered a series of heart-wrenching losses, including the death of Charlie, Maria's father and Carol's husband. By the time NKOTB reunited in 2008, the Carpinellas were ready for some fun. The shows seemed like the perfect opportunity to have a little adventure and relive more carefree times. Carol recalls, "It was one of the first happy things that had happened in our lives, and we were really, really so excited to be doing it together."

Infused with *joie de vivre*, the Carpinella ladies set off for ten shows during the first leg of the reunion tour. Having even more fun than they anticipated, they went to more shows during the second leg. And so it has continued since then. It's about more than just the show: it's about the chance to see the world, spend time together, and connect with new friends.

Carol and Maria also found ways to pay tribute to Mr. Carpinella's memory as they traveled. For example, while in Scotland, the duo visited St. Andrews Golf Course, which Charlie, an avid golfer, had always wanted to visit. Carol says, "They allowed us to go out on a very famous bridge on this golf course and take a picture and sprinkle some ashes. My husband was cremated, and we take a little bit of his ashes everywhere we go and put them somewhere. That's been a part of this tradition too."

Along the way, the ladies have struck up friendships with people all over the world, including Donnie, who refers to them affectionately as Pokermom and Pokerdaughter. Of this friendship, Donnie says, "We just clicked. One day I said, 'Pokermom, come here.' And that was it. She doesn't miss anything; I invite her to everything." This has been the icing on the cake of a wonderful journey for Carol and Maria. Carol says, "Donnie's just a really good person, and he's brought a lot of happiness to my and Maria's lives when we really needed it."

Stronger Than Ever

It's amazing. It's almost like going through life and then getting *another* chance at life, knowing what you know now.

—Jordan

With the *Today* show behind them, the ball was rolling fast and furious as the guys prepared to hit major venues across North America. With an eye toward pragmatism, the New Kids selected their dates carefully, initially skewing tour stops toward areas where their audience was the densest. Donnie says, "We always start small, with the hope of building bigger." The first run of the reunion tour did quite a bit of building, hitting primary markets in the United States and Canada. From there NKOTB did a few dates in Mexico, then went to Europe, and, finally, returned to the States to hit secondary markets. All told, the tour ran from September 2008 through May 2009.

NKOTB's reunion tour consisted of stops at high-profile venues, including New York's Madison Square Garden and the band's hometown TD Banknorth Garden. Once tickets were officially on sale, it was like déjà vu all over again: Madison Square Garden sold out in just six minutes; tickets for the opening show at Toronto's Air Canada Centre were gone in four.

As excitement built amongst fans, the group was hard at work getting ready to tour for the first time since 1994. NKOTB's rehearsal schedules were grueling as they fought to get themselves back in tip-top shape. Of that period, Jon says, "It was so much work. We put so much expectation on ourselves. I remember going on a diet and going to the gym like a madman and rehearsing, rehearsing, rehearsing, just trying to make everything as perfect as it could be, both physically and logistically."

Unlike earlier days, this time NKOTB had complete control of the entire show from start to finish. Jordan says, "To us, it's not just about recording music or about singing your song onstage, it's about finding the magic there. However it is that you get that done doesn't matter, as long as you do it. We're very hands-on with the whole thing because we don't want other people messing it up." Together they spent hours plotting to put together a performance that would blow audiences away. As Jon puts it, "Our objective was to bring back that feeling of being fifteen years old for the audience." It was a fine balance of incorporating the old with the new. While fans were obviously coming back to see the songs they had loved during their youth, it was also important to add a modern, fresh edge.

At the heart of it all was the music. The foundation of the new album was recorded with Nasri during those initial recording sessions with Joe, Jordan, and Donnie, and he also ended up playing a key role on the album as a whole. Jordan explains, "Nasri was a good thread all the way through the songs. He grew up listening to the New Kids and had a good sense of pop and R&B music. He's young, so he has a good sense of what sounds good on the radio. We had our battles with Nasri, but he was definitely instrumental in giving us that old, soulful New Kids sound, but putting it into 2008."

After signing with Interscope, NKOTB were introduced to Swedish producer and songwriter RedOne through Aimee

Nadeau. RedOne teamed up with NKOTB for several songs on the album, including "Dirty Dancing" and "Full Service." RedOne was also working with a then relatively unknown Lady Gaga. Aimee says, "When Donnie was in the studio writing and working on some new songs with RedOne, we were like, 'Well, why doesn't Lady Gaga come in and write some stuff too?' Donnie was very open to it even though she hadn't really had a hit, and no one knew who she was." The end result of this collaboration was "Big Girl Now," a track that Lady Gaga ultimately sang on as well. Jordan says, "I actually suggested that she do the duet with us. At first she was just going to be a writer. She's this dynamic personality with an incredible voice, was on Interscope, and they were ready to push her out, so let's do a duet. It fit right in."

In addition to "Big Girl Now," the album, *The Block*, incorporated acts such as R&B superstar Ne-Yo on "Single" and Nicole Scherzinger of Pussycat Dolls fame on "Grown Man." The song "Twisted" was written in conjunction with (and featured) famed producer Timbaland, who'd previously worked with artists like Justin Timberlake and Madonna. Additionally, NKOTB paid homage to their roots through a collaboration with fellow Boston boys New Edition on the track "Full Service."

Right before the tour launched, NKOTB released their first album since 1994's *Face the Music* on September 2, 2008. Fan Abbey Fisher says, "I bought *The Block* the day it came out, and I had to pinch myself because I couldn't believe I was buying a New Kids on the Block album in 2008." As would be expected, *The Block* had a more mature sound than NKOTB's previous albums and featured an up-to-date, dance-driven vibe. The lead single, "Summertime," was the one throwback to the earlier New Kids sound and also featured nostalgic, somewhat double-entendre lyrics, which could be applied not only to a relationship but also as a love song to fans.

With new music ready to go, tour dates scheduled, and countless hours of rehearsal behind them, it was time for NKOTB to hit the stage for the first of three shows in Toronto, Ontario, on September 18, 2008. Somewhat of a NKOTB hotbed, "Toronto is just beyond supportive," Danny says. "It was definitely a catalyst in launching the whole comeback. I don't know why, but in Toronto, you just get a completely different kind of energy." In the final moments leading up to the show, the five guys huddled under the stage as the lights went down. Together they listened as high-pitched screams at decibels more expected from thirteen-year-olds than from thirty-year-olds echoed throughout the sold-out twenty-thousand-seat arena. Backstage, Joe says, "There was such a feeling of camaraderie. Even though we were twenty years older, we got innocence back in that way. There was such an innocence about coming back. It felt like Christmas Eve and Christmas morning, those days in Toronto. We were all exhausted—people were sleeping in the catering area. It was nonstop. But once we hit the day of the show, it was really, really so special."

Onstage a video screen lit up, and the opening montage began to roll with messaging that perfectly encapsulated what so many in the crowd were feeling that night. Running in conjunction with nostalgic images of the past, the text read, "Fifteen years ago, they walked away. Tonight . . . the Block is back. Are you ready? It's time." As the video played, the screaming in the audience grew louder and more manic, exploding into one deafening roar as the soft piano overture of "Single" began. "It was a force," Joe remembers. "The crowd was so loud that you could feel it." Susy Medeiros, there that night, says, "I cannot even really begin to describe the feeling of that moment when the opening words came across the screen: 'The Block is back. Are you ready?' Our hearts were in our throats, and then up through the riser they came from under the stage. The screams were deafening as we stood there looking up at our boys and then at each other. We had tears in our eyes and goose bumps up our arms. I was suddenly a screaming, hysterical teenager and happier than I had ever been!" Of hearing this sound again after all this time, Jordan says, "It's slightly lower pitched. *Slightly*. It's still pretty damn intense, I tell you that." For his part, Danny says, "*That* sound was something that shocked me." Jon says, "The screaming is a little deeper now. That is the most amazing sound. I can understand why so many celebrities and singers miss the adulation of a crowd because it is a feeling like no other. I think so many entertainers and celebrities are lost souls that need and thrive off that. I'm starting to think it helped me out, too, later in life after being away. That feeling is a drug. It's a *legal* drug. I'm just glad I can appreciate it and know where it comes from and not take it for granted, because that's easy to do too."

Proud mom Marlene Putman was there to watch her sons' debut reunion performance that night. She remembers, "You just walked into that venue, and there was so much excitement because all those fans had been waiting. It's been all these years, and here we are! It was so funny to see the girls walking around with beers—so different. And then there's the countdown, and you know it's gonna start, and they've got the video going on the stage. Your heart's pounding. I never expected when NKOTB ended that they would come back big again. And then there they are, standing way up high, those five guys together again. I just burst into tears. I could hardly even watch it, I was crying so hard. I was like, 'We're off again! It's gonna happen again!'"

To this day, Jon says, it's almost impossible for him to wrap his head around what happened that night in Toronto. "It was *crazy*. An arena, after all these years. Back in an arena?" Joe's distended voice rang out through the dark venue, followed by Donnie's. A modernized NKOTB logo appeared on the screen above the stage. And then, as though they had never been gone, smoke billowed as the five guys rose up from below. It was utter pandemonium, with shrieking seldom found outside the teen idol sphere. Jordan remembers trying to remain in the zone as the riser emerged onstage. "I was trying to keep my composure, really. I was trying to make it less of a big deal than it really was in my head. I didn't want my excitement or my nervousness to take over, so I was just trying to control what I was doing and how I was feeling. But on the inside, I was saying, 'This is fucking *amazing!*'"

Of emerging onstage with his four cohorts that night, Jon says, "Just getting on that lift—we couldn't see the crowd, really, but we knew they were out there. I don't know how I made it through that show because the whole time in my head I was just like, '*Wow, wow, wow.* This is not happening.' It was like a *dream.* Like, how could that possibly be after all these years? Just coming up, and the sea of flashbulbs and lights. I'll always remember that."

To this day, Donnie can hardly think back to those initial seconds onstage in Toronto without getting emotional—in fact, he still watches a video to relive the moment. "It's the best thing I've ever watched," he says. "I've watched the opening of the reunion tour in Toronto more than any other video in my life. I cry almost every time I watch it. I get overcome because I think of every detail and putting it together and all the emotion. It was a huge moment in my life. Epic."

As they stepped off of the riser and descended the stairs onstage to approach the crowd, Joe remembers, "We started dancing, walking up and doing the slow choreography, and it really was a wall of sound. You were *hit* by it. It wasn't like it was 'Oh my God, it's loud' in your ears. It was a *force* that was pushing, coming like a wave. Coming from the audience, and we were walking into the wave. To say it gave you chills would be a huge understatement. You felt like you were floating. It was wild. That wave of sound actually had life to it. It had electricity. I guess sound is a wave; that wave had a physicality that night. It had a pulse."

It was as though the entire audience simultaneously checked all of its adult worries at the door and was transported to the more carefree days of its youth. Onstage the guys harmonized and synchronized better and with more precision than they had as youngsters. The chemistry and energy they shared collectively were still there, but this time it was accompanied by a concentration and smoothness that come only with age and experience. "We're tighter because we're more disciplined," Jordan explains. "We have the wisdom of all those years. We've learned from mistakes from the past. It's amazing. It's almost like going through life and then getting *another* chance at life, knowing what you know now. I think that has a lot to do with the tightness and the professionalism." "Single" transitioned into "My Favorite Girl," a frequent energetic opener of yore. Seamlessly, new and old fused into one.

The emotional impact of seeing NKOTB together onstage once again thudded rampantly throughout the audience. Cassie Meyer remembers, "It made me emotional because those memories of NKOTB are the very best childhood memories I have. Everything I remember doing or talking about—with my friends, at school, to my parents, to my sister—was in some way about the New Kids. When I think back to being ages four through eight, my only memories of those times are of me and the New Kids. The concert was epic. It sparked a whole new beast that is still alive and well to this day."

With a successful sold-out three-night stand in Toronto and another in Montreal under their belts, NKOTB made their American debut at the Izod Center in East Rutherford, New Jersey, on September 23, 2008. Again, the fan reaction was intense. Fan Kelly Kostanesky never had the chance to see NKOTB live during their initial run, but finally that opportunity presented itself in East Rutherford. "I saw all five guys together as one on that stage and honestly felt like my life was complete," she recalls. "I didn't know until that moment that there was a part of me that always wanted to say I had that moment of seeing NKOTB in concert. The reunion meant so much to so many of us, but those of us that never had the concert experience before appreciated it in ways we can probably never express. I remember standing just a few rows away from the stage when the introduction video began playing. I watched old and new images of the guys dance on the screen, and I've never cried tears of joy more than I did in that moment."

While the guys were soaking in every moment of this second go-round, they were also adjusting to the intense grind of being on the road, away from their normal lives and families, and living amongst one another again. With this period of assimilation came some growing pains. It was in East Rutherford that it seemed for a moment that all of Donnie's previous fears about reuniting with NKOTB surfaced. "We hadn't really learned the boundaries of backstage yet," he says. "I went to see a dentist, and he wanted tickets for the show, and he brought his staff, which was six women. We had a bunch of dressing rooms reserved, and they were in one of them—I didn't even know they were in there. Jon walked into the room and saw them and got upset. Jon was walking down the hallway, and he looked mad. I was always very dialed into Jon's emotional state and connected with him. I asked him what was wrong, and he said, 'Nothing!' I reached out to put my arm around his shoulder, and he pulled away from me and stormed off. And it was 1990 all over again. That's how we used to be. My reaction in 1990 would've been 'Fuck you!' Deep inside it would have been a very insecure reaction, like, 'What did I do wrong? Why is he mad at me?' But it would've come out as 'Fuck you.'"

From his point of view, Jon says, "I actually felt bad speaking up, but it was a *madhouse* backstage. I remember the first few shows, you would try to get away and would poke your head into a room to be able to take a breath and have nobody around. And it just seemed like there were people around in every single room and people in the hallways. It was a mess. It was weird that Donnie and I blew up at each other like that."

"When it came to the next day of a concert," Donnie continues, "we didn't speak at meet and greet. It was like 1990 all over again.

Every night backstage, we would gather, and the video would play, and we'd all sort of look up at it and talk and do a little huddle, and Danny would say a little speech, or someone would say something. Jon was kind of looming off to the side. Jared had called me maybe a half hour before the show and said Jon was really shaken up and feels horrible about what he did. I saw Jon over there alone, not in the huddle. The music's playing, the video's playing, it's showtime, and I just said, 'Hey! Are you gonna come in the huddle?' He came right over and hugged me, and that was it. It was gone. It was a blip, and nothing like that has ever happened again since." Jon agrees that was the end of that, saying, "Donnie has the biggest heart, and his intentions for having people come backstage is a beautiful thing. It continued throughout the tour, but he knew, 'Okay, if people are going to be back here, I need to respect the feelings of everybody else and contain it a little bit.' Once it was contained, it was perfect."

What started off as a troubling situation ended up exemplifying how maturity had shifted band members' relationships for the better. Of the difference in dynamics between then and now, Donnie explains, "We made up all the time as kids. All of us. We'd fight, and we'd make up. But I don't think we really forgave each other. I forgive Jon for that moment. It helped to know that he felt bad about it, and once I knew he felt bad about it, I felt bad for him. I don't want Jon to feel bad."

NKOTB's next reunion tour milestone occurred on September 26, 2008, on their two-night hometown stand at TD Banknorth Garden. The first night's crowd of nearly twenty thousand actually represented only a fraction of the people watching the show that evening; VH1 hosted a ninety-minute *Behind the Music Special Event* immediately followed by a live broadcast of the band's first three songs. Christina St. Arnaud attended the show that evening with her best friend from childhood, Nicole Palermo, which made the experience even sweeter. She recollects, "The crowd was electrifying, our boys were singing, and we were dancing together again after all those years apart. That night was like reliving our childhood. We were carefree and innocent. We were no longer concerned about jobs, mortgages, or bills. Instead our minds were preoccupied with the sight of our five favorite hometown boys as they were bringing down the house at the Garden, just as they had done so many years earlier."

For the New Kids, this hometown recognition means a lot. Joe explains, "There's so much love for this group in the city of Boston that it's really staggering. And Boston's a tough town—don't get too big for your britches, that whole thing. Around the reunion, there was a feeling of 'We're proud of you, and you did it right. Attaboy.' It *gets* us. We appreciate it so, *so* much. It's a love like no other."

Just as fans enjoyed revisiting the past, so too did the guys. Danny says that old standards like "The Right Stuff" have now taken on new meaning. "It just feels great to give the fans that moment, and it's also kind of a little bit of redemption. Seeing how much they love it makes me love doing it. There were times early on when we were kids that I hated doing that song. We had done it so many times. And then it became this moment during that time where you either loved us or hated us. Now, coming back around, it's not that love-hate thing. It's a completely different feeling. I have fun doing it, it's great."

Fan Helen Thompson remembers the impact of this chance to go back. "My first reunion show in Vegas on October 11, 2008, was an absolute dream come true. I couldn't believe my eyes when I saw them onstage together. During 'Tonight,' my sister Sara and I cried on each other's shoulders and reveled in the fact that NKOTB were our first loves, and we never thought we would see them again."

During the height of their fame in the eighties and nineties, NKOTB were in many ways unable to appreciate what was happening around them. But today it's a completely different scenario. According to Danny, "It's new all over again. Because of our ages when we first did it and how fast it happened, we couldn't soak it in like we do now. It's completely different for me." Jon feels similarly, saying, "God, I'm just so happy this happened as an adult. It's just so much better." With the benefit of experience, it's also less overwhelming and more manageable. Jordan concurs, "I enjoy this time around so much better. Not that I didn't enjoy it then, but I was a little shell shocked with all the attention and hysteria. It rattled me a little bit. I'm like an old warhorse now. You can scream in my ear, and it doesn't bug me. You can have a whole line of paparazzi in front of me taking millions of pictures, and I'm just like, 'Whatever.'"

There's also a new sense of pride based on the fact that they've been able to do things the way *they* want to this time around. Joe says, "To me, it was better than anything we've ever done. To be able to go at it as adults with plenty of time to reflect on our lives; to come back and be able to execute the way we really always wanted to be able to execute. To build it the way you want it, and to put it on the road and see it work the way you wanted it to work, and feel the commitment and feel the energy—there was a *lot* of satisfaction in that. And, of course, having the time of our lives. It was different. It was much different than back in the day."

Another big difference for the guys is that this time they have their own children to bring along for the ride. According to Jon, "Having kids on tour was an extension of the love we have for each other. The best part of having the kids around, for me, was seeing the other four guys be dads." Danny says, "Some of the first shows of the reunion tour, my kids were there, and they never had seen me onstage. They knew I was in a group of some kind, but that was it. I get a real different perspective because now I just walk by my daughters' room, and they're playing our music. I never pushed it on them, nothing. Having them along has been a giant bonus for me."

Jordan agrees. "It is the best of both worlds," he enthuses. "Having kids and a wife and family, you get to kind of share it with them, and it makes it a whole lot better. Dante, my eleven-year-old son, has been on tour with us a few times. He really likes it. Sometimes after he watches us perform, he'll do a couple of my moves. It's really funny seeing him do that. I would love to get in his mind and see what his take is on it."

"It's really one of the blessings of this time around. It's the great equalizer because you're a *dad*. Everybody's a dad," Joe says. "It's just so sweet. You've got Jordan sitting there with Dante playing the keyboard—that's just a beautiful thing. Dante looks like Jordan, and just to see him behind a keyboard in the dressing room is cool. And then Donnie's son Elijah comes in, and he has a very disarming and charming way—obviously, look at his dad. And then Jon, who doesn't have kids, probably loves kids more than anybody. So he grabs them right up instantly. He's just one of those guys that will swoop a baby up right away, and he has such great energy that they love it. That kind of stuff is so priceless, especially out on the road." At the wizened age of four, Joe's oldest son, Griffin, is practically a road veteran. Joe says, "He loves it. He likes to dress up, he likes to put on the outfits, he sees what I get into and really picks it up. On the last tour, he was able to walk around the stage with Jordan. Jordan was pointing things out and giving him a tour, showing him a couple of moves. Griffin loved all the guys, but he just gravitated toward Jordan. It was really, really sweet."

Donnie's ten-year-old son, Elijah, has also gotten into it. Donnie says, "He loves the tour bus, he loves the backstage, he loves the dressing room, he loves the guys. We sit on the sofas after the show, all five of us, and we eat. And *believe* me, we wouldn't have done that twenty years ago. But we do it now. You can feel the bond amongst the guys. Elijah wants to be in that dressing room when the five guys are eating after the show. He can feel it; he wants to be in that circle. He'll be with Danny's daughters the whole night, but he won't eat with them. 'I'm waiting for you. I wanna eat with the guys,' he says. But it's more than that. He can feel the spirit, that *thing* when we come off the stage after two and a half hours of cheering. There's just a heightened energy."

Fans want to soak up that heightened energy too. Kimberly Reed says, "In 2008 when I saw the guys at the Palace of Auburn Hills, I seriously thought it would be great and I would talk about it for a few days and tuck that love back in my heart. That night when the lights went down, it was as though I had time warped to a twelve-year-old version of myself. The feeling that came over me was something I had not experienced in years. Not even when I fell in love with a boy did I have this feeling. It was a giddy excitement I had not had in about fifteen years. All that love I tucked away came back with fifteen years of experience with it. It was the innocent, pure love that a twelve-year-old has, not the cynical version of my thirty-year-old self."

For as much as it's a chance for fans to go back to a simpler, earlier time, it is for the band members as well. Jordan explains, "A lot of girls thank us, like, 'You make us feel young again.' It's the same for us, though. It makes us feel young—makes us act young. We're really like five guys in the school yard trying to impress the girls. We're show-offs. We really love the admiration. We work hard to get the screams."

One of the most gratifying experiences for the guys this time around has been seeing the successful adults their fans have grown into. Danny says, "We're asking our fans what they do for a living, and they're doctors, lawyers, nurses, software developers. They're incredible. The majority are professional women that are independent and have made it alone and want their picture alone and want time with us."

Kimberly Reed explains why this love has transferred to adulthood, saying, "When you love something as a kid, you never stop loving it; you just tuck that love away in a different spot in your heart." Donnie explains this same phenomenon as a "spark." "When we decided to get back together, I think it lit a spark in the fans. The magic in all this stuff is when you plan all this out, and then when you actually get up and do it, things happen that you *didn't* plan. What's happened in this reunion is that we said, 'We're coming back,' it lit a spark in the fans, and they then lit a spark in us. They stoked the spark and kept it going."

As Donnie sees it, the spark has resulted in a back-and-forth that no one saw coming. The New Kids respond to fan reaction by taking it a step further, the fans respond in kind, and so it spirals from there. "We've gone to a level they didn't expect: we're tweeting, we're hugging, we're meeting and greeting. We just keep going. And they do too. They're screaming at the parts of the show they weren't supposed to, they're emotional, they're bringing out the signs and candles and pink hearts. They keep going to another level, and *we* keep going to another level, and it's going back and forth. The fans keep surprising us, they keep showing up; and we keep surprising them and not giving up."

Jared Paul has had a very unique vantage point on this relationship between NKOTB and their fans. He says, "It's not *normal*. You get used to working a certain way with the majority of artists who love their fans and treat them with respect, but it's not the same. They don't give fans passes to eat dinner backstage with them. They don't let them in their dressing room. They don't bring them on their bus because they need a ride. It just doesn't *happen*. I think it's a beautiful thing. I think I had a little bit of an awakening." On a day-to-day basis, Jared works to not only plan and make decisions that optimize the five guys' experience but also that of the ever-important sixth party: the fans. He says, "It's a very big part of my job to nurture that relationship. We *think* about the fans, and how are they going to react to this? How can we do our best to accommodate them?" Examples of extra steps taken to accommodate fans are rampant, and most recently include four town hall meetings in the spring of 2012. For these, members of NKOTB's Block Nation fan club were invited to various locations across the United States to participate in a brainstorming session with the New Kids and to provide input, feedback, and suggestions for future events.

It's because of this cyclical spark between NKOTB and their fans that what began as a reunion has transformed into a resurgence. NKOTB added a second leg to the initial reunion tour to hit Europe and then secondary US markets in the spring of 2009. After that, the tour was revamped, and NKOTB hit amphitheaters across the country during the summer months for their follow-up Full Service tour.

Before the Full Service tour began, promoters suggested that NKOTB bring on nineties boy band Backstreet Boys as an opening act. Donnie remembers discussing this possibility with Jared and saying, "I don't think Backstreet Boys are an opening act for us. I think that's a big tour." Donnie says, "In typical Jared fashion, I planted that seed in his head that we could coheadline a tour together. Why would we waste something that could be so cool? Two of the biggest bands in history. Why undervalue that with one of them as an opening band for the other one? It just didn't feel right. It felt like we were selling them short and selling the two groups together short. Jared ended up getting Jesse McCartney to open the tour, but he never let go of the idea of us and Backstreet Boys."

The Full Service tour went ahead without Backstreet Boys. At the final show in Houston on July 18, 2009, fans banded together to demonstrate their love and gratitude for NKOTB, fearing that this would be the end of the reunion that had provided them with so much. Heading up this effort, Jennifer Armstrong says, "I started a private Twitter account and quietly asked people to join to learn of the plan to hold up Thank You signs at the last show. The followers quickly grew from single digits to hundreds, and the plan was being passed back and forth at a rapid pace. We wanted to keep the plan a surprise, so the account was private, and I had to constantly check for new 'Follow' requests. I was getting so many at one point, I would just scan the list quickly for spammers, then approve everyone else."

Because Jennifer was receiving such a large response, she didn't even notice that one of the account's new followers was Jon Knight. She was surprised when, a few days before the show, she received a couple of messages in her in-box from Jon. Jennifer remembers, "Jon said I'd better 'mix up [my] plan soon!' because he was in the know about everything. A subsequent message from Mr. Knight suggested that we try candles instead of signs because that had never been done before."

Despite Jon's insider tip, it was a bit daunting to change the plan from signs to candles with so little time left. Nonetheless, Jennifer covertly asked fans to bring battery-operated candles to the show and to hold them up during "I'll Be Loving You (Forever)." "The response was simply amazing," Jennifer says. "People were sending in messages that they were buying five, ten, or twenty extra candles. To all of these fans' credit, we never spread the word that the candles were Jon's suggestion; we wanted people to do it because they understood our goal to create a moment for NKOTB that showed our appreciation."

After all of that planning, the night of the Houston show finally arrived. Hundreds of people came armed with candles for themselves and others in the crowd. Jennifer remembers, "I was so nervous because of the short amount of time we had to revise this plan. I worried the end result would be less than impressive." Jennifer had no reason for concern. Despite her fears, "As the opening notes of 'I'll Be Loving You (Forever)' started, the candles shot up all over. I watched as a few turned to hundreds, then to thousands. To see them swaying in the hot, Texas twilight was something I'll never forget. I could see the reactions of the guys onstage—it was extraordinary to behold. There was a cameraman onstage, and I could see Donnie and Joe repeatedly tell him to turn around and film the crowd. The large screens showed shots that panned the crowd, with many in the audience becoming extremely emotional through the song. As 'I'll Be Loving You' came to a close, the Woodlands Pavilion erupted in a roar that I've never really heard before. It was a mixture of joy and sadness, enthusiasm and tears. Everyone held up their Thank You signs, and the applause and cheers seemed like they would never end. After a few minutes, Donnie launched into one of those only-Donnie-Wahlberg-can-give pep talks—except this time, it was all about the future. On my way home from Texas, I received a message of thanks from Jon for the 'amazing' display."

From his point of view, Jon says, "Being the Twitter whore I am, I kind of ran into the plan. I knew it was coming and was actually kind of sad because I thought it would have less of an impact on me. But it turned out to be one of the most amazing moments of the reunion. It was very emotional for all of us because it was our last show, and we weren't sure if that was the end or if it would continue on. It was kind of a good-bye to the New Kids as we'd known it for the previous year. It's moments like that where the bond is felt between us five and our die-hard fans. Those candles and signs exemplified that bond."

Since the reunion began, fans have been braced for the announcement that the end is nigh. Jon says, "I think in general the fans are worried it's *all* gonna go away." When he first heard about the reunion, Jon, too, assumed it would be a temporary situation. He says, "I figured we'd do twenty-eight shows in the States, and that would be it. I told my business partner, 'I'm leaving for X amount of months, and I'll be back, and we can resume our company.' And since '08, I haven't really been back. He's not too happy about that, but what do you do?" For Jon or anyone else, predicting the ongoing reunion from the outset would have been virtually impossible, since there wasn't a preexisting model to emulate. Danny points out, "I think we're the only teenage group who's done this. I know the Eagles and bands like that have reunited, but we were *kids* the first time around, and that kind of phenomenon usually comes and goes. *Fifteen years.* That's why in the beginning I didn't expect much. I was just like, 'I don't know what the hell's gonna happen. I'm gonna work as hard as I can, and we'll see.'"

Despite fans' fears, the completion of the Full Service tour wasn't the end. In December 2009 NKOTB treated fans to an intimate one-off performance to ring in the holidays at Boston's House of Blues. The day of the show, a blizzard hit the city. Fan Jennifer Esbensen remembers, "Nobody was really expecting Joey to be there, with the birth of his son one week before and his having to travel from California to Massachusetts with flights being canceled. But the guys came out, and Joey was there. The crowd went crazy!" Of his somewhat surprise appearance that day, Joe says, "My wife had the baby on December 13, and the show was on December 20, so it wasn't that big of a stretch. The real drama was that my son was born with severe hearing loss, so we were in the throes of that and weren't at all close to telling everyone. I think there was a snowstorm hanging around, but it wasn't what it seemed. Donnie was working his razzle-dazzle showbiz: 'If there's a story to be told, let's tell one!' As in, 'He might not make it . . . he won't make it . . . he is not gonna make it . . . *Ladies and gentlemen, Joey McIntyre!!!*'"

Regardless, Joe's presence that night added to the festivity of the show, which featured NKOTB taking their old Christmas tunes from 1989 off the shelf and performing them with gleeful abandon; bringing New Edition veterans Johnny Gill and Ricky

Bell onstage to perform "Full Service"; and even a little bit of mistletoe action with crowd participation. Jon laughs, remembering, "When I saw the mistletoe going around, I was like, 'Hmmm, how can I shock the hell out of everybody?' So I made out with a chick." At the heart of it, the improvised show provided everyone with the chance to let loose and celebrate. Jon says, "There are shows where we're one hundred percent professional, and then there are shows where we like to just be ourselves and be goofy and kick back and have fun. House of Blues was one of those fun, goofy shows." Jennifer Esbensen agrees that this carefree quality was precisely what made the show so memorable. She says, "The guys joked around a lot onstage. It was very different from a regular concert, very impromptu, which made it that much better."

With that same sort of spirit, in summer 2010 NKOTB embarked on a short, weekend-only "nontour" of small theaters and casinos in what appropriately came to be dubbed the Casi-NO tour. It culminated in a three-night stand at New York City's Radio City Music Hall. For fans, this was a great opportunity to see a more stripped-down version of the band, closer up than they had the previous two years. Not only this, but with two and a half years under their belts, the Blockhead community had solidified, making the shows even more meaningful. Fan Shannon Thorne explains, "To me, the Casi-NO tour had something a little extra special about it. The social media boom had allowed us all to bond in a way that wasn't possible up to that point. We fans had begun to develop strong friendships with each other in spite of being scattered all over the globe. The guys themselves were getting to know many of us on a new level—sort of a cross between fans and friends. We were no longer a faceless mass; they were able to look into the audience while performing and see familiar faces with stories and memories attached to them. It was all very new and exciting on both sides, I think. It was a giant traveling festival of love and joy."

The show itself had a unique dance club vibe and began with a DJ rather than a more traditional opening act, allowing fans to hang out and party before the main event. A huge clock appeared, counting down to the guys' arrival and driving the crowd into a frenzy. Christine Darnell says, "For me, no matter how many times I see them, the excitement leading up to the first moment they are onstage is so great. It's like I'm seeing them for the first time every single show. All of a sudden on a huge video screen, a stopwatch-type countdown began in huge red digital numbers. When it reached a minute to showtime, the crowd went wild. The countdown reached zero, and the screen went black. What felt like an eternity passed while music started playing. About ten seconds or so later, a video montage began, and then the guys appeared onstage. They performed on a small stage with no crazy set. There was a DJ doing all the music, along with a mix during a brief intermission. As much as I love hearing a live band, I really enjoyed the DJ mixes that were incorporated into the show." In addition to the DJ, NKOTB also staged an acoustic set, which included Danny on guitar.

Shannon Thorne says, "The show still had flash—*lots* of flash, actually—but in a new way. This show, more than any before, was designed specifically for *us*, the fans. The guys knew exactly what we wanted because we had been given the opportunity to tell them. They listened, and they delivered. The feeling in that room was absolutely electric."

This intimacy allowed for more interaction between the group and its fans than ever before. Shannon explains exactly how up close and personal it got during one of the Hammond, Indiana, shows. "My favorite part of the show is always when the guys come out into the audience," she says. "The level of excitement goes through the roof. The first night of the Hammond run, I was seated at the very top of the first tier of seats. I couldn't see where anyone was for the longest time, and then, all of a sudden everyone around me was screaming and crowding toward the aisle, and I realized that Jon and Joe were coming up the stairs toward where I was sitting. When they got to the top of the stairs, Joe paused, uncertain where he was supposed to go. I held up a sign, and it caught his eye. He read it and started to walk away, and then he realized that he knew me. His face lit up like a little kid at Christmas, and he screamed 'Hi!' at me before telling his security that he had to hug me. At that point, Joe climbed over the railing and onto some empty seats so that he could give me a hug. He stayed there for the remainder of the song. *That* was the point when I realized that together NKOTB and their fans have built something that is truly special."

The pinnacle of the short but sweet Casi-NO tour occurred on NKOTB's final night at Radio City Music Hall. Looking back, fan Laurel Moffat laughs at the introduction of what was about to transpire. She says, "The way NKOTB set this up was really awkward. You could tell they didn't want to give their surprise away but hadn't really rehearsed it. Joe said something to Jordan, like, 'Okay, just sing the song now. Maybe you stop talking.'" NKOTB launched into a rendition of Backstreet Boys' "I Want It That Way." After a few lines, the curtain behind the New Kids went up. Laurel says, "And as soon as you could see feet, you knew what was going to happen. As soon as Backstreet Boys started singing, I thought the balcony was going to tear off the building. I went down to the edge of the balcony, and it felt like an earthquake under me. I ran back up because I really did think the balcony was going to come off the wall. You couldn't hear the song for a minute. I don't even necessarily think there's such a big crossover in their fan bases, but just that it was such a great surprise and they planned it so well, then kept it under wraps."

Based on the enthusiastic reception of that Radio City Music Hall performance, the seed of the NKOTB–Backstreet Boys collaboration that had been planted before the Full Service tour took root. In the fall of 2010, the two groups announced they would be combining their efforts into one mega–boy band act—NKOT-BSB—the following summer. The announcement caused a media stir, and long before summer set in, NKOTBSB made appearances on major televised events, including the American Music Awards, *Dick Clark's New Year's Rockin' Eve*, and *Dancing with the Stars*. They asked fans to determine each band's top five songs and packaged them on a joint NKOTBSB CD, which also included the original joint efforts "Don't Turn Out the Lights" and "All in My Head."

In May 2011 NKOTBSB set out on a tour of major venues throughout North America. The show featured a combination of mashups with all nine members of both bands onstage together as well as individual group time. The end result was a high-voltage, nonstop pop extravaganza that left audiences in a frenzy. For Joe, looking out at those crowds every night of the NKOTBSB tour was a sight to behold. He says, "It was like being in the Roman Colosseum every night—all of those cheers." The combination of all that excitement in the audience and the new experience of sharing the stage and volleying performances back and forth made for an incredible energy. Joe explains, "There was something about that NKOTBSB tour. Even though we were trading off, I gave it *all* every night. *Every* night I would come back under the stage and be drained and euphoric. Most of the time, it was like I just came back from a five-mile run, like, 'Oh, that felt great.'" Danny agrees that the entire experience was invigorating. "I think having nine guys there, everyone steps their game up."

The joint tour also gave both acts exposure to new audiences. Nicole Wandell says, "I never was a fan of NKOTB in the early years. I did listen to some of the singles off *The Block* on the radio but just thought, 'Eh, they're okay.' When they announced they would be touring with BSB, I became excited—because of BSB, not NKOTB. That all changed when I saw them in concert.

I absolutely fell head over heels in love with NKOTB once I saw them on the screen. The guys' emotions for their songs, their fans, and each other was just amazing. I have been to a lot of concerts, but that concert just left me in awe of both groups. I went to the NKOTBSB concert as a BSB fan, but I came away with love for both bands." Winning over new fans like Nicole was a gratifying experience for NKOTB. Danny says, "As it went on, we started meeting more of Backstreet Boys' fans, and they really enjoyed what we did."

In 2011 *Time* magazine voted NKOTBSB the number 2 "Comeback of the Year," second only to Arizona congresswoman Gabby Giffords (who survived an assassination attempt). In 2012 NKOTBSB went worldwide, playing arenas in Europe, Australia, Asia, and South America. For manager Jared Paul, who witnessed all of the hard work it took to get here, this unpredictable magnitude and longevity are the most gratifying parts of all. "They're in a position where they're a *very* prominent member of the music business now. They're returned, and they've returned with a vengeance. Four years later, they're an active band. I think that despite all their hard work, there were many times it could've been said that they couldn't get back together. Not only did they get back together, but they've had all this success. In my opinion, this many tours and this many successes later, they can't be perceived as some novelty, nostalgic artist. I certainly view them (and their fans view them) as a member of the music business community—and a very large one at that. That, to me, is not surprising, but I couldn't have said to you in 2007 that not only could they get back together but also that they could continue and *cement* their place in the business. Which is exactly what they've done."

A Little Bit of Bling

When Michelle Ball first gave Donnie a handmade Swarovski crystal–detailed ("blinged") Celtics jersey as a gift, she had no idea she was opening the door to adventure. This jersey led to a couple of requests from Donnie, including blinged Red Sox jerseys for the NKOTBSB Fenway show. Michelle also made five blinged Celtics jerseys for the New Kids to wear and/or sign, and then auction off to raise funds for Batting for Betty.

While driving from New York to Illinois for the opening show of the NKOTBSB tour, Michelle received a phone call from Donnie in the wee hours of the morning. The New Kids had decided to wear the blinged Celtics jerseys for the show finale, but they needed jerseys for the Backstreet Boys too. The catch? Michelle had less than twenty-four hours to make them. Not only did she have to do the tedious work of applying two thousand Swarovski crystals on each of the four BSB jerseys, but she also had to somehow manage to procure four jerseys—one for each of the group members' favorite football teams. "You can do this," Donnie told Michelle, even though it seemed impossible.

After a long, multistate scavenger hunt, Michelle managed to find the four jerseys. She then hit every Michaels arts and crafts store within a two-hour radius to gather enough crystals for blinging. Michelle laughs, remembering, "I'm in the front seat of the car, improvising with glue, paintbrushes, and Styrofoam plates. It's May, but we've got all the heaters on in the car to try to dry the glue."

With no time to spare, Michelle finished the jerseys backstage as the show was already under way. That night, she cried as NKOTBSB came out onstage outfitted in her wares.

As a reward for her hard work, at the end of the show, Donnie presented Michelle with an all-access pass for the remainder of the tour, bringing her on to work with NKOTB's wardrobe department. Throughout the summer, Michelle fulfilled various requests, including everything from blinged baseball hats to Celtics wristbands. She says, "I ended up getting pulled into their dressing room at one point to take orders from all of them as they were getting ready to go onstage. The love and appreciation from all of them was overwhelming."

A pinnacle for Michelle occurred at the end of the tour. She says, "Joe was always sarcastic and joking around—just Joe being Joe. But at the end of the tour, he came over to me and said, 'You can do anything you want to do. You need to believe in yourself more. You've got a lot of talent inside of you. I believe in you—why don't you?'" For Michelle, who had grown up loving Joe, this was a huge moment.

What began as a one-off gift to Donnie has turned into not only an adventure but also a new business endeavor. Since the NKOTBSB tour, Michelle's blinged creations have also been worn by singer Chris Brown and the freestyle trio TKA. She says, "This summer has taught me that *nothing* is impossible. Dreams are completely reachable. If you would've told me even two years ago that I would be backstage at a New Kids show and treated like family, I would've told you you were completely nuts."

Donnie views Michelle as a testament to the NKOTB fan base. "That's the kinda fans we have: I can call her when I need help."

Five Brothers and a Million Sisters

Back in the day, I didn't really know fans. I know
them now.

—Jon

While NKOTB and their fans have always been intricately connected, today their bonds are far more meaningful, authentic, and
interactive than they ever were in the 1980s and 1990s. "It's such a
profound relationship with us and the fans," Donnie says. "It really
is." Fans today are older and possess both the maturity and technology to build solid relationships with one another. They can also
interact with the band itself in ways that would have once been
unfathomable. After nearly thirty years together on this winding
ride of countless ups and downs, NKOTB and their fans have created a rich shared history. Though the music is important, it's this
sense of connection that really lies at the heart of the NKOTB
phenomenon.

It all starts with the fraternity between the New Kids themselves. The chemistry between the guys has been in place since
very early on and ultimately withstood the pressures and chaos

of success, as well as their long hiatus. Speaking with each one of them, you get the feeling that no matter how deeply fans love this band, no one is a bigger fan of each New Kid than his fellow bandmates. "I love them all," Joe says, simply. "They're amazing, *amazing* people. And thank God I'm at a place where I see that. The stuff I can learn from them literally without them saying a word is incredible." Jon agrees, saying, "Honestly, I consider my 'coworkers' more like brothers than my other two brothers. I don't know what you can compare it to because it's really not like college buddies or anything like that. Maybe it would be more like war buddies— just being in the trenches and being there for each other."

A greater maturity amongst the individual members and how they interact with one another has led to a greater faith in the group as a whole. Donnie explains, "I trust that collectively we'll make the right choices. When we first got back together in 2007, with a few more bad decisions and a few more arguments, we could've easily ended right back in the same place because we were still the same people. But we made choices. I think the maturing of each guy has somewhat shifted the dynamics."

Finding a balance and a way for everyone to be heard has played a big role in their general happiness this time around. For Donnie, this newfound ability to work together in truly respectful, productive ways has been a highlight of the reunion. "Our ability to manage the situations and not fight and take the worst route with each other, to be a little more respectful and patient and give each other a little more latitude and leeway to mess up—that surprises me and makes me happy." Seeing where they are today, Donnie believes wholeheartedly that the breakup was necessary— that without it, NKOTB would have never survived to make it to this point. "It would've been a disaster," he says. "There's no way we could've stayed together."

Today the guys have the time and space to be in the band *and* to have their own personal lives and individual creative pursuits.

As Jon explains, "The pace isn't backbreaking. There's no burnout. We can breathe now." This creates an idyllic, bizarre part-time job of sorts, in which the guys get a taste of pop stardom for a few months, then can immerse themselves in other facets of life. Jon says, "Honestly, my vision of myself is just a blue-collar, every-day kinda guy. And I think that's what makes this all so surreal; because one night I'm in the dressing room eating takeout after performing onstage, and then a week later I'm at one of my properties in New Hampshire ripping out a moldy carpet or smashing up a toilet. It's just weird how many experiences in life privileged people don't get to be involved in because of privilege."

"When I go home," Danny says, "I'm not a New Kid. I'm just Dad. It's no big deal. But we do talk about New Kids at dinner, and my sons will talk about what cities they want to come visit me at. I'm very lucky in that way. My sons are older and my daughters are younger, but they enjoy it in such a different way that it's made it so much more enjoyable for me. I can tolerate being away from them because I know that once they're on tour, it's gonna be amazing."

Since NKOTB reunited, Jordan, Joe, and Donnie have all worked on solo music and/or acting projects. In some cases, such as Jordan's *Unfinished* album and Joe's *Come Home for Christmas* album, bandmates have even made cameo appearances on one another's recordings. This support of one another's careers, Jordan says, "is probably a sign of growth. The New Kids is kind of like the mother ship, and then whatever else we do is a spin-off in terms of solo music. For me, it helps everything. It helps the solo albums, and it helps the group."

For fans, a big part of the allure to NKOTB is that much about both the band and the reaction it inspires has been preserved over the years. However, there are a few key differences between the early days and today. Amongst the most notable of these is a little technological advance called the Internet and, specifically, social networking. Though NKOTB fans were impressively adept at unearthing information about the band and its whereabouts and communicating with one another even before the advent of the World Wide Web, one key ingredient was missing: the New Kids were unable to participate in this conversation.

Back then, the group was reliant on media outlets to disseminate information. This was not the most optimal way of communicating with fans, for a few reasons, including the lag time and the media spin on NKOTB's messaging. Jordan says, "We're very much more connected with fans now than we were before. Twitter and social networking and everything else is perfect for a group like us. It's *incredible* that we get to talk to our fans and touch our fans on a daily basis, and they get to do the same thing to us. Back in the day, we'd have to wait for a network or publication to reach our fans. Now there's no middleman."

From a fan's perspective, Christine Darnell says, "Being a fan in this day and age is amazing. Growing up, I wrote letters all the time and read about NKOTB in magazines and watched them on TV, but *nothing* is like following them on Twitter. I follow a few other entertainers, and no one comes close to how NKOTB interact with their fans."

Jon marvels, "I can tell you a thousand stories about a thousand different things going on in fans' lives. Which, I think, is pretty amazing. I love Twitter. I think it's just the best invention ever. Now I know fans' names, I know they just moved out of their mother's apartment, I know they're having marriage problems, I know one is having a real bad time with depression, I know another's dog is chewing on the kid. The fans are all right here on my iPhone." All of this is somewhat remarkable for a band that was untouchable the first time around. For Jon, this newfound ability to really connect with fans in authentic ways has made the second time around so much sweeter. "This time is a lot more fun for me," he says, "because I think people know where I'm coming from. I think Twitter and everything else nowadays makes it easy to communicate, whereas back in the day, something would happen or you felt a certain way, and it wasn't easy to communicate that feeling to the masses. And now, *bam*! Instant feedback."

Twitter is also great for spontaneous gatherings. Jordan says, "Donnie doesn't like the party to end, and he likes greasy food. So the two combine into Waffle House after-parties." Danny laughs and says, "On tour, Donnie will tweet 'Meet us at the Waffle House,' and three hundred girls show up, and there's a party there. Oh my goodness, I hate the Waffle House. It's greasy, and nasty, and Donnie loves it. Usually I'm on the bus asleep, and he'll wake me up to tell me, 'We're stopping at the Waffle House.' And I'll get out, and there's hundreds of girls there, and they'll bring a boom box and party at the Waffle House. It's fun, definitely fun."

Fan Sarah Korte explains, "Once the Waffle House is found, word spreads, and it turns into a party both inside the restaurant and in the parking lot, with music coming from parked cars with the windows down and the stereo up. There's music playing inside, and Donnie leading chants such as 'When I say Waffle, you say House: Waffle! *House*! Waffle! *House*!' Donnie has been known to come in with a boom box held over his head with *The Block* blaring, leading the restaurant in singing 'Full Service' and 'Dirty Dancing.' He makes the rounds, dances with, sits down next to, speaks to, and hugs everyone, taking pictures with as many fans and employees as he can. Sometimes he's joined by another New Kid."

With changing technology, the music industry has evolved too. Whereas industry shifts worked to NKOTB's detriment during the *Face the Music* days, today's changes have worked to their benefit. Easier dispensation of information has allowed NKOTB to go direct to market with their fans in a way they couldn't before, when the rigid structures of radio, television, and print media were the only truly viable modes of communication. As Jordan sees it, "It's *great* for a group like us because we're all about our fans. We're not as much about trying to please the masses. We have our fans, and we know who our fans are. We don't have to have number one records and all that. We can just serve our fans with whatever we want and have a career."

Donnie agrees, emphasizing, "We don't try to convince the nonbelievers. We try to engage the believers." This focus on existing fans rather than detractors is a marked change from his experience the first time around and has allowed him to enjoy the experience even more. He says, "That's part of the maturity and part of the growing up. I was the fighter in the old days. I hated it when people disrespected us. I hated the press. I would argue and fight with writers and this, that, and the other. I had to grow up and learn that while I'm worrying about all the people who *don't* love us, I'm missing out on the people who do. I know what the truth is, and I don't even have to stand up for it. I just laugh. Before, someone would drive by and make a mean comment, and I would run and chase after their car. Now I'll smile and hug the fans tighter. I don't care what you say—these are my people."

As Donnie sees it, part of the allure to the group as a whole is the fact that each member adapts his own particular way of interacting with fans, based on his personality and style of doing things. "Each guy is comfortable being who he is with the fans. And the fans *know*. They know who's who, they know what's what. And they love us anyway. It's not like being a twenty-year-old kid, like, '*I'm* nicer to the fans. They should love *me* more.' They like who they like, and they like us all. They *love* us all. And when we're all together, that's what they like more than any one individual of us. I'm so grateful that we've *all* got the maturity to know that. That we've *all* come to that conclusion. But the fans get it, man. They see through everything. The fans are so sophisticated. And they're so, so smart about us. They're funny too. It's awesome."

Explaining the difference between NKOTB and some other artists, Donnie says, "There's a school of thought in the music business that if you give the fans too much, they won't come back. There's a school of thought that says you have to be elusive, you have to be the man behind the curtain." This is not, however, a theory that NKOTB have ever subscribed to—especially postreunion. "Back in the day," Jon says, "I didn't really know fans. I know them now. There's so many of them that do the sweetest things or say the nicest things." All of this contact and communication has also allowed fans to get to know the band in more real ways than in earlier times. Despite their celebrity, these are open guys, not fuzzy figures shrouded in mystery. What you see is what you get. Jon explains, "I think there's not that much fans don't know about us. We're open and honest with them. What wouldn't they know? Nothing! They know everything! They're the CIA."

In addition to technology, the other big game changer in band-fan interaction has been the incorporation of meet and greets and VIP access at shows. Reflecting on this modern-day access, fan Shea Brock says, "During the old days, there were no VIP packages to buy. There was no cruise. If you wanted to meet the boys in person, it came down to two things: either you knew someone who had connections, which we didn't, or you used your imagination and determination to get you what you wanted. Fortunately, we had imagination and determination in spades. We scoured malls, mapped out venues, and got kicked out of our fair share of hotels. But it was worth it. We met the boys on a few occasions, all on our own."

Incorporated since the initial 2008 reunion tour in conjunction with VIP Nation (formerly I Love All Access), fans now have the opportunity to purchase packages that afford them opportunities to meet and take pictures with NKOTB in addition to other perks, such as prime seats and early access to shows. Fan Kelly Stammel says, "To meet any celebrity is a special event, but to meet someone that you have admired and adored for over twenty-five years is a dream come true."

As the head of VIP Nation, Colibri Evans has had the chance to see NKOTB and their fans interact on a firsthand basis over the past few years. "For me," she says, "it's been the *best* working with New Kids because they're so wonderful to their fans. They meet two hundred fifty people a night. It's amazing. Their dedication to the fans blows me away every time I come out on the road. It's not just the time they spend with fans, it's how much attention they pay to their fans. We have to peel them off the fans. It's really genuine." Of their desire to connect with fans, Danny says, "We have a very unique bond with the fans. Especially having been away for the fifteen years and then to come back. We're getting to relive all this, and they get to relive it too. The stories go on and on and on."

There tends to be an abundance of spiritedness at these sessions. For instance, when NKOTB incorporated the Ultimate VIP Package into their meet and greets (a high-tier package that allows a single fan to meet the guys alone as opposed to going in with a group of other fans), Colibri says with a laugh, "I thought, 'Okay, these meetings will go really quick.' But these guys go *over the top*. I mean, whatever these girls want, the guys do it. At one show, the guys suggested, 'Why don't we make a pyramid and put a girl at the very top?' I mean, who does that? In the beginning, they were just taking a photo or two. Now these girls are having individual photo shoots backstage. They could have *easily* limited it to one photo per the package details, but it's these guys. They're just doing *so* much more. And they have so many other things going on too: they have press here, press there, a show to put on, and rehearsals." As Joe sees it, "It's nice to slow it down. I think we're good at slowing it down as much as possible. As much as we have to meet a lot of people, we know when it's getting too quick."

Most of the time, the guys are having just as much fun as their fans at meet and greets. This is a far cry from the meet and greets of the old days, which were more stilted affairs. According to Jon, "We didn't like them back in the day. They were just such a chore. But I think it was just being overworked and overtired. It was totally different. You were thrown in a room with tons of people, and it was sort of just a free-for-all. There was no conversation, it was just, 'I love you.' Now we're talking to humans, not hormones." They are also a rewarding experience now. Donnie says, "There is a moment every night—every *single* night—meeting those fans, when I say, 'This is why I'm here.'"

Meet and greets have not only allowed the fans to get up close and personal with the guys but also have allowed NKOTB another avenue through which to become acquainted with some of the fans rather than simply seeing a blur of faces from onstage. Fan Heather Slawinski marvels, "Yesterday I saw a woman who has met me many times in the past, yet she still didn't recognize me or realize we had met before. This got me thinking: I am not a memorable person. I bet half of my high school would say they had never seen me before. This is a huge reason why Joe McIntyre remembering who I am is so meaningful to me. It took me a long time to even believe he knew who I was. My mind couldn't accept that a man who sees thousands of women each night could recognize me, while people who were in my math class of thirty people did not. I will never forget the first time he proved he knew me; I was floored. If I hadn't been a Joe girl already, I sure would have been after that moment.

"NKOTB are amazing," Heather continues. "It's as if they have this wonderful ability to pinpoint our insecurities and boost us up. Feel unmemorable? Joe will remember you. You think you're ugly? Donnie will tell you you're beautiful. You think your handmade bracelet for them is cheesy and lame? Danny will put it on immediately and love it. Having trouble sleeping at night because of all of your problems? Log on to Twitter and chat with Jon—he'll lighten your mood. I think that is one of the reasons we have embraced them so eagerly: they have given us so much of what we have needed. Not only an escape from our troubles but also love, support, and confidence. NKOTB make so many of us feel like the most special person in the room."

Most fans are quite cognizant of the effort NKOTB put forth, and they're grateful for it. Cynthia Bruneau says, "More now than then, we can feel their love for us, even when they are exhausted from touring and trying to maintain life at home and work away from NKOTB. To give so much, it really makes them extraordinary. You can see when they are tired, when they need a break, when they are missing home and family. But you can also see that they are really enjoying being a group again, and doing the shows, being onstage, the meet and greets, the cruises, the screaming—it's where a part of them will always belong."

Annual cruises have also become a prime opportunity for fans to connect with the band. Since 2009, NKOTB have embarked on an ever-growing seaborne adventure from Miami to the Bahamas. What began as a four-day cruise with 2,000 fans has grown into a five-day cruise with 2,700 cruisers. Rose Tours owner Billy Roseman says, "It took an hour to sell twenty-seven-hundred tickets. We sold out in *one* hour. That is not the norm. It was so unbelievable that our system crashed the first time we ran it. We couldn't handle the calls."

When Jared initially approached the guys with the idea of a cruise, they were somewhat apprehensive based on their previous cruise experience in 1990, which was so intense that Jordan actually escaped the boat midway through. Of that first sailing, Jon says, "We were locked in the cabin, like, 'Oh my God, get me off this boat!' There were two boats, side by side, so we weren't even on the fans' ship. It was too much." But this time around, the cruise has been an entirely different experience and, arguably, the highlight of the year for both fans and NKOTB. The cruise has presented a unique opportunity for them to party together intimately and to really let their hair down in a way that's not possible at a single concert. Every evening, the band stages a theme night and comes out to party with its fans on the lido deck. These nightly parties have become something of legend. The guys get up close and personal with their fans, crowd surfing and mingling with the masses on podiums set out in the middle of the deck. These parties often extend to the wee hours of the morning, with Donnie generally being the last to leave as the sun is about to rise.

Days are filled with various quirky events, such as yoga (also known as "stretchify") with Jordan and bingo with Jon. Each year the band hosts a tongue-in-cheek game show, such as New Kids–themed *Double Dare* or *Jeopardy*. And then, of course, there are the performances. In this kind of setting, the guys really have the chance to venture out in ways they normally don't onstage. The 2011 cruise, for instance, featured the Joe and Acoustic Wood Show, in which Danny played a stripped-down acoustic set, while Joe walked fans through his childhood and career with a series of show tunes and storytelling. The ship docks for a concert on the beach, and afterward NKOTB play a series of beach games with fans. From the first year, fans have taken it upon themselves to decorate cabin doors much like their bedroom walls were decorated in the eighties and nineties. The guys can often be found prowling the hallways to check out the various decorations, meet fans, and leave random commentaries and autographs on the doors.

You never know what's going to happen on the cruise. Fan Chanda King remembers her delight when Jon suddenly made an appearance in her friend's cabin. She says, "Jon's head popped out of his room all of a sudden. He came walking out in the hall in his pajamas because he was trying to take a nap and ended up talking to us for about an hour. He just plopped down on the bed and talked to us. It was so funny because Jon has this thing where he doesn't tell security where he is. You could see security walking by the room and walking back, on his walkie-talkie, like, 'Where's Jon? Has anybody seen Jon? I lost Jon!' He just talked to about seven girls in there. Just the fact that he came in there and laid down on the bed, like, 'What's up?'" The guys love all of this mixing and mingling too. Of the cruise, Jon says, "If we could just do a cruise a year for the rest of our lives! It's kind of a crime that we get paid to do four days' worth of just hanging out and having fun."

Billy Roseman—who has the benefit of seeing other entertainers interact with their fans on similar cruises—finds the New Kids' connection with fans particularly impressive. "The thing that gets me the most is the concerts at night when they all get out in the crowd," he says. "They get on those platforms right there with their fan base, and they're singing and signing autographs, and connecting personally. New Kids have a following that is just unbelievable. They don't *have* to be out there, but they are out there because they just *love* the fans. The fan base feels that; the fan base *knows* when you're real and when you're not. And I think that's their success."

For all of these events and occasions, it's not just fans making memories; it's the guys too. Donnie says, "It really is cool. It's not just them and their little 'never forget' moments. They may not all be the same as mine, but I got a whole bunch of them too. I got a *whole* bunch." To this day, when interacting with fans, Donnie still looks back on the day in 1984 when his dad told him he'd better not ever change. "Part of my accessibility is because of that very statement. I thought about it every time I met people. I think about it to this very day. I will never be that guy that walks out of a building and doesn't stop and say hi to people."

For their part, fans seize meet and greets and the cruise as their opportunity to have actual conversations with the guys and, in many cases, to say things they've wanted to say for many, many years. Of the powerful sentiments they've heard from fans, Jordan says, "A lot of girls tell us that we got them through tough times. We were kind of the Band-Aid, we were the soothing blanket that got them through a *lotta* stuff, like child abuse, sexual abuse, death in the families, all that kind of trauma. We get so many letters, and a lot of girls that come to our meet and greets tell us, 'Because of you guys . . . ' So that's pretty damn touching. It makes you feel like there's a lot of purpose for what you do. It's almost like we're the lucky ones that she picked, and thank God. And why us? We were their happy place through all of the pain and chaos of the world, through all the confusion and trauma. There's *tons* of that."

Of course, there's a lot of levity too. Chrissy LaBrecque says, "We have changed, yes. We are grown women. We are wives. We have children and careers. We drive our own giddy selves to the concerts and have a beer while we are there. But the feeling has not changed. The camaraderie. The excitement. The innocence. I often wonder if the five men responsible can even begin to understand how much we appreciate that gift."

VIP Nation's Colibri Evans believes it's the band's sense of gratitude and appreciation for fans that underlies this sort of emotional reaction. "They are definitely different from other bands I work with," she says. "I don't know if it's because it's their second time out that they're so gracious and humble, but I've heard that even back in the day, they were this way with their fans. I feel like they really get it that without the fans, they wouldn't be here, and I can't say that about every band on the road. But they *so* value their fans, and it's like this give-and-take. They just give so much to their fans because they realize they wouldn't be here without them. I just feel like it's a phenomenon on its own, seeing the dynamic between them and their fans. It's very alive, and it's very organic. It reminds me of why I do this: It's refreshing. It's not always a community. This is *such* a community."

Indeed, it *is* a community. Whereas other fans may come out for a show or two for other groups, Colibri has had the opportunity to see the vast difference between Blockheads and fans of other groups. "It's interesting because it's more than just coming to a show," she says. "They just travel around. The cool thing, too, is that you look at the message boards, and you see the fans started out coming alone, and then they made friends, and they call each other sisters, they travel together. It's turned into this whole phenomenon. It's not just, 'I like this band, I'm going to go see a show.' This is a *lifestyle*. They plan their summers around it."

Many fans didn't see all of this coming. When they went to see NKOTB play their first round of reunion shows, it was with the intention of having a one-off night. But then, unexpectedly, it turned into something bigger—something more. Jill Price had precisely this experience. She says, "I never expected to feel the way I did after the show. The moment we got home, we were checking tour dates to see if there were any other shows we could get to. It didn't take long for us to make it a reality and start planning the trip. This started us on many road trips together to see them. And we met some other amazing fans along the way."

The dedication of NKOTB fans is an anomaly in pop music. The lifestyle element of all of this is more frequently found in the jam-band scene, with bands such as the Grateful Dead and Phish, where fans travel long distances from one venue to the next, chasing ever-rotating set lists. While NKOTB shows are infused with a sense of spontaneity, the actual foundation of the show generally remains static throughout the tour. So, for their fans, this willingness to travel great distances and see multiple shows per summer has more to do with soaking in the atmosphere and excitement than seeing a different show every single night. Fan Kelly Stammel explains, "It doesn't matter how many times you see them perform during a tour, every show is unique in its own way. They don't just go through the motions; they pour every fiber into making sure each fan has a special and fantastic time. They give a thousand percent of themselves."

Fan Stacey Bahr says, "I've traveled to New York City, Chicago, Ohio, Atlanta, and Ontario with these ladies. I've cried with them, laughed with them, celebrated the birth of children, mourned the death of loved ones, and have felt closer to them than friends I have known for the majority of my life. It is a bond that is unexplainable. I don't know why or how, but for some reason, I felt at home with the Blockheads. They are the most generous people, with huge hearts: offering a place to stay, a ride, an offer to be the one who takes on the great stress of buying tickets for the group when they go on sale—all for someone they hardly know. To outsiders, it sounds crazy, and my 'regular' friends don't get it, but if you're a Blockhead, you know exactly what I'm talking about and have a million stories just like this. No matter where I go or how long it's been since I've seen them, it always feels like I'm coming home when I get to talk to them or see them."

Another big draw to shows is the fact that even in an arena setting, the guys are extremely interactive with fans, even from the stage. Danny says, "We get up there, and we want to connect. We want to look people in the eye and see that they're happy, see that they're enjoying themselves." Fan Karen Alexander says, "Non-Blockheads often ask me how I can see the same show twelve times a year and never get tired of it. Each show takes on its own personality and feels like it's the start of a whole new tour, even though they are performing the same set and sticking to a similar script when they chat with the crowd between songs. It's the smaller things that seem to matter most. I get to see the guys communicate with one another while onstage. (Nothing in life is more adorable than watching Danny crack himself up onstage or watching Joey turn to Jordan to point out something funny in the crowd.) I get to see the guys read the hilarious signs Blockheads hold up in the crowd and respond to them. I get to see their subtle glances, smiles, and smirks as they recognize faces in the crowd. Like many Blockheads, I've had my fair share of moments with each guy onstage when they lock their eyes on you during a particular song and the rest of the world seemingly fades away, or they point or wink or generally do something so amazing and adorable that it makes me weak in the knees. There is no other place on earth I can go where all my stress completely fades away, and I can sing and dance and be completely free for a few hours, with everything else in the world completely blocked out. It's a ride, a journey, an experience."

Jordan understands this appeal. He says, "It's more about the people than the incredible level of skill. We're more than music, and we're more than dancing, and we're more than singing voices. We connect with people from the heart and with our personalities. People love that Jon has two left feet. People love that he's shy. People love that. They love when they see him goof up with dance steps or when someone else onstage tries to help him. Because everyone can connect with and relate to that. You know, who hasn't made a mistake? Who isn't insecure? When you see that live onstage—and we're not ashamed of it, but we accept what it is— then it becomes strength. It's not all about the slick dance moves and the number one songs. It's about connecting with our fans and being *real* and letting them know who we are as people. Really connecting with them and not taking them for granted or just looking at them as a ticket sale or a record sale." Fan Laura Barr couldn't agree more. "Their real personalities come through, and they're not perfect," she explains. "The guys are perfectly imperfect."

For as much as many NKOTB fans have been caught off guard by how much this has all meant, so too have some of the guys. Donnie says, "It was a surprise to me how fulfilling it was. It was a surprise to me how emotional it was, how rewarding it was. And, quite frankly, how wrapped up in the fans I am. I'm not caught up in the hype. I don't need it. I don't need some fulfillment. I can live without it. But I don't want to. I *love* making people smile. I *love* sharing myself. I love the feeling of making people happy. I love the fact that, for whatever reason, I've been put in a position to change people's lives in a simple way. I'm not healing diseases. But I can make someone happy, even for a short time.

"It's hard to broadstroke the fans," he goes on, "but they *really* are just incredible. They're funny, and they get it. Like, we can't really put one over on them. It eventually becomes our sisters watching us. They're willing to be impressed by us. They're willing to indulge us. They're able to poke fun at us. And we *need* that. We need to sort of come down."

Though many outside of this insular little universe don't understand exactly why this all matters that much, for Blockheads, that's okay. They *do* understand, and that's part of the bond. Shannon Thorne surmises, "People think it's strange and that we fans are a bit delusional. For me, it's all about surrounding myself with the kind of people that I aspire to be myself. I know that Joe, Jordan, Jon, Donnie, and Danny are not my best friends. I get that I am paying them money, and they are providing a service. I also know that they are truly kind and generous people who care about their fans. They have dedicated a huge portion of their lives to making people smile. Those five men have indirectly changed the course of my life; they opened up a whole new world to me that I never would have been a part of if they hadn't decided to give it another shot. I have new friends all over the world and a new sense of self-confidence. For that, I will be forever grateful to them."

The Mutual Inspiration Society

Over the past few years, Danny has used Twitter as a supportive virtual environment for weight loss and healthy living. "I've worked out since I was nineteen or twenty years old," he says. "I realized I could use Twitter to communicate with some of our fans about how to live a bit healthier. Since that started, I've literally had hundreds of girls sending me before and after pictures. Some of these girls have lost up to 150 pounds. It's just very, very touching."

Valerie O'Shea is one of the women who have been deeply affected by Danny's encouragement, ultimately shedding 132 pounds. At her husband's suggestion, she brought before and after pictures to show Danny on the 2011 NKOTB cruise. She remembers, "Danny was on the lido deck taking pictures with fans. I was so nervous. I wasn't nervous about meeting him, but I was nervous to show him my before picture. I was embarrassed by that picture and what I had looked like, but was proud of all I had achieved. Danny played a big part in helping me lose that weight. His reaction was the best—I definitely shocked him. He looked at the picture and then looked at me. He did this at least a half a dozen times. Finally, he said, '*Wow!* Keep it up. You look amazing!' I had a hard time forming a coherent sentence."

A couple of days later at the cruise photo op, Valerie says, "Danny was the last one I hugged. So, I hugged him and turned to walk out of the room. Out of the corner of my eye, I saw him do a double take of me. He asked the girl next to him to hold on, and he yelled, 'Wait, hold on. Come back!' I stopped dead in my tracks, turned, and went back to him. He looked at me and said, 'Your before picture is amazing. You are truly an inspiration.' He made it hard for me to breathe; all I could hear was Danny Wood calling me an inspiration. That moment meant everything to me. He has sealed a very special place in my heart forever."

The appreciation is mutual. Danny says, "Fans are always telling me I inspire them. Now, I work at my fitness even more than I used to because they inspire me. Their stories are incredible and I admire anyone who makes a life change like that."

This Love Will Last Forever

What's *really* cool is when you're sixty years old
and hanging out, or onstage, or at the Rock and
Roll Hall of Fame . . . and you're *still together*. I
realize that now.

—Donnie

The journey of five ragtag Boston kids who found their collective
musical roots in a run-down Roxbury house has been nothing if
not unpredictable. Over the course of their career, they've given
birth to the boy band movement and written their own rules.
While they've certainly worked hard for everything they attained,
in some ways it seems there also has to be a little bit more to it all.
Donnie says, "In interviews I always used to say, 'It was destiny.'
And the guys would say, 'Oh, destiny. What an idiot.' I know they
hated it when I said that. But, part of it is like, what else could
it be? We were bussed to Roxbury. Maurice lived right up the
street from the school we were bussed to. We had to have gone
through that to be 'the guys.' All this stuff, it all came together.
That doesn't mean it didn't take hard work, commitment, and a

belief against *all* odds. We just kept showing up, man. So do I think it was meant to happen? It happened."

Perhaps even more impressive than "showing up" the first time around was showing up the second, with all of that history behind them—both in terms of the group in general and their relationships with one another. Accomplishing that, Donnie says, "was a process. We had to relive everything in 2007 and 2008. For some of us, it was all smooth sailing. For some of us, it wasn't. We had to relearn it—or learn it for the first time, in some cases." Tearing up, Donnie says *that* part of it all has been a big victory. "It's *huge*. Huge. If you watch old videos of us, you'll hear Jon saying, 'The cool part is, we're all friends.' We weren't always friends. Some of us stopped being friends. Some of us weren't really ever friends. Well, we are now. We made it." For Donnie, the bonds they've formed amongst the five of them are one of the group's biggest accomplishments. "If you look at the Beatles, the Stones, New Edition, or any other group, they all went through this. But what's *really* cool is when you're sixty years old and hanging out, or onstage, or at the Rock and Roll Hall of Fame, or whatever, and you're *still together*. I realize that now."

Ironically, it's now clear that an important part of making it to this point was the New Kids' demise in the 1990s. Looking back, Joe says, "Everyone always asks, 'How'd you survive the fall?' Well, thank God for the fall! What did you want us to do? Be on life support? We got the *opportunity* of falling off the map."

For most of the New Kids, it all boils down to things that are quite simple. Jordan muses, "People always ask us, 'What's the highlight of your career?' I don't know. Some of the guys would say Fenway, but that was not a highlight of my career. It's a milestone for the New Kids, but those big moments aren't really the *moments* to me." For him, the greatest parts have been "all the little inside jokes that we had; those little things are the best. Winning an American Music Award, that was cool; but to me, that doesn't stand out when I think about the New Kids. Just hanging out. We were so crazy, we had so much fun, we were so close."

Over the years, the New Kids have mastered being in the moment and rising to the occasion, whether at the Apollo in 1988 or in Rockefeller Plaza in 2008. "We first came up being competitive," Danny says. "We were white kids performing for all-black crowds. So that part of me is always still there. I look forward to getting up on that stage and being the best group every night." There are always mountains to climb, no matter how many milestones they've attained. Joe says, "You think something like Fenway is it, but there'll be other things that we get to create for our fans, and our fans are gonna show up again and surprise us. Sometimes I talk about how it's like a good marriage. You wanna come home with a rose and surprise her, and she's gonna do something for you that makes you feel great. That's the kind of relationship we have with our fans."

Today the New Kids exemplify the kind of gratitude that can come only with experiencing the full spectrum of victory and defeat over time. This time around, Joe says, "*Now* we can soak it in. *Now* we can really grasp it." As Donnie puts it, "Right now, when I look at things, I *really* wouldn't want to be anywhere else. I'm immensely grateful. I'm grateful every day. For *all* of it."

For guys who have been around the sometimes punishing sphere of show business for so long, there's still a refreshing sense of wonderment about it all, even today. Jon shakes his head, saying, "This time around, I've just been in awe the whole time. There's not a night I don't look out at the audience in amazement. It's been that way since '08: I just say 'Wow' and count my blessings. I'm always like, 'All these people are here to see us! *Why?*'"

For NKOTB's die-hard fans, the last few years have represented a time of reconnecting, reliving, and redemption. This band, which was supposed to be an adolescent phase, has turned into so much more. And because of all that's happened, it seems that the New

Kids will continue to impact their lives from here on out. Abbie Vicknair says, "We know at any point it could be over. But even when this is all over, it's not really going to be over because there's this new connection that's formed between them and us, and it's always going to be there. Even when it ends as a group, it's not gonna be over."

For the guys, Donnie says, "I think in some ways we've accomplished what we set out to do. We altered the legacy of the group for the better. We changed it. The goal was to come back, play an arena tour, and be great. And do an album and make it count and be proud of it. And, selfishly, yeah, to rewrite our history. We want to control the final chapters of this book. Not the outsiders, the people who don't know. *We* want to write the last chapters of New Kids and what our legacy is going to be." Altering the band's legacy took more than just the five band members. Donnie says, "We couldn't have written the new chapters without the fans. So we can't write any more without them. That's the deal. It's a partnership now. Whatever happens, it has to involve them." As for what comes next, as Donnie puts it, "If you can stick around long enough, you can do it all."

Perhaps most important of all this time around, it's *fun*, both for NKOTB and for their fans. Joe explains, "We certainly don't want it to end right now. We want to keep it fresh and exciting because that's what it's about. We do it for that fire and excitement. It's been a real, real blast."

acknowledgments

First and foremost, I'd like to thank Andrea Diaz-Vaughn—for a lot of reasons that span a couple of decades. But most of all, because without her and her sage Ice Cube quotes, this whole thing probably wouldn't have gone much further than Florida.

Thanks to my agent, Coleen O'Shea, and to my wonderful editor, Michelle Howry, who has made this whole process more fun than any job should be. Also, the crackerjack team at Simon & Schuster: Stacy Creamer, David Falk, Sally Kim, Marcia Burch, Kiele Raymond, and Cherlynne Li.

"Phenomenal" is a huge understatement for the delightful group at AGP, CAA, and VIP Nation who have made my life incredibly easy: Jared Paul, Josh Russack, Janelle Lopez, Simon Green, and Colibri Evans. If there's a more first-class, class-act team in the business, I certainly don't know who they are.

This book never could have been written without the help of more Blockheads than I can even begin to count. Your contributions were alternately hilarious, touching, intelligent, and insightful.

Huge heapings of thanks to Celia McConnell, Maria Gagliano-Scalora, Rick Seabolt, and Rob Banagle, all of whom helped me get this off the ground. To Phil Cordano, for his assistance with the early research of this project. Also, to Grandma Hallissy, who has been a huge source of support.

To my beloved brother, Nicholas, a massive, unabashed New Kids fan: this one's for you, my friend. On that note, big thanks to

Lindsey Murray and Ira Skinner, who appreciated this project on Nick's behalf.

Dad and Mom—it's hard to know where to start. Thanks for (literally) coming along for the ride and for cheerfully and adeptly reading all bazillion versions of this manuscript. I love you.

Most of all, huge thanks to the New Kids themselves for being so helpful and all-around awesome: Danny, Donnie, Joe, Jon, and Jordan. It's such an anomaly to find five guys in your position who truly are exactly what they appear to be: grounded, humble, appreciative, intelligent, and pretty damn funny too. I can't think of anyone who deserves success as much as you do. It's been a privilege to tell this story.

index

McPherson, Greg, 117, 156, 157
Menino, Thomas, 10
Merry, Merry Christmas, 109, 117, 118
Mexico, 210
Miami, Fla., 171
Michael, George, 89
Milli Vanilli, 6, 105, 145, 156
Mission Control Studios, 54, 64, 66, 69
Monroe, Marilyn, 52
Montgomery County Fair, 85–86
Moon, Tom, 6
MTV, 77, 91, 176, 178, 181, 182, 183
MuchMusic, 163
Music for the People, 172
music videos, 75, 76, 89–91, 101, 108, 150, 163
    for "Please Don't Go Girl," 70, 74, 76–77, 108
    for "You Got It (The Right Stuff)," 76, 89–91
"My Favorite Girl," 68, 69, 88, 216

Nasri, 187–88, 189, 192, 193, 211
Nassau Coliseum, 114
National Academy of Recording Arts and Sciences, 145
NBC, 3, 197
Neighborhood Children's Theatre of Boston, 9–10, 44
"Never Let You Go," 163, 164, 165, 202
New Edition, 30, 31, 32, 35, 38, 44, 45, 96, 212, 227, 254
New Kids on the Block (album), 56, 70, 126, 160
    in creating first small fan following, 58
    delayed chart success of, 108–9
    demo tracks recorded for, 54–55
    first single released on, 56–57
    lackluster response to, 57–59, 60, 63, 67
    track listing of, 56
New Kids on the Block (NKOTB), 1948–1994:
    age gap between Joe and other members of, 45–46, 60–61, 66, 79, 82

albums and recordings of, *see specific albums and songs*
American Music Awards and, 123, 151–53, 231, 254
Apollo Theater performances of, 71–74, 88–89, 131, 255
awards earned by, 1, 102, 123, 254
award show appearances by, 110–11, 122–23, 151–53, 231
backlash against, 123, 124, 125–26, 145, 146, 149, 152
"beginning-of-the-end" of 1990s run for, 133, 144–45, 146, 147, 149, 153
beginning rise in popularity and fame of, 75–76, 85, 87–88, 92–95, 97
bickering and rifts between bandmates in, 47, 82, 83, 130, 133, 146–48, 151, 155–56, 159, 169, 191, 217–18, 254
bodyguards and security for, 83, 84, 115, 135, 137, 154, 157, 158, 167, 245
boy band descendants of, 176–77
breakup of, 2, 5, 162, 168–70, 172–73, 236
as broken down into archetypes, 94
budget constraints in early days of, 59, 70, 83
camaraderie and closeness in, 16, 60–61, 65, 82, 114, 168, 213, 221–22, 235–36, 254–55
as catering to specific demographic, 127–28
CBS Records' near-ousting of, 60, 63, 64, 75
CBS Records' signing of, 55–56
celebratory concert atmospheres of, 8, 14–15, 105, 114–15, 228, 248, 250
celebrity encounters of, 88–89, 136, 141, 152
chart success and record sales of, 1, 5, 57, 74, 84, 87–88, 89, 90, 91, 99, 102, 106, 108–9, 110, 118, 129, 146, 155, 202

New Kids on the Block (NKOTB),
1948–1994 (*cont.*)
1992 tour of, 157–60
nonstop work schedule of, 5, 91,
100, 107, 109–10, 122, 126,
130–31, 145, 146, 213
official fan club of, 100–101, 169
onstage antics and spontaneity of,
13–14, 51–53, 78, 85–86, 96, 105,
114, 135, 157, 167–68, 206, 227,
228, 248, 249, 250
opening acts for, 113, 224
as opening act for Tiffany, 77–80,
82–88, 104, 131, 160, 194
original small following of, 58,
59–60
perceived "wholesome" teen image
of, 125, 152–53, 164–65
as positive role models, 102–3, 134
radio station auditions of, 71
random shows and weekend gigs
of, in wake of first album, 59–60,
61, 63
rapid ascent of, 5, 100–101, 103,
104, 108, 111
regaining of creative control by,
149–51, 159, 162
rowdy crowds faced by, 95–96,
154–55, 157–59
second Tiffany tour of, 103–5, 109,
110, 114
songwriting contributions of, 56,
67–68, 109, 125, 162
as source of solace and inspiration
for fans, 61–62, 80, 95, 128–29,
160–61, 173–74, 201, 209,
246–47, 251–52
sparse road conditions in early days
of, 3, 59, 82–83, 84
staged theatrics and special effects
in shows of, 10, 12, 15–16, 114,
129, 130, 134, 135, 198–99,
214–15, 229
Starr's disorganized and laid-back
approach to, 32–33, 49–50, 55,
67, 68
Starr's dwindling presence with,
110, 155

Starr's loving relationship with,
50–51, 55
Starr's split from, 155–56
Starr's studio as refuge and hangout
for, 32–35, 50, 65–66
Super Bowl XXV halftime show of,
152–53
superstardom of, 4, 5, 6, 111, 122,
125, 133–34
teen magazine coverage of, 89, 93
television appearances and
performances by, 3, 88, 106–7,
110–11, 117–18, 141–42, 156–57,
167, 196–200, 202, 203, 205–8,
210, 218, 231
in thoughtful gestures to fans,
41–42, 80–81, 132, 143, 183
wardrobe worn by, 53, 57, 83, 88,
101–2, 107, 206, 233–34
young fan base of, 5, 85, 108, 116,
149
youthful and playful dynamic in
appeal of, 13, 14, 76–77, 85–86,
90, 94–95, 97, 107, 114, 228
see also specific band members
New Kids on the Block (NKOTB),
2008 and beyond, reunion of, 4,
6–8, 184–251, 254, 255–56
annual fan cruises and, 42, 121,
244–46, 252
beginning talks on, 6–7, 184–88,
191
BSB's joint headlining tour in, 10,
11–12, 98, 161, 224, 230–34
building up hype for, 196, 197
"Casi-NO" tour (2010) and,
228–30
children of bandmembers brought
on tour in, 98, 220–22, 237
conflicts among bandmembers in,
217–18
creative control in, 211, 220
failed outsider attempts in
instigating of, 181
fan nostalgia and, 161, 203, 205,
207–8, 213, 215–17, 219, 222–23
fan-orchestrated demonstrations of
love and gratitude for, 224–26

about the author

A California native, at age seventeen, Nikki traded in her flip-flops for Ugg boots and headed out to the East Coast. She graduated from Harvard with an ALB in Liberal Arts and worked at a wide range of media companies, including *The Boston Globe* and Random House. She has been a freelance writer and editor since 2008 and is the author of *So Much to Say: Dave Matthews Band—20 Years on the Road*. When she's not writing, Nikki can usually be found at shows, on road trips, hiking, and/or continuing her ongoing quest to find the world's most perfect slice of pizza. She lives in Boston, Massachusetts.

If anyone knows where this perfect pizza slice exists, please visit www.nikkivannoy.com to let Nikki know where to find it. She will be most appreciative.